Mark

ONE JUMP AHEAD

THE TOP NH HORSES

TO FOLLOW FOR **2025/2026**

THE AUTHOR

Mark Howard is 50 and graduated from Manchester University with a BA Honours Degree in History. For the last 32 years, he has written the National Hunt horses to follow book *One Jump Ahead*. He also writes the Flat racing equivalent, *Ahead On The Flat*. In addition, he appears as a pundit on *Racing TV* (Sky Channel 424) and, prior to that, *Attheraces*. He is also a regular contributor to sportinglife.com and has written for *The Irish Field, Sports Advisor and Racing & Football Outlook (Borderer & Trainer File)*. He is Ambassador for the successful syndicate ValueRacingClub.co.uk

FRONT COVER: **JAGWAR,** ridden by Jonjo O'Neill jnr, winning the TrustATrader Plate Handicap Chase at the Cheltenham Festival in March for owner J.P.McManus and trainer Oliver Greenall & Josh Guerriero.

BACK COVER: **BANBRIDGE** (Advised @ 33/1 in last year's *One Jump Ahead*) winning the King George VI Chase at Kempton on Boxing Day under Paul Townend.

Front cover photograph supplied by STEVE CARGILL PHOTOGRAPHY.
www.stevencargill.com.

Back cover photograph supplied by HEALY RACING Ltd.
Listowel, Co.Kerry. Ireland. V31 PVO7. Telephone: 00 353 6821680.

Published by *Mark Howard Publications Ltd.* 69, Fairgarth Drive, Kirkby Lonsdale, Carnforth, Lancashire. LA6 2FB.
Telephone: 015242 71826
Email: mark.howard@mhpublications.co.uk
Website: www.mhpublications.co.uk

(Please note: If you are currently NOT on the *Mark Howard Publications* mailing list and you would like to be, and therefore receive all information about future publications then please post / email / phone your name and address to the above).

Printed by REEDS (Cumbria) LTD. Southend Road, Penrith, Cumbria CA11 8JH.
Telephone: 01768 864214. www.hhreeds.co.uk

ISBN: 978-1-0687418-0-7

CONTENTS

INTRODUCTION

For National Hunt enthusiasts, it is impossible not to be excited about the winter ahead. If the prospect of Final Demand, Kopek Des Bordes and Lulamba going over fences for the first time doesn't set the pulse racing, nothing will. Last spring saw the major prizes shared amongst some fresh faces with Golden Ace grabbing her opportunity after Constitution Hill and State Man gift wrapped the Champion Hurdle to Jeremy Scott's mare, while the former's stablemate Jonbon blundered away his best ever chance to win the Queen Mother Champion Chase. Marine Nationale read the script though and ensured there wasn't a dry eye in Gloucestershire with memories flooding back of the late Michael O'Sullivan, who tragically lost his life a month earlier following a fall at Thurles. The mighty Galopin Des Champs was dethroned, too, with the twelve times Grade 1 winner missing the opportunity to emulate Best Mate and win the Cheltenham Gold Cup for a third time. Instead, it was a new kid on the block, Inothewayurthinkin, who justified his connections' decision to supplement the seven year old at a cost of £25,000, and claim steeplechasing's holy grail.

Familiar faces dominated the training ranks though with Willie Mullins ensuring the British trainers' title remained in Ireland for a second consecutive year, but only just. On the morning of the first day of the Cheltenham Festival, the Closutton team were in 56th position in the table, £2,265, 421 in arrears of Dan Skelton. By the end of the week with another ten Festival winners added to his tally, including his 100th courtesy of Jasmin Des Vaux in the Albert Bartlett Novices' Hurdle, Mullins had narrowed the gap to £1,214,778. Not for the first time, the Grand National at Aintree proved the game changer with Ireland's 19 times champion trainer being responsible for the first, second, third, fifth and seventh home. The deficit between Skelton and Mullins had shrunk to £122,026. That amount had been whittled down to £1,431 by the time the latter had witnessed Captain Cody emulate stablemate Macdermott twelve months earlier by winning the Scottish National at Ayr. Even though Paul Nicholls' former assistant had built his advantage back up to £68,483 going into the final day of the season at Sandown, there was a feeling of inevitability about what was about to happen. The rest, as they say, is history.

In total, Mullins won 34 Grade 1 prizes during 2024/2025 - 21 of the 35 in Ireland and 13 of the 38 in the UK. It is fair to say that both Mullins and Skelton have led the way in terms of recruitment during the spring/summer, closely followed by messrs Elliott, De Bromhead and Nicholls. As the pages ahead will hopefully testify, the superpowers amongst the training ranks have got even stronger during the 'off season.' That comment also applies to the major owners. J.P.McManus was crowned champion owner in Britain for a seventeenth time - and for the nineth consecutive year - plus, for the 22nd time in Ireland. Robcour will ensure the green and gold don't get everything their own way though following huge investment, especially from France. Expect Brian Acheson's squad to improve upon their fourth position in last year's Irish title.

Gigginstown House Stud finished runners-up behind McManus in Ireland with their maroon and white silks being responsible for four Grade 1 winners. Six years ago, Michael O'Leary announced that he was scaling back his interest in National Hunt racing and wouldn't be buying any more young horses. Along with threatening to charge customers for the use of the toilets on his Ryanair flights, he has had a change of heart. Willie Mullins returned to their trainer's roster following a six year exodus in 2022, while the O'Leary investment in equine talent has accelerated during the last twelve months. Their purchases at the Cheltenham March & April and Aintree Grand National Sales alone, included Keep Him Company (£220,000), Generous Risk (£250,000), Lemmy Caution (£250,000), Lultimatom (£225,000), In A Sonnet (£135,000), With Nolimit (£250,000), The Irish Avator (£200,000), Wyoming Line (£275,000), Ballyfad (£175,000) and Low Kick (£170,000).

Congratulations to Olly Murphy and his team who enjoyed a magnificent season. Fifth in the table with a personal best 141 winners and an impressive strike-rate of 25%, which was the best in the business, Gordon Elliott's former assistant's monthly tallies between November and April were 24, 20, 13, 19, 15 and 16. A model of consistency throughout the winter and spring, Olly is another to have added to his team with some hefty purchases amongst the Irish pointing ranks. It won't be long before the quality is added to the quantity and, having the champion jockey Sean Bowen partnering most of them, isn't a hindrance either.

On a sad note, we lost the legendary Edward O'Grady, who passed away at the age of 75 in late July. Four times champion trainer in Ireland, the Tipperary native was responsible for 18 Cheltenham Festival winners and just shy of 1,700 winners throughout his illustrious career. The memory of the brilliant Nick Dundee parting company with Norman Williamson at the third last in the Royal & Sun Alliance Chase at Cheltenham in 1999 has never faded. Leading owner John Hales also died in January at the age of 85. Born in Erdington, Birmingham, he was a highly successful businessman through his company Golden Bear Toys who were responsible for the Teletubbies, and he enjoyed some magnificent days on the racecourse. One Man provided Hales with his first winner at Ayr on the 12th November 1993, having bought the dashing grey for £68,000 earlier that year. The Gordon Richards trained gelding won 17 times over fences, including the King George twice and Queen Mother Champion Chase before he was tragically killed at Aintree in April 1998. Ironically, Hales enjoyed his biggest success of all at the same track when Neptune Collonges captured the Grand National fourteen years later. Having part owned Grade 1 winners from last season, Caldwell Potter and Kalif Du Berlais, his legacy lives on.

Enjoy the winter

Mark Howard

FOREWORD
by Nick Luck

9 times Broadcaster of the Year

"Please could you send an updated photo," wrote Mark eventually. The amusement of seeing a twenty-something ***Foreword*** writer beaming maniacally out of the front cover had clearly worn as thin as my hair. Duly noted.

And while it's true to say that the polite annual request to fill this page - usually as Mark and I weigh up the field for the Nunthorpe - is a stark reminder of the passage of time, it is equally a source of comfort.

When *One Jump Ahead* arrives pristine in its Jiffy bag on the doormat, it transports me instantly to the period in my life where racing really grabbed hold, and would distract me before much else: when the Ladbrokes in Burleigh Street held the attention longer than the seminar rooms on the other side of the Strand, and when the joy of buying the Evening Standard on the Tube home was to open from the back and see tomorrow's declared runners for the first time - that is, unless I'd had a chance to glance at Ceefax during the day.

Racing in the ***Standard*** sadly followed the law of ever diminishing returns, and went the same way as one of London's friendliest betting shops. But ***One Jump Ahead*** (of its time), which had brilliantly tapped into the increasingly fevered sense of anticipation for the 'winter game' around the turn of the millennium, is going strong.

And unsurprisingly so, given both the insatiable appetite for preview on the ever lengthening path to the Cheltenham Festival and the quality of insight and foresight provided within these pages. You don't have to go back too far either to unearth the nugget of all ante-post nuggets, as twelve months ago Mark confidently suggested that Banbridge was the King George bet at 33/1. His intuition, combined with a carefully cultivated network of contacts, told him not only that this would be the target, but also how he would arrive there off a slightly unorthodox preparation.

Understanding the way that trainers think and operate has always been one of the strengths of this book. It is one thing to assert rather lazily that "trainers are creatures of habit", but it is another to appreciate their methods and why each curates the careers of horses slightly differently.

The identification of Puturhandstogether as last season's Fred Winter winner would be one such example as - let's face it - there were plenty to choose from in that academy. Similarly, Willie Mullins and Dan Skelton had literally hundreds of promising and unexposed novices this time last year. But why did Kopek Des Bordes and The New Lion stride confidently into Mark's *Top 40* Prospects in late summer?

Regular readers of Mark's ***Updates*** know that it never ends there: the Cheltenham November meeting missive yielded 6 winners from 13 selections, while the 8/1 about Joyeuse for the William Hill at Newbury looked money well bought from the second the tapes went up.

And if ever there was evidence that, for all its necessary freshening, this book will always return you to something reassuringly familiar, let's welcome back that up and coming trainer Philip Hobbs (alongside Johnson White) back to the ***Talking Trainers*** section. Lovely stuff.

Here we are again, folks. I'm ready for my close up, Mr Howard.

TYPE OF TRACK

AINTREE	National Course	Left-Handed, Galloping
	Mildmay Course	Left-Handed, Tight
ASCOT		Right-Handed, Galloping
AYR		Left-Handed, Galloping
BANGOR-ON-DEE		Left-Handed, Tight
CARLISLE		Right-Handed, Stiff / Undulating
CARTMEL		Left-Handed, Tight
CATTERICK BRIDGE		Left-Handed, Tight / Undulating
CHELTENHAM		Left-Handed, Stiff / Undulating
CHEPSTOW		Left-Handed, Stiff / Undulating
DONCASTER		Left-Handed, Galloping
EXETER		Right-Handed, Stiff / Undulating
FAKENHAM		Left-Handed, Tight / Undulating
FFOS LAS		Left-Handed, Galloping
FONTWELL PARK	Chase Course	Figure of Eight, Tight
	Hurdle Course	Left-Handed, Tight
HAYDOCK PARK	Chase Course	Left-Handed, Galloping
	Hurdle Course	Left-Handed, Tight
HEREFORD		Right-Handed, Tight
HEXHAM		Left-Handed, Stiff / Undulating
HUNTINGDON		Right-Handed, Galloping
KELSO		Left-Handed, Tight / Undulating
KEMPTON PARK		Right-Handed, Tight
LEICESTER		Right-Handed, Stiff / Undulating
LINGFIELD PARK		Left-Handed, Tight / Undulating
LUDLOW		Right-Handed, Tight
MARKET RASEN		Right-Handed, Tight /Undulating
MUSSELBURGH		Right-Handed, Tight
NEWBURY		Left-Handed, Galloping
NEWCASTLE		Left-Handed, Galloping
NEWTON ABBOT		Left-Handed, Tight
PERTH		Right-Handed, Tight
PLUMPTON		Left-Handed, Tight / Undulating
SANDOWN PARK		Right-Handed, Galloping
SEDGEFIELD		Left-Handed, Tight / Undulating
SOUTHWELL		Left-Handed, Tight
STRATFORD-UPON-AVON		Left-Handed, Tight
TAUNTON		Right-Handed, Tight
TOWCESTER		Right-Handed, Stiff / Undulating
UTTOXETER		Left-Handed, Tight / Undulating
WARWICK		Left-Handed, Tight / Undulating
WETHERBY		Left-Handed, Galloping
WINCANTON		Right-Handed, Galloping
WORCESTER		Left-Handed, Galloping

IRELAND

BALLINROBE	Right-Handed, Tight
BELLEWSTOWN	Left-Handed, Tight / Undulating
CLONMEL	Right-Handed, Tight / Undulating
CORK	Right-Handed, Galloping
DOWNPATRICK	Right-Handed, Tight / Undulating
DOWN ROYAL	Right-Handed, Tight / Undulating
FAIRYHOUSE	Right-Handed, Galloping
GALWAY	Right-Handed, Tight / Undulating
GOWRAN PARK	Right-Handed, Tight / Undulating
KILBEGGAN	Right-Handed, Tight / Undulating
KILLARNEY	Left-Handed, Tight
LEOPARDSTOWN	Left-Handed, Galloping
LIMERICK	Right-Handed, Galloping
LISTOWEL	Left-Handed, Tight
NAAS	Left-Handed, Galloping
NAVAN	Left-Handed, Galloping
PUNCHESTOWN	Right-Handed, Galloping
ROSCOMMON	Right-Handed, Tight
SLIGO	Right-Handed, Tight / Undulating
THURLES	Right-Handed, Tight / Undulating
TIPPERARY	Left-Handed, Tight
TRAMORE	Right-Handed, Tight
WEXFORD	Left-Handed, Tight

ACKNOWLEDGEMENTS

I would like to thank all the following trainers who have given up their time, during the summer, to answer my inquiries:

Talking Trainers: Harry Derham, Josh Guerriero, Philip Hobbs, Gary Moore, Olly Murphy, Paul Nicholls OBE, Jonjo O'Neill (plus Jonjo O'Neill jnr & Joe O'Neill), Ben Pauling, Nicky Richards, Lucinda Russell, Dan Skelton & Jamie Snowden. Plus, Joseph O'Brien & James Owen. Thank you also to the following secretaries for organising the appointments/answering queries: Hannah Roche (Paul Nicholls) and Kelly (Nicky Richards).

Thank you to Anthony Bromley, David Minton & Bernice Emanuel *(Highflyer Bloodstock),* Nick Luck (Foreword), Declan Phelan, James Reveley, Mags O'Toole, Rich Ricci, Joe Chambers (Racing Manager), Robcour (Brian), Alex Elliott, Michael Shinners & Joanna Wild (Skybet), Fran Berry *(Racing TV),* Bobby O'Ryan, Mick Meagher, Kevin Blake, James Couldwell (ValueRacingclub.co.uk).

The TOP 40 PROSPECTS FOR 2025/2026

ARCADIAN EMPEROR (FR)

4 b g Kamsin (GER) – Allegro Lady (GER) (Santiago (GER))
OWNER: J.P.McMANUS
TRAINER: Willie MULLINS. Closutton, Co.Carlow.
CAREER FORM FIGURES: 1
CAREER WIN: 2025: Mar LISRONAGH Yielding PTP 3m

Willie Mullins' 7 winners (from 53 runners) at the Dublin Racing Festival at Leopardstown, 10 winners (from 76 runners) at the Cheltenham Festival and 15 winners (from 74 runners) at the Punchestown Festival during the 2024/2025 season all featured the unbeaten Bambino Fever who completed a rare treble with three Graded bumper successes. The Jukebox Jury gelding was providing the Closutton team with their fourteenth victory in the Festival bumper at Cheltenham. J.P.McManus has won the same event twice (Mucklemeg (1994) & A Dream To Share (2024)) and the pair may have a leading contender for the 2026 version courtesy of winning pointer Arcadian Emperor.

Irish point expert Declan Phelan believes: **"€30,000 store with plenty of Flat winners in the family tree, including the dam, plus the likes of Arctic Fire. A relatively light framed dark bay, medium sized and athletic. Entrusted with market favouritism for his sole point start at Lisronagh in March when representing the local Tipperary based stable of Sam Curling. Jockey David Doyle decided to drop in stone last for the opening half of the race, his mount consenting to do so. Steadily improving his position on the concluding circuit, Arcadian Emperor eased his way to the front at the second last with a slick jump and thereafter shot away for a smooth win without his jockey getting serious. He illustrated a lovely racing style and the ability to change up into higher gears when desired. Joining Mullins on a private deal, he certainly looks a surefire bumper winner, and should he manage to muscle up his frame, he might be a live candidate for the 2026 Cheltenham Festival bumper."**

Remarkably, thirty two individual stallions have been responsible for the 33 winners of the Cheltenham Festival bumper – Flemensfirth is the only one to have sired two winners – and there is a possibility Kamsin will become the thirty third in March. Arcadian Emperor hails from the same source as the Queen Mother Champion Chase winner Marine Nationale, namely Sam Curling, who sent out a personal best 34 point winners last season finishing second in the table behind Colin Bowe.

POINTS TO NOTE:
Probable Best Distance - 2 miles
Preferred Going - Good/Soft
Connection's Comments: "We've had a few nice horses by Kamsin, including subsequent Grade 2 winner Kamsinas. He got a very good ride. We had planned to sit upsides in front, but David said he was green going to the start, so he dropped him in and educated him." Sam CURLING at Lisronagh (23/3/25)

GOING:	R	W	P	TRACK	R	W	P
Yielding	1	1	0	Left-Handed	1	1	0

TRIP:	R	W	P	JOCKEY:	R	W	P
3m	1	1	0	D.Doyle	1	1	0

BALLYCOMMON BOY (IRE)

4 b g Harzand (IRE) – Atasha (GER) (Soldier Hollow)
OWNER: Mrs D.L.WHATELEY
TRAINER: Olly MURPHY. Wilmcote, Stratford-Upon-Avon, Warwickshire.
CAREER FORM FIGURES: 1
CAREER WIN: 2025: Apr DROMAHANE Good/Yielding PTP 3m

As discussed in the *Introduction*, Olly Murphy had a superb campaign with 141 winners from 570 runners (25%). Strong Leader provided Gordon Elliott's former assistant with more Graded success, while Go Dante (Imperial Cup) and Resplendent Grey (Bet365 Gold Cup) rounded off a memorable season with big handicap wins at Sandown in the spring.

Not one to rest on his laurels, the Warwickshire based handler has added to his burgeoning squad with a number of expensive recruits from Ireland. Arguably the most exciting addition is the unbeaten pointer Ballycommon Boy. Expert Declan Phelan comments: **"Muscular bay gelding: the distaff side of his pedigree are German Flat horses, his dam won on the level in Germany at the trip of a mile. Raced for Tipperary handler Tom Keating at Dromahane in early April. One of the best maidens staged by the premier point track this past spring, consisting of eleven runners, a solid gallop was set from the start. Ballycommon Boy tracked the pace setters, minding his own business, until he was produced four deep round the outside as the bunched field took the home bend with three to jump. Landing in front over the third last, he kept up the revs and refused to yield: he survived a stumble on landing at the final fence and ran most honestly to the line to post a smart two and a half lengths success from The Irish Avatar (sold for £200,000 to join Willie Mullins). The notion on the day of an upper-class effort was subsequently backed up, as three horses in behind all managed to win their own four-year-old maidens in the following weeks. Unlike the majority of UK based trainers, Olly Murphy took the trouble to travel over on some Sundays to Ireland to view the point action with his dad Aiden, and they were quick off the draw to secure this budding prospect via a private deal. In general, progeny of Harzand prefer soft/heavy: with a win on a sound surface already bagged, Ballycommon Boy could be versatile on the going front. He has the ability to quicken and the hunger to please. One would expect him to elevate to 140-150 class as a hurdler and chaser and he may bag a Graded race as a novice hurdler, time may solve the issue of his optimum distance, he could easily win at both two and three miles."**

POINTS TO NOTE:
Probable Best Distance - 2m – 2m 4f
Preferred Going - Good/Soft
Connection's Comments: "He's a lovely horse that has always done everything very nicely and I think that he will win a bumper." Tom KEATING at Dromahane (6/4/25)

GOING:	R	W	P	TRACK	R	W	P
Good/Yielding	1	1	0	Left-Handed	1	1	0

TRIP:	R	W	P	JOCKEY:	R	W	P
3m	1	1	0	A.Feeney	1	1	0

BIG TICKET

4 b g Soldier of Fortune (IRE) – Twenty Eight Guns (Black Sam Bellamy (IRE))
OWNER: Mr R.TREDWIN
TRAINER: Nigel & Willy TWISTON-DAVIES. Naunton, Gloucestershire.
CAREER FORM FIGURES: 1
CAREER WIN: 2025: May STOWLIN Good/Yielding PTP 3m

Nigel Twiston-Davies has been a huge supporter of Irish pointing over the years – Grade 1 winners Blaklion, Fundamentalist, Imperial Commander and Potters Charm all began their careers down that route. Along with his son Willy, the Naunton based operation have been busy acquiring fresh talent from the same source with Hot To Go (£165,000), Leader Crik (£165,000), Shabalko D'Herm (£140,000), Shotgun Rider (£155,000) and Un Sens A La Vie (£180,000) added to the Grange Hill Farm team. Perhaps the jewel in the crown though will be the former Jonathan Fogarty trained four year old Big Ticket, who was purchased for £155,000 in May.

Declan Phelan writes: **"Chunky bay gelding with a white star on his forehead: second produce of the five-times winning mare, Twenty Eight Guns (120 rated at her peak). Turned out by Jonathan Fogarty for a competitive maiden at Stowlin in early May. Took closer order from halfway, managing to jump to the front at the second last and, in a matter of strides, sealed the deal, powering clear for a sixteen lengths winning verdict. Given seven horses were in close contact at the third last, the manner in which he spreadeagled the field at the death was commendable and noteworthy. A bid of £155,000 at Doncaster May Sales assisted a move to Nigel & Willy Twiston-Davies. The animal enjoyed the sound underfoot conditions at the Galway venue and the owner of a nice blend of speed and stamina, he ought to make his presence felt as a smart middle distance novice hurdler during the coming season and he may be competitive in Graded events. His slick jumping suggests, he will have plenty to offer as a novice chaser at a later date."**

There were two divisions of the four year old maiden and the Twiston-Davies's are now training both winners – the Simon Munir and Isaac Souede owned Masked Man won the second division and he, too, has arrived in Gloucestershire. Seven years earlier, dual Cheltenham Festival winner Monkfish won the same event before establishing himself as a Grade 1 performer for the Ricci's and Willie Mullins. Can lightning strike twice?

POINTS TO NOTE:

Probable Best Distance	-	2m 4f
Preferred Going	-	Good/Soft

GOING:	R	W	P	TRACK	R	W	P
Good/Yielding	1	1	0	Right	1	1	0

TRIP:	R	W	P	JOCKEY:	R	W	P
3m	1	1	0	B.Stone	1	1	0

BILL JOYCE (IRE)

6 b g Mahler – Bettys Delight (IRE) (Flemensfirth (USA))
OWNER: DAN WALKER
TRAINER: JONJO & A.J.O'NEILL. Temple Guiting, Gloucestershire.
CAREER FORM FIGURES: 1 – 110 – 1133F0
CAREER WINS: 2023: Feb LISRONAGH Yielding PTP 3m: 2024: Jan WARWICK Soft NHF 2m; Feb EXETER Heavy NHF 2m; Nov CARLISLE Good/Soft NH 2m 4f; Dec SANDOWN Soft Grade 2 NH 2m 4f

Jonjo O'Neill, along with his son A.J. who shares the licence, is a trainer to be feared when it comes to the staying handicap chases at the Cheltenham Festival, especially when choosing to run his novices. Wichita Lineman (2009) and Holywell (2014) both won the Ultima Handicap Chase during their first season over fences, while Monbeg Genius had the misfortune to bump into Corach Rambler and Fastorslow in the 2023 version. Similarly, Johnnywho was denied by a neck in the Kim Muir last spring on only his fifth outing over the larger obstacles.

Jackdaws Castle inmate Bill Joyce looks a prime candidate to do something similar next spring having developed into a high-class novice hurdler last winter. A point-to-point winner who cost £225,000, he won bumpers at Warwick and Exeter during his first season under Rules before scoring twice over timber during the 2024/2025 campaign. Following in the hoofprints of the aforementioned Johnnywho, he broke his duck over hurdles at the first time of asking at Carlisle in November readily seeing off seven opponents by upwards of three and a half lengths. Elevated in class, the Mahler gelding produced a smart effort to beat Quebecois by five lengths in the Grade 2 Winter Novices' Hurdle at Sandown's Tingle Creek meeting in early December. The O'Neill trained runner handled the surface better than most ploughing through the testing conditions. An excellent third in the Grade 1 Challow Novices' Hurdle at Newbury three weeks later, he couldn't match The New Lion's finishing kick, but it was still a career best performance. While Bill Joyce failed to recapture that level of form during the second half of the season, Jonjo O'Neill jnr feels he would have gone close on his handicap debut at Aintree's Grand National meeting when falling six out (first down the backstraight on the final circuit).

Officially rated 136, Bill Joyce ran in four of the same races which Johnnywho (rated 138) contested as a novice hurdler. Therefore it won't be a surprise if the six year old follows a similar path over fences, culminating in a trip to Prestbury Park in March.

POINTS TO NOTE:
Probable Best Distance - 3 miles +
Preferred Going - Soft
Connection's Comments: "Bill Joyce is a lovely big horse and we always thought he'd go well for an obstacle. He is a chaser in the making, so anything he does now is just a bonus." A.J.O'NEILL at Sandown (6/12/25)

GOING:	R	W	P	TRACK	R	W	P
Heavy	1	1	0	Left-Handed	6	2	0
Soft	4	2	0	Right	4	3	0

Good/Soft	2	1	0	Galloping	3	1	0
Yielding	2	1	0	Stiff/Undul.	4	2	0
Good	1	0	0	Tight	1	0	0
				Tight/Undul.	1	1	0

TRIP:	R	W	P	JOCKEY:	R	W	P
2m	3	2	0	J.J.O'Neill jr	7	3	0
2m 4f	4	2	0	A.J.O'Neill	1	1	0
2m 7f	1	0	0	R.McLernon	1	0	0
3m	2	1	0	T.P.Roche	1	1	0

BLOFELD (IRE)

6 ch g Diamond Boy (FR) – Sorcillera (Anzillero (GER))
OWNER: Miss MARIA D MYCO
TRAINER: Rebecca MENZIES. Sedgefield, County Durham.
CAREER FORM FIGURES: 1
CAREER WIN: 2025: Feb AYR Heavy NHF 2m

Northern jump racing lost one of its stalwarts last Autumn when news broke that former trainer John Wade had passed away at the age of 80. Based in the North East, Wade was a self-made man who developed his own skip hire, waste recycling, earthworks and waste disposal businesses. The John Wade Group acquired a Newton Aycliffe quarry in the 1970s and operated the site under 2023. In addition, Wade trained more 200 winners until retiring in 2016. He became landlord of Howe Hills Stables near Sedgefield racecourse with Rebecca Menzies taking over the reins.

Menzies, who was assistant trainer to the late Ferdy Murphy, has developed into one of the north's leading dual purpose handlers in recent times with her seasonal tallies over jumps over the last four years registering 31, 40, 32 and 36 winners.

Arguably the best prospect currently residing at her County Durham base is the once raced six year old Blofeld. Owned by Wade's long standing assistant Maria Myco, he is a big strapping gelding by Diamond Boy measuring over 17hh who is set to go novice hurdling this winter. A €12,000 foal, promising conditional William Maggs steered him to an emphatic victory on his debut in a five runner bumper at Ayr in February. Encountering testing conditions, he overcame his inexperience to lead inside the final quarter of a mile before powering clear to score by seven and a half lengths. From the family of Irish National winner Commanche Court, he looked a relentless galloper devouring the bottomless ground in the process – he covered two of the last three furlongs in 12.99 and 13.72 seconds. The runner-up Triple Crown Ted is well thought of and he was put firmly in his place. Due to contest the Grade 2 championship bumper at Aintree in early April under Brian Hughes, the lively ground ruled him out. The triple champion jockey rode him in a gallop on the all-weather at Newcastle beforehand.

Having contacted Blofeld's trainer in early September, he has reportedly thrived during the summer and will reappear in a middle distance maiden/novice hurdle before tackling something like The French Furze Novices' Hurdle at Newcastle (29th November). Provided he stays healthy, he could be one of the best horses Menzies has handled thus far.

NB. Rebecca also issued a positive bulletin regarding former winning Irish pointer **KLONDIKE**. A ready winner at Cragmore (Yielding/Soft) in late January when trained by Donnchadh Doyle, the Bathyrhon gelding was bought privately on behalf of Caspian Racing Limited and the five year old is one to keep an eye on.

POINTS TO NOTE:

Probable Best Distance	-	**2m 4f +**
Preferred Going	-	**Soft**

GOING:	**R**	**W**	**P**	**TRACK**	**R**	**W**	**P**
Heavy	**1**	**1**	**0**	**Left-Handed**	**1**	**1**	**0**
				Galloping	**1**	**1**	**0**

TRIP:	**R**	**W**	**P**	**JOCKEY:**	**R**	**W**	**P**
2m	**1**	**1**	**0**	**W.Maggs**	**1**	**1**	**0**

BOSSMAN JACK

5 b g Jack Hobbs – Lindeman (IRE) (Presenting)
OWNER: M.W.LAKE & Exors of the Late N.W.LAKE
TRAINER: Dan SKELTON. Shelfield Green, Alcester, Warwickshire.
CAREER FORM FIGURES: 1
CAREER WIN: 2025: Jan WINCANTON Good/Soft NHF 1m 7f

Runner-up in the trainers' championship for a second consecutive year, it is only a matter of time before Dan Skelton goes one better. Paul Nicholls' former assistant enjoyed another superb campaign with his 179 domestic winners, including three at the highest level, accumulating total prize-money of £3,374,474. Skelton led the title by £68,483 before racing on the final day until Willie Mullins sent out three winners, including Graded successes for Gaelic Warrior and Il Etait Temps, plus the Closutton outfit were responsible for the second, third, fourth and fifth in the Bet365 Gold Cup, at Sandown Park and retained his crown.

Team Skelton are blessed with a tremendous team of youngsters for the 2025/2026 season, which has been swelled during the spring/summer with a huge intake of new recruits. The stable sent out 26 bumper winners from 98 runners last term, including the well bred Bossman Jack who created a favourable impression on his sole start.

Bred by Richard & Lizzie Kelvin-Hughes, he is a half-brother to the dual Grade 2 winner and 155 rated chaser Gidleigh Park and was bought for £50,000 as a three year old store at the Goffs UK Spring Sale. Making his debut in a twelve runner bumper at Wincanton in mid January, the Jack Hobbs gelding was confidently ridden by Fergus Gillard. Anchored in rear, he made smooth headway leaving the backstraight before taking charge approaching the final quarter of a mile. Pushed out to readily see off the challenge of the well regarded Necronaut (fourth since), the third and sixth (three times) have scored subsequently. The *Race Iq* data highlights the fact Bossman Jack covered two of the last three furlongs in 12.93 and 12.77 seconds. Given time since, he is quick enough for two miles and looks Graded material.

POINTS TO NOTE:

Probable Best Distance	-	**2m – 2m 4f**
Preferred Going	-	**Good/Soft**

GOING:	**R**	**W**	**P**	**TRACK**	**R**	**W**	**P**
Good/Soft	**1**	**1**	**0**	**Right**	**1**	**1**	**0**
				Galloping	**1**	**1**	**0**

TRIP:	**R**	**W**	**P**	**JOCKEY:**	**R**	**W**	**P**
1m 7f	**1**	**1**	**0**	**F.Gillard**	**1**	**1**	**0**

CLONDAW PARK (IRE)

4 b f Walk In The Park (IRE) – Zamani (IRE) (Teofilo (IRE))
OWNER: Mrs CERI FELL
TRAINER: Harry DERHAM. Boxford, Berkshire.
CAREER FORM FIGURES: 1
CAREER WIN: 2025: Feb LISRONAGH Heavy PTP 3m

Leading stallion Walk In The Park became the first horse to sire the Cheltenham Gold Cup (Inothewayurthinkin) and Grand National (Nick Rockett) winners since Cottage, a former Coolmore sire, in the 1950s. The son of Montjeu was owned by Michael Tabor and trained in France by John Hammond finishing runner-up in the Epsom Derby behind Motivator twenty years ago. Coolmore are keen to get a horse by Walk In The Park to stand as a stallion - they bought eight foals in 2022 and their first three year crop have been running over hurdles in France this year. He is also the sire of this potentially smart mare who won her point-to-point in Ireland for Mick Goff before being bought by rising star Harry Derham for £320,000 at the Cheltenham Festival Sale.

"Racy lady, bay with a white spot on her crown: related to Nichols Canyon: a €30,000 buy back at a 2024 store sale. Pitched up racing for the Mick Goff yard for one of the first mares' only four-year old maidens of the spring, held at Lisronagh in February. In a 12 runner contest, Harry Goff, son of the handler, was obviously confident this mare knew her job, as he elected to front run from the beginning and his mount was sharp in every department, including jumping. Given the desperate underfoot conditions, Clondaw Park set a steady tempo for most of the race and moving away from the third last, the remainder of the field were stacked in behind her. Young Goff, then turned the screw approaching the second last and, in the matter of 20 yards, opened up a winning advantage with the mare finding gears to put daylight between herself and the rest. Eventually scoring by eight lengths, it was a visually impressive conclusion and Harry Derham was taken by the effort, as he made a winning bid of £320,000 when purchasing her at the Cheltenham Tattersalls Sale in March. In the cold light of day, one could question the substance of the form as none of the eleven defeated mares won a point during the remainder of the spring: the style was indeed persuasive, and Clondaw Park will make waves as a hurdler given her gears: achieving Grade 3 status (130/135) should be within her range as a novice hurdler, she may require a rate of progression to climb to the higher echelons of the sport. She is likely to be versatile in terms of trip, more than capable of winning over two miles. The poser of whether she must dominate a race from the front, remains unresolved," reports expert Declan Phelan.

Clondaw Park has the option of contesting mares' bumpers or going straight over hurdles. Either way, she looks a terrific prospect for a stable who endured a tough winter - Derham's gallop was flooded after 74mm of rain fell in less than 40 hours thanks to Storm Bert towards the end of November. Despite that, by the end of the season, the yard had enjoyed a personal best campaign with 57 winners at a strike-rate of 21%.

POINTS TO NOTE:
Probable Best Distance - 2m - 2m 4f
Preferred Going - Soft
Connection's Comments: "It was a flick of a coin whether I was going to run her or not. She is a very, very good mare and was foot perfect today. She has a very good pedigree, so she'll be top drawer wherever she goes." Mick GOFF at Lisronagh (23/3/25)

GOING:	R	W	P	TRACK	R	W	P
Heavy	1	1	0	Left-Handed	1	1	0

TRIP:	R	W	P	JOCKEY:	R	W	P
3m	1	1	0	H.P.Goff	1	1	0

DERRYHASSEN PADDY (IRE)

6 b g Arctic Cosmos (USA) – Kerrie Girl (IRE) (Golan (IRE))
OWNER: MORRISON-BELL & RUSSELL
TRAINER: LUCINDA RUSSELL & MICHAEL SCUDAMORE. Kinross, Perthshire.
CAREER FORM FIGURES: 11 - 113
CAREER WIN: 2023: TATTERSALLS FARM Heavy PTP 3m: 2024: Feb AYR Heavy NHF 2m; Nov UTTOXETER Soft MH 2m 4f: Jan WINDSOR Soft NH 3m

Lucinda Russell, with the assistance of her partner Peter Scudamore, has won the Grand National twice, trained three Grade 1 winners and four Cheltenham Festival winners feature on her glittering CV. Ahoy Senor and Corach Rambler developed into top flight staying chasers and, in all likelihood, the lightly raced Derryhassen Paddy will reach a similar level over fences. Featured in Declan Phelan's *Irish Pointers* last year, he is rated 143 over hurdles winning twice and finishing a gallant third in the Grade 1 Albert Bartlett Novices' Hurdle at the Cheltenham Festival.

A point winner for Ian Donoghue, brother of jockey Keith, in Ireland in December 2023, the six year old wasn't hard pressed to follow up in a bumper at Ayr a couple of months later on his first run for his new connections. Switched to hurdles last winter, the Arctic Cosmos gelding stayed on stoutly to defeat Farland by a length and a half at Uttoxeter - the Scottish raider hit the line strongly covering two of the last three furlongs in 13.18 and 13.87 seconds, according to *Race Iq*. Back in action 54 days later, he outmuscled the Listed winning mare Honky Tonk Highway in a driving finish at Windsor's Winter Million Festival in January, relishing the step up to three miles in the process. Craig Nichol's mount prevailed by a nose with eight and a half lengths back to the 129 rated third. Drying ground ruled Derryhassen Paddy out of a Grade 2 staying novices' hurdle at Haydock the following month. Given his lack of experience, he ran a cracker at the Festival in March only seven lengths behind Jasmin De Vaux. Having been bought by new owners beforehand, Derek Fox partnered him for the first time in public and he was in the firing line throughout. Headed before the last, he stayed on to grab a well deserved bronze medal. Peter Scudamore remarked afterwards: **"He's a horse we think a lot of and I wish he'd been able to run at Haydock last month. He's more than a tough horse, he's got a good level of ability."**

Put away afterwards to be prepared for his chasing career, he is an outstanding prospect who will hopefully develop into a leading contender for the Brown Advisory Novices' Chase at the Cheltenham Festival.

POINTS TO NOTE:
Probable Best Distance - 3 miles
Preferred Going - Soft
Connection's Comments: "I've always thought he was phenomenal. With the stride he has, they can hardly live with him. He's really a chaser and he needs soft ground. We'll look after him because it's all about chasing next year." Lucinda RUSSELL at Windsor (17/1/25)

GOING:	R	W	P	TRACK	R	W	P
Heavy	2	2	0	Left Handed	3	2	1
Soft	2	2	0	Right	1	1	0
Good/Soft	1	0	1	Figure of 8	1	1	0
				Galloping	1	1	0
				Stiff/Undul.	1	0	1
				Tight	1	1	0
				Tight/Undul.	1	1	0

TRIP:	R	W	P	JOCKEY:	R	W	P
2m	1	1	0	D.R.Fox	1	0	1
2m 4f	1	1	0	P.Wadge	1	1	0
3m	3	2	1	C.Nichol	2	2	0
				D.Lavery	1	1	0

DOCTOR DU MESNIL (FR)

5 b g Doctor Dino (FR) – Saint Grace (FR) (Saint Des Saints (FR))
OWNER: OVER THE STICKS SYNDICATE
TRAINER: Willie MULLINS. Closutton, Co.Carlow.
CAREER FORM FIGURES: 1
CAREER WIN: 2025: Apr CORK Yielding NHF 2m 3f

Jody Townend was crowned champion Lady jockey in Ireland for a fifth time last season. Brother of Paul, who became champion National Hunt jockey in Ireland for a seventh time in 2024/2025, the 28 year old formed a formidable alliance with the leading bumper horse Bambino Fever winning Grade 1 events at the Cheltenham and Punchestown Festivals. The unbeaten mare is set to play a significant role in the top novice hurdles this winter.

Townend also partnered the potentially high-class Doctor Du Mesnil to victory on his debut in a bumper at Cork on Easter Sunday. On an afternoon when Willie Mullins sent out six winners and, twelve months earlier, subsequent *Sky Bet* Supreme Novices' Hurdle winner Kopek Des Bordes made a winning start to his career, the five year old produced a striking display putting thirteen rivals to the sword in the two miles three event. Well bought at €55,000 and from the family of Grand National Trial winning chaser Lord Du Mesnil, he was sent off 11/8 favourite. Positioned in midfield, Townend's mount moved stealthily into contention rounding the hometurn before setting sail for home approaching the two marker. Powering clear, the Doctor Dino gelding won easily by eleven lengths from Thedeviluno (runner-up again since). Doctor Du Mesnil hit a topspeed of 35.04mph and covered the third and second last furlongs in 12.92 and 12.78 seconds, according to *Race Iq*.

While stamina isn't an issue, Doctor Du Mesnil is likely to begin his hurdles career over two miles and should have no trouble winning his maiden hurdle. Graded events beckon and the five year old looks Turners Novices' Hurdle material.

POINTS TO NOTE:
Probable Best Distance - 2m - 2m 4f
Preferred Going - Good/Soft
Connection's Comments: "He's going to be a good horse. He's so relaxed. You can ride him any way you want. He's actually even a different horse on grass compared to at home. He picked up, in two strides I had them covered. It's a long way up the straight and I knew I had them covered whenever I wanted. If he can get off the ground at all over a jump, he'll be a very good horse. He's a big chaser in the making. I liked the way he quickened up." Jody TOWNEND at Cork (20/4/25)

GOING:	R	W	P	TRACK	R	W	P
Yielding	1	1	0	Right	1	1	0
				Galloping	1	1	0

TRIP:	R	W	P	JOCKEY:	R	W	P
2m 3f	1	1	0	J.Townend	1	1	0

DUTCH CORNER (IRE)

4 ch g Getaway (GER) – Lightning Breeze (IRE) (Saddlers' Hall (IRE))
OWNER: CROWE BROTHERS
TRAINER: Dan SKELTON. Shelfield Green, Alcester, Warwickshire.
CAREER FORM FIGURES: 3

A half-brother to four times Grade 1 and dual Cheltenham Festival winner Yorkhill, Dutch Corner is bred to be a useful performer. Placed in his only bumper at the Skelton's local track Warwick in the spring, he is expected to leave that form behind once plying his trade over obstacles this campaign.

A €50,000 foal, the four year old was sent off 3/1 favourite for a 'newcomers' event at the Midlands track towards the end of March. Ridden with the utmost confidence by Harry Skelton, the Getaway gelding tanked through the contest and, having moved up ominously behind the leaders, looked set to score at the first time of asking. However, his passage in the homestraight wasn't trouble free before staying on to fill third position. Three lengths behind Warren Greatrex's winner Liam Mera Kai, the second, fourth, fifth and seventh have all run creditably in defeat since. According to *Race Iq*, Dutch Corner hit the highest speed of all twelve runners, recording 38.04mph during the penultimate furlong – the four year old covered that furlong in 11.84 seconds, which is the fastest of any runner in the whole field.

Team Skelton were no doubt disappointed that Dutch Corner didn't make a winning start but it won't be long before he redresses the balance. One for the future, he can develop into a smart two mile novice hurdler.

POINTS TO NOTE:
Probable Best Distance - 2m – 2m 4f
Preferred Going - Good/Soft

GOING:	R	W	P	TRACK	R	W	P
Good	1	0	1	Left Handed	1	0	1
				Tight/Undul.	1	0	1

TRIP:	R	W	P	JOCKEY:	R	W	P
2m	1	0	1	H.Skelton	1	0	1

EL CAIROS (FR)

5 ch g No Risk At All (FR) – Linda Queen (FR) (Linda's Lad)
OWNER: DAVID MAXWELL
TRAINER: GARY & JOSH MOORE. Lower Beeding, Sussex.
CAREER FORM FIGURES: 1 - 152
CAREER WINS: 2024: Apr CURRAGHMORE Yielding PTP 3m; Nov NEWBURY Good NHF 2m

It was announced in mid September that dual amateur champion jockey David Maxwell has retired from the saddle at the age of 47 on medical advice. He rode 75 winners in the UK during his career and plans to sell his string of 16 horses at a sale in Cheltenham on the 24th October. These include the potential top notch novice hurdler El Cairos who had some smart form in bumpers last season.

A five year old by No Risk At All, he won an Irish point in April 2024 before being bought by Maxwell for €200,000 at the Punchestown Festival Sale the following month and dispatched to Gary and Josh Moore. A half-brother to eight times winning staying chaser Wasdell Dundalk, he displayed an explosive turn of foot to win a bumper at Newbury on his Rules debut in November. Leading over two furlongs out, he quickened clear to score by six and a half lengths (third and fifth have won since). The statistics courtesy of *Race Iq* suggest it was a taking display – he hit a top speed of 37.84mph and covered two of the last three furlongs in 12.15 and 12.03 seconds. Absent for 125 days, he reportedly worked very well under Jamie Moore in a racecourse gallop at Lingfield prior to taking his chance in the Cheltenham Festival bumper. Five lengths fifth at Prestbury Park, he was unlucky not to finish closer having met trouble in running in the homestraight. Withdrawn from the Grade 2 championship event at Aintree in April owing to the quickening underfoot conditions, his misfortune continued at the Punchestown Festival. Taking on eleven rivals in a strongly contested event, David Maxwell's mount travelled strongly before hitting the front over a furlong out. However, he soon hung to his left and ended up on the stands rail gifting the race to Alan King's Baron Noir. Beaten a length and a half, he still managed to finish six lengths clear of the third.

Regardless of who purchases the five year old at the pending sale towards the end of October, El Cairos is a tremendous prospect for both the short and long-term. He possesses a sharp turn of foot and will benefit from the assistance of a professional jockey. Fingers crossed he is lining up in the *Sky Bet* Supreme Novices' Hurdle next spring.

POINTS TO NOTE:
Probable Best Distance - 2 miles
Preferred Going - Good/Soft
Connection's Comments: "El Cairos was impressive and he's a nice horse. He's always shown that at home, but the proof is in the pudding here today and it was a rare turn of foot." Gary MOORE at Newbury (7/11/24)

GOING:	R	W	P
Yielding	2	1	1
Good/Soft	1	0	0
Good	1	1	0

TRACK	R	W	P
Left-Handed	2	1	0
Right	2	1	1
Galloping	2	1	1
Stiff/Undul.	1	0	0

TRIP:	R	W	P
2m	3	1	1
3m	1	1	0

JOCKEY:	R	W	P
D.Maxwell	3	1	1
S.Staples	1	1	0

EL CLAVEL

5 b g Spanish Moon (USA) – Lucky Flower (FR) (Soldier of Fortune (IRE))
OWNER: MISOL RACING & ECURIE DE ROEBECK
TRAINER: NOEL GEORGE & AMANDA ZETTERHOLM.
CAREER FORM FIGURES: 1 – 2122 - 1
CAREER WINS: 2024: Apr COMPIEGNE Heavy Hdle 2m 2f; Nov AUTEUIL Heavy Hdle 2m 2f: 2025: May AUTEUIL Very Soft Grade 1 Hdle 3m 1f

The exciting El Clavel provided Noel George with his first Grade 1 winner in France when capturing the Grande Course de Haies d'Auteuil - the French Champion Hurdle - at Auteuil in May. It was a second victory in the three miles one event for triple champion jockey James Reveley, ten years after Un Temps Pour Tout's success for David Pipe. Bought as a yearling for €38,000, the five year old has won three of his six races over hurdles and his connections believe he will make an even better chaser. Following the impact stablemate Il Est Francais has made in the UK during the last couple of seasons, the Spanish Moon gelding is one to look forward to.

A thirteen lengths winner at Auteuil in November, he returned in the spring finishing runner-up twice in Listed and Grade 2 events at the same track. Beaten eight lengths by Losange Bleu on the latter occasion in April over two miles five, Dominique Bressou's charge made all and El Clavel, who was ridden by Baptiste Le Clerc, could only stay on at the one pace. However, it was a different story the following month in the Grande Course de Haies. Reunited with Reveley and tackling three miles plus for the first time, he sat in behind his old rival before being asked for his effort in the homestraight. Taken wide, he led marginally at the last and, with the assistance of the stands rail, the Noel George and Amanda Zetterholm trained runner beat Losange Bleu by a length and a quarter with the pair wide apart across the track. It was eight lengths back to the third. A big strong horse, El Clavel still looked green and can only improve. **"He's just a very good horse. James and I have always said that, if we have a Cheltenham Gold Cup winner around the place, it will be him,"** remarked Noel George afterwards.

The plan is for El Clavel to have another run in France during the Autumn before embarking on a novice chase career in the UK. The Grade 1 Kauto Star Novices' Chase at Kempton on Boxing Day, which Il Est Francais won in such devastating fashion a couple of years ago, is a possibility followed by the Brown Advisory Novices' Chase in the spring. His British debut is eagerly anticipated.

POINTS TO NOTE:
Probable Best Distance - 3 miles +
Preferred Going - Soft
Reveley's Remarks: "The plan is for him to have another run over hurdles in France during the Autumn before going over fences in the UK. I think he will make an even better chaser and he could be anything."

GOING:	R	W	P	TRACK	R	W	P
Heavy	4	2	2	Left-Handed	6	3	3
Very Soft	2	1	1	Galloping	6	3	3

TRIP:	R	W	P	JOCKEY:	R	W	P
2m 2f	3	2	1	J.Reveley	5	3	2
2m 5f	2	0	2	B.Le Clerc	1	0	1
3m 1f	1	1	0				

GRANGECLARE PARK (IRE)

4 b g Walk In The Park (IRE) – Burkes Lady (IRE) (Westerner)
OWNER: KTDA Racing
TRAINER: Gordon ELLIOTT. Cullentra, Longwood, Co.Meath.
CAREER FORM FIGURES: 1
CAREER WIN: 2025: Apr CURRAGHMORE Soft PTP 3m

Envoi Allen and Samcro were dual Cheltenham Festival winners for Gordon Elliott winning 8 Grade 1 races between them during their time at Cullentra. The pair began their careers by winning a point-to-point for Colin Bowe before being sold for £400,000 and £335,000 respectively. The triple Grand National winning trainer returned to the same source to purchase privately the potentially top-class Grangeclare Park, who made a lasting impression 'between the flags' at Curraghmore on Easter Sunday.

Declan Phelan believes: **"One of the star turns out of the 2025 four-year-old spring pointing contingent. Tall, rangy elegant bay, home bred by Joey Logan, a sibling to two modest track winners. Logan had prepped the horse and Colin Bowe was entrusted to finish off the job: with Bowe for under three months, he travelled to Curraghmore at Easter for his debut in a competitive maiden. Patiently ridden by Barry O'Neill, who was keen to educate the art of competitive racing to his mount, in a true run affair, the combination knifed**

through the field during the closing mile. Towering over most of his rivals, he swept to the front after the second last and for minimum force readily drew clear to win by 20 lengths: a classy polished display from a professional equine athlete. By all accounts, he changed hands privately for a sum in the £400,000-500,000 ballpark and has joined Gordon Elliott under the ownership of the UK based KDTA partnership. He is the full package as a racing unit: he has the size, the engine and a lovely relaxed racing style: 2m 4f and upwards will be his eventual playground as a hurdler/chaser and he has that instant appearance of Graded material. In the past nine years, Irish trained horses have won all the Cheltenham Festival bumpers, with six victors for Closutton, one for John Kiely and two for Gordon Elliott. When Jamie Codd was at the steering wheel of the Elliott bumper runners, he bestowed a big advantage, Codd in my view the best bumper jockey of all time. Since Jamie has retired, the Elliott results in the premier bumpers have not been as positive. The Elliott barn has stocked up heavily once again from the pointing academy and will likely make a play at the 2026 Festival bumper. If chosen to exclusively stick to bumpers this coming winter, I fancy Grangeclare Park will be the number one seed for the stable and he has the talent to make a serious impact come Cheltenham in March."

Gordon Elliott won the Cheltenham Festival bumper with Fayonagh (2017) and the aforementioned Envoi Allen (2019), and Grangeclare Park's new owners KTDA Racing went close with Romeo Coolio in 2024. The partnership may have an outstanding candidate for the 2026 renewal.

POINTS TO NOTE:

Probable Best Distance	**-**	**2 miles**
Preferred Going	**-**	**Soft**

GOING:	**R**	**W**	**P**	**TRACK**	**R**	**W**	**P**
Soft	**1**	**1**	**0**	**Right**	**1**	**1**	**0**

TRIP:	**R**	**W**	**P**	**JOCKEY:**	**R**	**W**	**P**
3m	**1**	**1**	**0**	**B.O'Neill**	**1**	**1**	**0**

HERON IN THE PARK (IRE)

5 b m Walk In The Park (IRE) – Night Heron (IRE) (St Jovite (USA))
OWNER: The JEKYLL
TRAINER: Tom GEORGE. Stroud, Gloucestershire.
CAREER FORM FIGURES: 11
CAREER WINS: 2024: Dec BORRIS HOUSE Good PTP 3m: 2025: Mar NEWBURY Soft NHF 2m

Tom George trained ten Grade 1 winners in Britain and Ireland between 2002 and 2019. It has been slim pickings for his Stroud based operation during the last few years though with seasonal tallies of 11, 6 and 6. However, owner Damian Tiernan paid £280,000 for the Donnchadh Doyle trained point winner Heron In The Park in December and she looked a fine prospect when defeating five rivals in a mares' bumper at Newbury last spring on her first start for George. She looks a high-class mare in the making with aspirations of going close in the Grade 2 Dawn Run Mares' Novices' Hurdle in March.

"Rangy and muscular bay lady: originally sold through the ring as a €40,000 foal, the Monbeg outfit purchased her as a three-year-old for €50,000: sibling to three track winners, including the 2022 *Betfair* Hurdle winner, Glory And Fortune. Debuted at Borris House in December, encountering eight opponents. Initially dropped out the back for nearly two miles, she advanced forward during the final circuit, pressing the leaders three out, and then taking control off the home bend as they faced the second last. She drew away to score unbothered by nearly ten lengths. The performance enhanced her currency and a few weeks later she proved to be the sales topper at the Tattersalls Cheltenham December auction: a bid of £280,000 on behalf of owner Damian Tiernan decisive. Given that Tom George has almost dropped off the map of trainers in recent years, six winners recorded in 23/24 & 24/25, the fact he received the mare to train was a mild surprise. The new handler pitched up the mare for a decent mares' bumper at Newbury (Soft) on the first day of March and the booking of Harry Cobden was almost a statement of intent. Cobden is not found wanting if he has the material underneath him: he anchored the mare in last place as the field entered the home straight, and then steadily the partnership eased their way to the front and in the end Heron In The Park won without Cobden moving a muscle: a visually appealing triumph, and a ride likely to fill the mare with confidence: a fine athlete, one with a high cruising speed and apparently lots of scope: she has impressed over two and three miles and one would imagine is the stable star turn at George's barn. One could justify the spend on her compared to other winning pointers. Anything other than at least a Listed/Graded mares' novice hurdle this winter will represent failure: very classy and one liable to produce her best in true run races over galloping tracks. Given she functions to real effect with hold up tactics, probably 2m 4f will witness her in a better light than two miles as a hurdler," believes Declan Phelan.

The £45,000 Listed mares' novice hurdle at Newbury's Winter Festival (29th November) looks an ideal first half of the season target before Heron In The Park's sights are raised in the New Year.

POINTS TO NOTE:
Probable Best Distance - 2m - 2m 4f
Preferred Going - Good/Soft
Connection's Comments: "She did everything we hoped for and expected really. She took a while to settle in when she arrived after winning her point-to-point in Ireland, and we've just taken it steady and have taken her away a couple of times to work and she has proved everything we thought. I would like to believe she is going to be a top-class hurdler and then chaser beyond that." Tom GEORGE speaking in March 2025

GOING:	R	W	P	TRACK	R	W	P
Soft	1	1	0	Left-Handed	2	2	0
Good	1	1	0	Galloping	1	1	0

TRIP:	R	W	P	JOCKEY:	R	W	P
2m	1	1	0	H.Cobden	1	1	0
3m	1	1	0	Rob James	1	1	0

IN MY TEENS (IRE)

3 b f Camelot – Jer's Girl (IRE) (Jeremy (USA))
OWNER: J.P.McMANUS
TRAINER: Gavin CROMWELL. Balrath, Co.Meath.
CAREER FLAT FORM FIGURES: 212
CAREER WIN: 2025: June DOWN ROYAL Good Mdn 1m 2f

Cheltenham Gold Cup winning trainer Gavin Cromwell's first Grade 1 winner was Jer's Girl at the Fairyhouse Easter Festival in 2016. The daughter of Jeremy belonged to J.P.McManus and she was the first horse the 22 times champion owner sent to Cromwell. She only raced twice on the Flat before embarking on her hurdling career, which yielded four victories, two at the highest level and total prize-money of £151,415.

The thrice raced In My Teens is the second foal out of her illustrious mother and hopes are high the daughter of Camelot could achieve something similar over obstacles this winter. Fitted with a hood each time, she didn't make her debut until June when a staying on second behind Dancing Teapot in a fillies' maiden over a mile at Gowran Park. Beaten a length by Joseph O'Brien's winner (sixth in Listed company since), she reappeared less than three weeks later running out an emphatic six and a half lengths winner at Down Royal. Stepped up to ten furlongs, Gary Carroll's mount led two out before stretching away to beat the 86 rated Valencia (fourth, sixth and seventh won since). It was her jockey's first winner in the famous green and gold silks. Ironically, his father Raymond partner J.P.McManus' first ever winner. In My Teens covered the last three furlongs in 11.54, 11.91 and 12.49 seconds, according to *Race Iq*. Absent for 72 days, she returned in a ten furlongs conditions event at Roscommon in September and ran a cracker considering she raced keenly for much of the contest. Backed into 11/10 favouritism, the Cromwell filly was still on the bridle early in the homestraight. Bumped inside the final furlong, she was beaten a neck by the 88 rated Viking Invasion with the pair four and a half lengths clear of the third Vorfreude (rated 92).

Yet to race beyond a mile and a quarter on the Flat, In My Teens is bred to stay much further and, provided she learns to relax, she could be a potent force in the juvenile hurdles this term. Indeed, she could be Triumph Hurdle material. She is bred to be.

POINTS TO NOTE:
Probable Best Distance - 2 miles
Preferred Going - Good/Soft
Connection's Comments: "She did things right today and, as time goes on, she will learn more. She's nice to look forward to. Always a good sign (took a while to pull her up in Gowran and today), she hit the line well. Hopefully, there is more to come. I'll just give her a chance and she could be nice." Gavin CROMWELL at Down Royal (21/6/25)

GOING:	R	W	P
Soft	1	0	1
Good	2	1	1

TRACK	R	W	P
Right	3	1	2
Tight	1	0	1
Tight/Undul.	2	1	1

TRIP:	R	W	P
1m	1	0	1
1m 2f	2	1	1

JOCKEY:	R	W	P
Gary Carroll	3	1	2

JAGWAR (FR)

6 b g Karaktar (IRE) – Quizas Jolie (FR) (Video Rock (FR))
OWNER: J.P.McMANUS
TRAINER: OLIVER GREENALL & JOSH GUERRIERO. Malpas, Cheshire.
CAREER FORM FIGURES: 2 – 25145 - 11311
CAREER WINS: 2024: Feb CARLISLE Heavy NH 2m 3f; Oct WETHERBY Good/Soft HC 2m 3f; Nov BANGOR Soft HC 2m 4f: 2025: Jan CHELTENHAM Soft NHC 2m 4f; Mar CHELTENHAM Good/Soft Grade 3 HC 2m 4f

"Jagwar should keep getting better with time – he still looks weak almost now and has some strengthening to do yet," commented Josh Guerriero after the ex-French gelding had won the TrustATrader Plate Handicap Chase at the Cheltenham Festival in March. The giant six year old proved a revelation once switched to fences last season winning four of his five starts with his official rating escalating from 118 to 148. Featured in the *Top 40* during the 2023/2024 campaign, he has plenty more to offer and it is not beyond the realms of possibility the Karaktar gelding could develop into a Cheltenham Gold Cup contender.

Previously trained in France by Emmanuel Clayeux and runner-up on his hurdles debut at Auteuil in October 2022, he proved frustrating to follow during his first season with Olly Greenall and Josh Guerriero. Despite running well at Aintree on his British debut and recording a workmanlike win at Carlisle, he failed to settle over the smaller obstacles racing too keenly.

Last season was a different story though winning handicap chases at Wetherby and Bangor, including a three lengths victory from the subsequent Grade 2 runner-up Lowry's Bar at the latter off a mark of 123. Connections felt Jagwar was below par when losing his unbeaten record over fences in a novices' handicap chase at Uttoxeter in December behind Grade 2 winner Jingko Blue. However, he regained the winning thread in a novices' handicap chase at Cheltenham's Trials meeting readily defeating stablemate Billytherealbigred by two and a half lengths off 132. The Bet365 Gold Cup winner Resplendent Glory was nearly fifteen lengths behind in fourth. Seven weeks later, the J.P.McManus owned runner provided Greenall & Guerriero with their second Cheltenham Festival winner since holding a joint licence when accounting for nineteen rivals in a fiercely competitive handicap on the third day. Sent off 3/1 favourite and racing off a mark of 139, he didn't jump with the same fluency compared to his previous win but still proved too good. Overcoming a mistake at the last, he powered up the hill to win by around three lengths.

Reported to have thrived physically during the summer at Martinstown Stud in Ireland, he is bred to stay further being a half-brother to a 3m 5f winner. Considered superior to 152 rated Festival winning stablemate Iroko, who was beaten four lengths by Gold Cup winner Inothewayurthinkin in a Grade 1 novice chase at Aintree last year, he may emerge as a threat to the best staying chasers this winter. The Paddy Power Gold Cup at Cheltenham (15th November) may be his first target but don't be surprised if Jagwar becomes the first northern trained winner of the Cheltenham Gold Cup since Jodami in 1993. This time last year, the 2025 Gold Cup winner had won a Festival handicap as a novice and wasn't the most fluent of jumpers either.

POINTS TO NOTE:

Probable Best Distance	-	**3 miles +**
Preferred Going	-	**Good/Soft**

Connection's Comments: "Jonjo (O'Neill jnr) said he had plenty of horse underneath him. He made a mistake at the last, but he's won with his ears pricked. He's just a big baby. He's the biggest horse we've ever had, he measures 18hh, so he's still fairly weak and needs to muscle up behind. Once he does, I think his jumping will improve." Olly GREENALL at Cheltenham (13/3/25)

GOING:	R	W	P
Heavy	4	1	1
Soft	4	2	0
Good/Soft	3	2	1

TRACK	R	W	P
Left-Handed	10	4	2
Right	1	1	0
Galloping	3	1	1
Stiff/Undul.	3	3	0
Tight	3	1	1
Tight/Undul.	2	0	0

TRIP:	R	W	P
2m	1	0	0
2m 2f	1	0	1
2m 3f	2	2	0
2m 4f	6	3	1
2m 5f	1	0	0

JOCKEY:	R	W	P
J.J.O'Neill Jr	9	5	1
J.Reveley	1	0	1
K.Brogan	1	0	0

JET OF STARS (IRE)

4 b g Jet Away – Gilt Ridden (IRE) (Heron Island)
OWNER: FYFFE & RUSSELL
TRAINER: LUCINDA RUSSELL & MICHAEL SCUDAMORE. Kinross, Perthshire.
CAREER FORM FIGURES: 1
CAREER WIN: 2025: Feb OLDTOWN Yielding PTP 2m 4f

Three times champion jockey Brian Hughes will be riding the bulk of owner Jimmy Fyffe's burgeoning string of horses this winter. The Scottish businessman, who is a director of JF Kegs Limited and Dundee United Football Club, has invested heavily in equine talent during the last few years, including the unbeaten Irish pointer Jet of Stars. Fyffe owns him in partnership with trainer Lucinda Russell and the four year old could be the dual Grand National winning handler's next young star.

Irish point expert Declan Phelan writes: **"Tall, lengthy bay gelding with a white stripe on face: son of an unraced dam, who has bred multiple winners, including Johns Spirit, The Game Changer and the infamous Morgan (dead horse which caused Gordon Elliott all the problems). Joined Denis Murphy via the store sales for €60,000. He was targeted at the highly competitive 2m 4f maiden at Oldtown in the middle of February: a race containing a selection of touted runners, Jet Of Stars having cruised comfortably, moved up to press for the lead at the third last. In front two out, he was in control when making a final fence mistake: managing to quickly recover his momentum, he won by four lengths and was value for more. The third and fourth were to win their own maidens, giving a fair boost to the form. Judged on the display, he has natural gears and a relaxed high cruise gallop and more than a whiff of quality. The Lucinda Russell yard paid a near record transfer fee for the Scottish establishment when collecting the gelding for a bid of £230,000 at**

the Cheltenham Festival Sale in the aspiration he can develop into a flagship high-class candidate. Given how comfortable he proved over 2m 4f, you never know, he could be a Ryanair player in future years. In the short term, a campaign this coming winter over hurdles should yield a few minor wins, with the concentration on bringing him along steadily, in the hope of much higher yields as a chaser." The Oldtown point-to-point has been won by subsequent Graded winners Asterion Forlonge (2018) and Jingko Blue (2023). Brian Hughes has plenty to look forward to with Jet of Stars and Grade 2 winning novice hurdler Jet To Vegas who is set to go chasing.

POINTS TO NOTE:
Probable Best Distance - 2m 4f
Preferred Going - Good/Soft
Connection's Comments: "His homework was savage, that's why we came here to one of the best tracks in the country. I was a little nervous watching him coming over the last, but thankfully he picked up." Denis MURPHY at Oldtown (15/2/25)

GOING:	R	W	P	TRACK	R	W	P
Yielding	1	1	0	Right	1	1	0

TRIP:	R	W	P	JOCKEY:	R	W	P
2m 4f	1	1	0	J.W.Hendrick	1	1	0

JURANCON (FR)

6 b g Free Port Lux – Bamox (FR) (Coastal Path)
OWNER: BROCADE RACING
TRAINER: David PIPE. Nicholashayne, Somerset.
CAREER FORM FIGURES: 5 – 1121 - 21211
CAREER WINS: 2023: Oct PORTRUSH Soft PTP 3m; Dec CHEPSTOW Heavy NHF 2m: 2024: Mar HEREFORD Soft NHF 2m; Nov CHEPSTOW Good/Soft MH 2m: 2025: Jan NEWBURY Soft NH 2m; Mar NEWBURY Soft HH 2m

There is every possibility former point winner Jurancon will be tackling fences at some stage this season but the six year old still has unfinished business over timber and can win a major handicap hurdle before then. Officially rated 132, the Free Port Lux gelding hasn't raced beyond two miles under Rules. However, being a half-brother to Git Maker, who was placed in the Scottish National last year, he is bred to excel over further.

Successful in one of his two point-to-points for Colin Bowe in Ireland, he was acquired privately on behalf of Brocade Racing, of Native River fame, and was a dual bumper winner during the 2023/2024 campaign. Sent hurdling last Autumn, he developed into a useful novice registering three victories at Chepstow and Newbury twice. David Pipe's charge beat subsequent Grade 2 winner Tripoli Flyer by a length and a quarter at the former track in October and defied his penalty at the latter in January. Returning to the Berkshire venue for his handicap debut in early March, he looked well ahead of the assessor when brushing aside five opponents by upwards of two and a half lengths off 127. His trainer remarked: **"The further Jurancon went, the better and his formlines are strong. He's got a great attitude."** The winning time was nearly four seconds quicker than the 0-120 novices' handicap hurdle run earlier on the card.

Entered in a competitive two and a half miles handicap hurdle at Aintree's Grand National meeting, Jurancon was ruled out due to the drying ground. His connections are evidently thinking about stepping him up in distance this term. There are a whole host of options during the Autumn – the Silver Trophy or Welsh Champion Hurdle at Chepstow (11th & 12th October), and the £100,000 Greatwood Hurdle at Cheltenham (16th November). The Pond House team have won the last named event five times. Alternatively, the six year old could be aimed at the 0-140 Paddy Power Intermediate Handicap Hurdle over two miles five the previous day – fifteen years ago, another Pipe inmate Grands Crus proved a good thing off 126.

POINTS TO NOTE:
Probable Best Distance - 2m – 2m 4f
Preferred Going - Soft
Connection's Comments: "We've always thought plenty of Jurancon. He settled and travelled nicely and kept going strongly. On soft ground, two miles is fine but he'll stay further in time." Jack TUDOR at Newbury (15/1/25)

GOING:	R	W	P	TRACK	R	W	P
Heavy	1	1	0	Left-Handed	8	5	2
Soft	7	4	3	Right	2	1	1
Good/Soft	1	1	0	Galloping	4	2	2
Good	1	0	0	Stiff/Undul.	3	2	1
				Tight	1	1	0

TRIP:	R	W	P	JOCKEY:	R	W	P
2m	8	5	3	Jack Tudor	7	4	3
3m	2	1	0	G.Harney	1	1	0
				B.O'Neill	2	1	0

KAISER BALL (FR)

5 br g Nom De D'La (FR) – Voix De Montot (FR) (Voix Du Nord (FR))
OWNER: Mrs MARIE M COSTELLO
TRAINER: Willie MULLINS. Closutton, Co.Carlow.
CAREER FORM FIGURES: 1
CAREER WIN: 2025: Feb FAIRYHOUSE Soft NHF 2m

"We bought him as a foal and he's a very high-class horse," enthused amateur rider Thomas Costello having steered his mother's Kaiser Ball to an impressive debut win in a Fairyhouse bumper in February. A seven and a half lengths winner of a contest which had previously been won by subsequent Grade 1 winners Fury Road (2019) and Ferny Hollow, the five year old trained by Willie Mullins looked smart.

A €15,000 yearling, the Nom De D'La gelding is a full-brother to the aforementioned 129 rated hurdler Juby Ball and also a sibling to the *Betfair* Hurdle runner-up Fifty Ball. Patiently ridden by his inexperienced jockey (ridden 3 winners under Rules, including twice aboard the family's useful hurdler/chaser Asian Master), he made good headway on the outside before leading with quarter of a mile to travel. Pushed clear, he won unextended from the highly regarded

Eachtotheirown - his trainer Barry Connell believes the runner-up is **"a top-class horse with a big future."** The fifth, Sticktotheplan, who was beaten over 26 lengths, has won twice over hurdles since, including at Listed level, and is rated 133 (joined Olly Murphy). Kaiser Bell unseated Costello after the line with Willie Mullins commenting: **"He just ducked at a gate and the saddle slipped. Luckily horse and rider are fine. He's always shown he's a nice horse at home."**

Entered in the Grade 1 bumper at the Punchestown Festival, the son of Nom De D'La is evidently held in lofty esteem at Closutton. While the jockey situation is not ideal with bigger and better things on the horizon, he is a hugely promising young horse with aspirations of winning at Graded level and competing at the major spring Festivals.

POINTS TO NOTE:
Probable Best Distance - 2m - 2m 4f
Preferred Going - Soft
Connection's Comments: "The last day he was due to run was in Thurles. We were going out to the gallop that day and Michael O'Sullivan was beside me. He said to me 'do you know what is the only thing that can get that horse beat today?' I said, 'what is that Michael?' and he said 'yourself." Thomas COSTELLO at Fairyhouse (22/2/25)

GOING:	R	W	P	TRACK	R	W	P
Soft	1	1	0	Right	1	1	0
				Galloping	1	1	0

TRIP:	R	W	P	JOCKEY:	R	W	P
2m	1	1	0	Mr T.Costello	1	1	0

KEEP HIM COMPANY (FR)

5 b g Walzertakt (GER) – Anais Collonges (FR) (Dom Alco (FR))
OWNER: GIGGINSTOWN HOUSE STUD
TRAINER: Gordon ELLIOTT. Cullentra, Longwood, Co.Meath.
CAREER FORM FIGURES: 1
CAREER WIN: 2025: Mar KILDORRERY Soft PTP 3m

An impressive four lengths winner of a point-to-point at Kildorrery at the beginning of March, Keep Him Company hails from the famous Costello family at Fenloe House in Newmarket-on-Fergus, Co.Clare. The late Tom Costello's graduates included the triple Cheltenham Gold Cup winner Best Mate. His son John is now at the helm and he produced the Walzertakt gelding to made a sparkling debut at the Co.Cork venue – the ill-fated Festival winner Corbetts Cross won the same maiden three years earlier. Purchased by Gigginstown House Stud for £220,000 at the Cheltenham Festival Sale in March, he joins Gordon Elliott and could return to Prestbury Park next spring for the Turners Novices' Hurdle.

Declan Phelan comments: **"Medium lithe bay: lots of winners (Flat & jumps) in his continental brood. €27,000 foal from the Arqana Sale in 2020. Dam a full sister to Whitbread winner, Quentin Collonges. Housed with John Costello, and his tall son Conor was trusted to steer for his only start between the flags at Kildorrery in early March. Prominent in the first**

four from the beginning and slick and polished in the jumping department, careered away rounding the final bend and won apologising by four lengths: apparently, in a different league to his rivals, clocking the fastest time on the card. Given he won without his jockey having to exert any real pressure, and signalled an ideal blend of crisp jumping and gears, he instantly instilled confidence in the idea he had a bright future ahead for track racing and at a minimum will land Grade 2 or 3 races as a hurdler or chaser, and may make a fair fist of matters, if tested, in Grade 1s. Deserved to make decent money at the sales, with Gordon Elliott and Gigginstown House Stud combining for a winning bid of £220,000. Given his sheer class, he may function over a variety of distances and he is simply a very good horse and one to pay a healthy respect towards."

POINTS TO NOTE:
Probable Best Distance - 2m - 2m 4f
Preferred Going - Soft
Connection's Comments: "We always thought that he was a nice horse, but he hadn't been away for a schooling race." John COSTELLO at Kildorrery (1/3/25)

GOING:	R	W	P	TRACK	R	W	P
Soft	1	1	0	Right	1	1	0

TRIP:	R	W	P	JOCKEY:	R	W	P
3m	1	1	0	C.J.Costello	1	1	0

KINGBEL DU LION (FR)

5 b g Non Rien De Rien (FR) – Tazabelle Du Lion (FR) (Passing Sale (FR))
OWNER: Mrs S.RICCI
TRAINER: Venetia WILLIAMS. Kings Caple, Herefordshire.
CAREER FORM FIGURES: 73 - 1
CAREER WIN: 2025: Feb BANGOR-ON-DEE Heavy MH 2m 3f

Royale Pagaille provided Venetia Williams with her eleventh Grade 1 winner of her illustrious training career when winning the *Betfair* Chase at Haydock Park in November for a second time. It proved an even more notable milestone for the ten year old's owners, Rich and Susannah Ricci, because it was the pair's one hundredth success at the highest level. The Ricci family now have four horses in training at Aramstone in Herefordshire, including another ex-French gelding Kingbel Du Lion.

Jerome Delaunay handled the five year old in his native country running twice over hurdles and fences. A gelded son of Non Rien De Rien, he debuted in the prestigious Prix Emilius, a conditions hurdle, at Auteuil in October 2023. Weakening after the second last, he trailed in seventh around fifteen lengths behind Dazodream and Funiculi Funicula (rated 141). Absent for 149 days and switched to fences, he stayed on in third behind the mare Kroisade in a four year old chase at the same venue in March last year. Bought shortly afterwards, Kingbel Du Lion joined the Grand National winning handler and was given plenty of time to develop physically. He made his British debut 346 days later in a maiden hurdle over two miles three at Bangor in February. Partnered by Charlie Deutsch, the Ricci's new recruit made short work of his two rivals throwing in some prestigious leaps along the way. Leading after the third, he galloped on strongly drawing away after the second last to beat the 110 rated Winchmore Hill (runner-up again since) by a dozen lengths.

Allocated an opening mark of 123, he is bred to stay three miles and will switch to fences this winter. With only three runs on his CV, Kingbel Du Lion is open to significant improvement for his new connections and can rack up a sequence in novice handicap chases this term.

POINTS TO NOTE:

Probable Best Distance	-	**2m 4f - 3 miles**
Preferred Going	-	**Soft**

GOING:	**R**	**W**	**P**
Heavy	**3**	**1**	**1**

TRACK	**R**	**W**	**P**
Left-Handed	**3**	**1**	**1**
Galloping	**2**	**0**	**1**
Tight	**1**	**1**	**0**

TRIP:	**R**	**W**	**P**
2m 1f	**1**	**0**	**1**
2m 2f	**1**	**0**	**0**
2m 3f	**1**	**1**	**0**

JOCKEY:	**R**	**W**	**P**
C.Deutsch	**1**	**1**	**0**
W.Lajon	**2**	**0**	**1**

LASCAR DU MATHAN (FR)

4 b g Doctor Dino (FR) - Delice Nouba (FR) (Turgeon (USA))
OWNER: ROBCOUR
TRAINER: Gordon ELLIOTT. Cullentra, Longwood, Co.Meath.
CAREER FORM FIGURES: 11
CAREER WINS: 2024: Nov COMPIEGNE Heavy Hdle 2m 1f: 2025: Mar AUTEUIL Heavy Hdle 2m 1f

Brian Acheson and Robcour have made significant investment during the spring/summer on fresh equine talent and arguably their most exciting addition is the unbeaten French gelding Lascar Du Mathan. Twice a winner over hurdles when trained by Noel George and Amanda Zetterholm, the four year old was bought privately off David Maxwell and has joined Gordon Elliott. A chaser in the making, he is expected to compete in conditions and Graded hurdles this season before developing into a top-class horse over fences.

Bought for €100,000 as a two year old at the Arqana Autumn Sales in 2023 on behalf of Maxwell, he made his debut in a conditions hurdle for unraced horses at Compiegne in November. Partnered by James Reveley, Lascar Du Mathan was immediately dropped out in last position and given a beautiful educational ride. Still in rear with a circuit to travel, he crept into contention leaving the backstraight. Around seventh jumping the penultimate flight, he made up ground before a slight error at the last. The three times champion jockey didn't have to resort to the whip though as his mount led close home to prevail by a short neck. The runner-up won his next two starts. Off the track for four months, the Doctor Dino gelding returned to action in the Prix Ventriloque, another conditions hurdle, at Auteuil in early March with his owner in the saddle. Sharing the advantage early on with Lucky D'Olva, David Maxwell's mount took charge on the final circuit and, despite showing signs of inexperience after the second last, the four year old powered away on the run-in from some useful rivals. A five and a half lengths winner, there were three previous winners behind him and the second, third and fourth (Listed) have won subsequently.

James Reveley has partnered some top-class horses during his glittering riding career, including the aforementioned El Clavel, Gaelic Warrior and Il Est Francais amongst others, and is of the opinion Lascar Du Mathan is one of the best he has ridden and regards him as a future Gold Cup horse. Gordon Elliott may have inherited a superstar.

POINTS TO NOTE:
Probable Best Distance - 2m - 2m 4f
Preferred Going - Soft
Reveley's Remarks: "One of the nicest horses I've ever ridden, he is top-class and could be a Gold Cup horse one day. He has plenty of speed and could run over any trip. He is a big horse with a lot of class."

GOING:	R	W	P	TRACK	R	W	P
Heavy	2	2	0	Left-Handed	2	2	0
				Galloping	2	2	0

TRIP:	R	W	P	JOCKEY:	R	W	P
2m 1f	2	2	0	J.Reveley	1	1	0
				D.Maxwell	1	1	0

LEMMY CAUTION (FR)

4 gr g Tunis (POL) – Albain Champenoise (FR) (Lavirco (GER))
OWNER: GIGGINSTOWN HOUSE STUD
TRAINER: Gordon ELLIOTT. Cullentra, Longwood, Co.Meath.
CAREER FORM FIGURES: 1
CAREER WIN: 2025: Mar MONKSGRANGE Yielding/Soft PTP 3m

"Tall angular steel grey: produce of an unraced dam, little known French bloodline, sourced in France by Walter Connors, who sent him to Colin Bowe for pointing. He lined up for one of the four-year-old gelding races at Monksgrange and left a very positive impression. Hidden in midfield during the early exchanges, his jockey Barry O'Neill allowed him to find his feet: asked to improve after four out, he swiftly progressed to challenge the leaders and, once over the second last, he drew clear like a smart individual. He has a relentless gallop. Sold to Gordon Elliott for £250,000, one could see him figuring in the upper-class staying novice events as a hurdler and chaser: may not be a natural bumper horse," believes expert Declan Phelan. Only four, it will be interesting to see whether he goes down the bumper route or straight over hurdles. Either way, the grey is one to very much look forward to.

POINTS TO NOTE:
Probable Best Distance - 2m 4f
Preferred Going - Good/Soft
Connection's Comments: "I was at the point-to-point and I really liked him, he was a lovely individual. We have been lucky buying from Colin Bowe in the past with the likes of Samcro and he recommended this horse strongly, so hopefully he will be successful." Eddie O'LEARY, of Gigginstown House Stud, at the Aintree April Sale (3/4/25)

GOING:	R	W	P	TRACK	R	W	P
Yielding/Soft	1	1	0	Left-Handed	1	1	0

TRIP:	R	W	P	JOCKEY:	R	W	P
3m	1	1	0	B.O'Neill	1	1	0

LORD DES BORDES (FR)

4 b g Cokoriko (FR) – Bossa Nova (FR) (Network (GER))
OWNER: Mrs J.DONNELLY
TRAINER: Willie MULLINS. Closutton, Co.Carlow.
CAREER FORM FIGURES: 1
CAREER WIN: 2024: Aug ARGENTAN Good/Soft Mdn 1m 4f

French trainer Daniela Mele has been a rich source of future stars, as far as Willie Mullins is concerned. Cheltenham Festival winners Majborough and State Man have won 15 Grade 1 races between them since arriving at Closutton. Capodanno and Zenta have also chipped in with one apiece.

The Swiss born handler, who is based with her partner Guy Cherel at Gavray-sur-Sienne in Normandy, is also responsible for the once raced Lord Des Bordes, who was previously owned by Walter Connors. Out of a mare who won over hurdles and fences at Auteuil, the son of Cokoriko made his debut in a fourteen runner Flat race at Argentan in August last year. Sporting a noseband, he raced handily on the rail before being produced with his effort in the short homestraight (400 metres). Pushed along to lead, he is a big imposing horse who can only improve with time and experience. A narrow scorer, the third has won twice since and the winning time was four and a half seconds quicker than the victor of the AQPS Flat race on the same card. The original plan was for Lord Des Bordes to go hurdling last Autumn but Mullins stepped in and acquired him privately on behalf of patron and Joe and Marie Donnelly. The British and Irish champion trainer invariably leaves his three year old recruits off until the following season and this is another example having been gelded since arriving. He could be a high-class novice hurdle prospect.

POINTS TO NOTE:
Probable Best Distance - 2 miles
Preferred Going - Good/Soft
Connection's Comments: "We are surprised in a good way because the colt is immature and we had to see how he would behave over the 2,500m distance. He still needs to gain experience. Daniela Mele did a great job." Former owner Walter CONNORS at Argentan (26/8/24)

GOING:	R	W	P	TRACK	R	W	P
Good/Soft	1	1	0	Right	1	1	0
				Tight	1	1	0

TRIP:	R	W	P	JOCKEY:	R	W	P
1m 4f	1	1	0	T.Bachelot	1	1	0

LULTIMATOM (FR)

4 b g Cokoriko (FR) – Vultip (FR) (Fragrant Mix (IRE))
OWNER: GIGGINSTOWN HOUSE STUD
TRAINER: Willie MULLINS. Closutton, Co.Carlow.
CAREER FORM FIGURES: 1
CAREER WIN: 2025: Mar PORTRUSH Yielding PTP 3m

Willie Mullins has trained seventeen Grade 1 winners for Gigginstown House Stud but none since Apple's Jade won the Champion Four Year Old Hurdle at the Punchestown Festival in 2016. The pair went their separate ways later the same year before being reunited in 2022. The Closutton team and the O'Leary's combined at the Aintree April Sale purchasing Pat Turley's point winner Lultimatom for £225,000. He could be Cheltenham Festival bumper material.

"Handy sized bay with white stripe on face: €50,000 store, dam unraced, French stock. Based with Paddy Turley, he debuted in a six-runner maiden at Portrush in March and was well found in the market. He dictated the race from the front, fluctuating the tempo at times, making a couple of minors jumping errors along the way. Once the field rounded the home bend and viewed the second last, he was given the office, readily quickening and drawing away for an untaxed eight lengths success. Sold to Willie Mullins at a price of £225,000 at the Goffs Aintree sale and with natural boot, he certainly strikes as one likely to win a bumper and could be Graded standard in that discipline. It could be he will prosper as a middle-distance hurdler/chaser, and it is feasible we may be dealing with a 135+ equine athlete," concedes Declan Phelan. Turley introduced the hugely talented but enigmatic King of Kingsfield to win the same maiden in 2022. Its roll of honour also features Grade 1 winner Finian's Oscar (2016).

POINTS TO NOTE:

Probable Best Distance	-	**2 miles**
Preferred Going	-	**Good/Soft**

Connection's Comments: "He jumped and travelled brilliantly. He has a lot of class and his homework was very good, he's extremely straightforward. We jumped off in front and did everything easily, he was only in second gear. I steadied up to the second last and then he went on again. We were flying down to the last, but he's a very good horse." Declan LAVERY at Portrush (22/3/25)

GOING:	R	W	P	TRACK	R	W	P
Yielding	1	1	0	Left-Handed	1	1	0

TRIP:	R	W	P	JOCKEY:	R	W	P
3m	1	1	0	D.Lavery	1	1	0

Please see pages 191-197
for details of the
One Jump Ahead Updates

MANLAGA (IRE)

3 b f Maxios – Tornada (FR) (Ballingarry (IRE))
OWNER: J.P.McMANUS
TRAINER: Nicky HENDERSON. Lambourn, Berkshire.
CAREER FORM FIGURES: 1
CAREER WIN: 2025: Mar AUTEUIL Heavy Hdle 1m 7f

Nicky Henderson has won the Triumph Hurdle on a record breaking seven occasions. However, the Seven Barrows team haven't had much good fortune in the Grade 1 event during the last couple of years. The unbeaten Sir Gino was denied the opportunity to line up when ante-post favourite in 2024, while stablemate and compatriot Lulamba was headed in the shadows of the post by 100/1 hurdling debutant Poniros last spring. Granted better luck, the tide could turn next March following the acquisition of another French three year old, Manlaga, who was purchased by J.P.McManus following her impressive win at Auteuil in March. The Prix Auricula is the first race of the season over hurdles for three year old fillies at the Parisian track.

Trained by Marcel Rolland, who also handled another good mare, dual Grade 2 winner Allegorie De Vassy (in foal to the now deceased Jukebox Jury), she was a €35,000 foal and is a half-sister to Venetia Williams' 141 rated chaser Martator. Fitted with a hood and tongue tie, she faced eleven opponents and was ridden by Ludovic Philipperon. Racing enthusiastically on the outside, she was positioned in midfield before moving up towards the end of the backstraight. Still in fourth jumping the final flight, Manlaga picked up strongly to lead on the run-in before bounding clear to score by three lengths. The fourth (Olga De Kiev), who was beaten eight lengths, has won at Grade 3 level since. The fifth and sixth have also won subsequently.

Two fillies, namely Burning Victory (2020) and Lossiemouth (2023), have won the Triumph Hurdle during the last six years and Manlaga could make it three next spring. J.P.McManus and Nicky Henderson have been responsible for some top-class hurdlers over the years, including Binocular, Buveur D'Air, Epatante and My Tent Or Yours. They may have unearthed another one.

POINTS TO NOTE:

Probable Best Distance	-	**2 miles**
Preferred Going	-	**Good/Soft**

Reveley's Remarks: "The Prix Auricula is always a very good race and the form is strong. I rode Action Du Berlais, who is a nice horse, and we were beaten a fair way."

GOING:	R	W	P	TRACK	R	W	P
Heavy	1	1	0	Left-Handed	1	1	0
				Galloping	1	1	0

TRIP:	R	W	P	JOCKEY:	R	W	P
1m 7f	1	1	0	L.Philipperon	1	1	0

MISTER PESSIMISTIC (IRE)

4 b g Westerner – Gracemount (IRE) (Beneficial)
OWNER: NIALL O'LEARY / LUCKY IN LIFE SYNDICATE
TRAINER: Henry DE BROMHEAD. Knockeen, Co.Waterford.
CAREER FORM FIGURES: 1
CAREER WIN: 2025: Apr LOUGHANMORE Good/Yielding PTP 3m

"Athletic bay with white stripe on forehead: Sean Doyle enjoyed success with the dam, Gracemount (4 wins), and he was also in charge of this offspring when he ventured up to Loughanmore on Easter Saturday for a quality four-year-old maiden. In a race run in a fast time, Mister Pessimistic knew his job: locking onto the leaders from early doors, he was in control from two out and went clear under hands and heels once asked the question, to dominate his opponents in recording an emphatic four lengths victory. Owner of a high cruising speed, expect him to make an instant impact as a hurdler and he will be mixing in Graded company over timber this winter. In time, he will be an exciting novice chase prospect. Regarded as one of the top Monbeg four-year-olds from the spring, he sold for good money in private and will be a significant addition to the Henry De Bromhead team. He is bound to showcase his talent at the major Festivals at future dates," reports expert Declan Phelan. Despite the fact Mister Pessimistic is only a four year old, Henry De Bromhead's charge is likely to embark on his hurdle career this winter and develop into a high-class novice over two and two and a half miles. Owned by Niall O'Leary, he is a youngster with a big future.

POINTS TO NOTE:

Probable Best Distance	-	**2m – 2m 4f**
Preferred Going	-	**Good/Soft**

GOING:	**R**	**W**	**P**	**TRACK**	**R**	**W**	**P**
Good/Yielding	**1**	**1**	**0**	**Left-Handed**	**1**	**1**	**0**

TRIP:	**R**	**W**	**P**	**JOCKEY:**	**R**	**W**	**P**
3m	**1**	**1**	**0**	**J.Scallan**	**1**	**1**	**0**

MYDADDYPADDY (IRE)

4 b g Walk In The Park (IRE) – Debdebdeb (Teofilo (IRE))
OWNER: DERMOT HANAFIN
TRAINER: Dan SKELTON. Shelfield Green, Alcester, Warwickshire.
CAREER FORM FIGURES: 1
CAREER WIN: 2025: Mar HUNTINGDON Good/Soft NHF 2m

The New Lion developed into the leading British trained novice hurdler last winter with the unbeaten six year old earning an official rating of 159. A dual Grade 1 winner, the Kayf Tara gelding became the first horse to win the Challow Novices' Hurdle at Newbury and follow up at the Cheltenham Festival when beating the best of the Irish in the Turners Novices' Hurdle in March. Purchased by J.P.McManus after his win at Newbury over Christmas, the six year old will be campaigned as a Champion Hurdle contender this season.

Stablemate Mydaddypaddy has a long way to go before he can be mentioned in the same breath but there was a lot to like about his winning debut in a bumper at Huntingdon last spring. Indeed, it evoked memories of The New Lion's initial success in a similar contest at Market Rasen eleven months earlier. Homebred, the four year old son of Walk In The Park is out of the Listed placed and 137 rated jumper Debdebdeb. All the rage for his racecourse bow in a fourteen runners affair at the Cambridgeshire track in early March, Dan Skelton's charge was ridden with supreme confidence by the trainer's brother Harry. Snuggled in behind at the rear of the field, he floated passed rivals towards the end of the backstraight before hitting the front over two furlongs out. Going clear along the stands rail, he effortlessly pulled away to win eased down by eleven lengths. It was a demolition job outclassing inferior opponents. The four year old hit a top speed of 36.71mph inside the penultimate furlong and covered the last two furlongs in 12.54 and 12.65 seconds, according to *Race Iq*. Olly Murphy purchased the runner-up Lirion for £60,000, while the eighth has won twice since on the Flat and is rated 76. Grade 1 winning hurdler Crambo won the same contest three years earlier.

Held in the highest esteem, Mydaddypaddy was arguably the most exciting of Dan Skelton's 26 bumper winners last term. He has the potential to be a top notch novice hurdler and develop into a strong contender at the Cheltenham Festival in March.

POINTS TO NOTE:
Probable Best Distance - 2m - 2m 4f
Preferred Going - Good/Soft

GOING:	**R**	**W**	**P**	**TRACK**	**R**	**W**	**P**
Good/Soft	**1**	**1**	**0**	**Right**	**1**	**1**	**0**
				Galloping	**1**	**1**	**0**

TRIP:	**R**	**W**	**P**	**JOCKEY:**	**R**	**W**	**P**
2m	**1**	**1**	**0**	**H.Skelton**	**1**	**1**	**0**

NARCISO HAS (FR)

3 b g Doctor Dino (FR) – Chegei Has (FR) (Kahyasi (IRE))
OWNER: J.P.McMANUS
TRAINER: Willie MULLINS. Closutton, Co.Carlow.
CAREER FORM FIGURES: 1
CAREER WIN: 2025: Apr AUTEUIL Very Soft Hdle 1m 7f

The Prix Wild Monarch, a conditions hurdle for unraced horses at Auteuil in April, has produced some top-class horses in recent years, including State Man (runner-up in 2020), Gaelic Warrior (sixth in 2021), Sir Gino and Salvator Mundi (first and second in 2023). Willie Mullins is training three out of four of those Grade 1 winners and he has taken charge of the 2025 winner Narciso Has, who looked every inch a Triumph Hurdle prospect when winning on his debut in the spring.

Homebred, he was a stablemate of the aforementioned Manlaga and made a similarly striking impression at the Parisian track. A big imposing three year old who will jump fences in time, he was always to the fore sharing the advantage throughout. Headed at the second last, Ludovic Philipperon's mount picked up well between the final two flights and pulled away on the run-in. A length and a quarter victor, Narciso Has looked a strong stayer and recorded a winning time of 3m 47.75 secs (Very Soft), compared to Manlaga who covered the same C&D in 3m 50.13 secs (Heavy).

Like Manlaga, Narciso Has was bought by J.P.McManus who seemingly has a formidable team of three year olds for the 2025/2026 campaign. Likely to make his Irish debut in a Graded event, he has joined a stable who have won five of the last six Triumph Hurdles.

POINTS TO NOTE:

Probable Best Distance	-	**2 miles**
Preferred Going	-	**Soft**

GOING:	**R**	**W**	**P**	**TRACK**	**R**	**W**	**P**
Very Soft	**1**	**1**	**0**	**Left-Handed**	**1**	**1**	**0**
				Galloping	**1**	**1**	**0**

TRIP:	**R**	**W**	**P**	**JOCKEY:**	**R**	**W**	**P**
1m 7f	**1**	**1**	**0**	**L.Philipperon**	**1**	**1**	**0**

NO DRAMA THIS END (IRE)

5 gr g Walk In The Park (IRE) – La Segnora (FR) (Turgeon (USA))
OWNER: McNEILL FAMILY And CHRIS & GILES BARBER
TRAINER: Paul NICHOLLS OBE. Ditcheat, Somerset.
CAREER FORM FIGURES: 1 - 19
CAREER WINS: 2024: Feb BADBURY RINGS Soft PTP 3m; Dec WARWICK Soft NHF 2m

Prolific winning owner and dairy farmer Paul Barber sadly died in June 2023. Aged 80, he won the Cheltenham Gold Cup twice courtesy of See More Business and Denman and was instrumental in Paul Nicholls becoming one of the greatest National Hunt trainers of all time having owned Manor Farm Stables in Ditcheat.

Barber's birthday was on the 31st December and it was therefore fitting that promising winning UK pointer No Drama This End donned his famous green and white silks when making his Rules debut in a bumper at Warwick on New Year's Eve. A 23 lengths winner of a maiden point at Barbury Rings in February last year when trained by Will Biddick, the €26,000 store was subsequently sold for £160,000 to join the fourteen times champion. Off the track 317 days, Harry Cobden's mount was sent off 100/30 second favourite behind Dan Skelton's Irish point winner Keops Des Bordes who was well touted beforehand. The four year old raced handily from the outset and, having pressed the leader turning for home, the Ditcheat runner went to the front over a furlong out before pulling away to score impressively. A three and a half lengths victor, No Drama This End hit a top speed of 37.05mph inside the penultimate furlong and the sectionals made for good viewing, too. The Walk In The Park gelding covered the last two furlongs in 12.26 and 13.02 seconds.

Following an absence of 71 days, No Drama This End finished a respectable ninth in the Cheltenham Festival bumper. Racing on ground which was arguably fast enough, the big strapping gelding held every chance on the home bend before fading thereafter. Beaten nine lengths, he is set go novice hurdling and will benefit from stepping up to two and a half miles. One could envisage him starting off at Chepstow (5th November) before being campaigned towards the Grade 1 Challow Novices' Hurdle at Newbury (29th December), a race his stable have won six times. He is an exciting young prospect.

POINTS TO NOTE:

Probable Best Distance	-	**2m 4f**
Preferred Going	-	**Soft**

Connection's Comments: "It would've been Paul Barber's 82nd birthday. He'd have been Paul's type of horse, as he's a big strong chasing type. He did a very nice racecourse gallop a few weeks ago and we thought he'd run well, but that blew us away." Paul NICHOLLS at Warwick (31/12/24)

GOING:	R	W	P	TRACK	R	W	P
Soft	2	2	0	Left-Handed	3	2	0
Good/Soft	1	0	0	Stiff/Undul.	1	0	0
				Tight/Undul.	1	1	0

TRIP:	R	W	P	JOCKEY:	R	W	P
2m	2	1	0	H.Cobden	2	1	0
3m	1	1	0	W.Biddick	1	1	0

PROACTIF (FR)

3 b g Masked Marvel – Balder Phenix (IRE) (Presenting)
OWNER: J.P.McMANUS
TRAINER: Willie MULLINS. Closutton, Co.Carlow.
CAREER FORM FIGURES: 1
CAREER WIN: 2025: Sept AUTEUIL Very Soft Hdle 2m 2f

While most of the racing world were watching Scandinavia provide Aidan O'Brien with a ninth victory in the St Leger at Doncaster in mid September, the Prix Finot, a conditions hurdle for unraced three year olds, was being staged at Auteuil during the same afternoon. The two miles two event has kickstarted the careers of many high-class National Hunt horses over the years. Grade 1 winners L'Ami Serge (3rd in 2013), Min (4th in 2014), Protektorat (2nd in 2018), Ptit Zig (9th in 2012), Saint Roi (3rd in 2018) all made their racecourse debuts in the prestigious contest.

The colts and geldings version was won impressively by Proactif who stretched away after the last from an 18 strong field looking a high-class prospect. Owned and trained by Daniela Mele and ridden by Lucas Zuliani, the Masked Marvel gelding raced in behind the leaders along the rail until pulled out halfway down the backstraight. Jumping to the front with a bold leap at the second last, he stayed on strongly to beat the promising **APOLON DE CHARNIE** by six lengths. A half-brother to Gavin Cromwell's three times winning chaser Tyre Kicker (rated 128), the time was a second and a half slower than the fillies' version (won by Maskina), which was staged later on the same card. Willie Mullins was reportedly quick off the mark and secured the gelding for a hefty six figure sum from a stable who have supplied him with some top-class ammunition in recent years, namely Majborough and State Man.

Daniela Mele and partner Guy Cherel invariably run quality three year olds in the Prix Finot – the latter was responsible for Irish Saint (won it in 2012), the aforementioned Saint Roi (2018) and Saphir Du Rheu (3rd in 2012) – and Proactif looks cut from the same cloth. A big, scopey individual, he could be very smart and develop into a household name. Expect him to make his Irish debut in a Graded contest after Christmas before a tilt at the Triumph Hurdle. Don't forget where you heard about him first.

POINTS TO NOTE:
Probable Best Distance - 2 miles
Preferred Going - Sof
Reveley's Remarks: "I rode the fifth (Milord D'Alesa) and we like our horse. Daniela Mele likes to run a good horse in the Prix Finot and I suspect the winner is very good."

GOING:	R	W	P	TRACK	R	W	P
Very Soft	1	1	0	Left-Handed	1	1	0
				Galloping	1	1	0

TRIP:	R	W	P	JOCKEY:	R	W	P
2m 2f	1	1	0	L.Zuliani	1	1	0

REAL QUARTZ (IRE)

5 bb g Soldier of Fortune (IRE) – Miss Elderberry (IRE) (Yeats (IRE))
OWNER: GED MASON & Sir ALEX FERGUSON.
TRAINER: Dan SKELTON. Shelfield Green, Alcester, Warwickshire.
CAREER FORM FIGURES: 1
CAREER WIN: 2024: Nov BOULTA Yielding PTP 3m

Owners Ged Mason and Sir Alex Ferguson have a huge amount to look forward to with Grade 1 winning novice chasers Caldwell Potter and Kalif Du Berlais in training with Paul Nicholls. The pair are also involved in Grade 1 and Cheltenham Festival winning duo Monmiral and Protektorat. The latter, who won the Ryanair Chase in 2024, is trained by Dan Skelton who is also in charge of winning pointer Real Quartz. A gelded son of Soldier of Fortune, he was a four and a half lengths scorer at Boulta in November before being bought a week later at the Goffs UK Coral Gold Cup Sale for £190,000.

Declan Phelan reports: **"Rangy bay gelding: €45,000 store, dam half-sister to Joncol, sibling Alan De Banks won two bumpers in 2024. Housed with Sam Curling, he made one appearance in Irish points: his port of call, Boulta in November. Running through rank rotten weather, he was one of ten runners in the maiden: ridden by Derek O'Connor who elected to hold up his mount. He gradually closed ranks in the final mile, moving into contention two out. He challenged for the lead at the final fence and found generously to win going away by over four lengths, showing fine resolve when it counted. Purchased by Ged Mason & Sir Alex Ferguson and sent into training with Dan Skelton, he had plenty of upside. He consented to settle, and had the appetite to compete when it mattered, therefore he will be a horse certain to win his quota of races: bound to be trip versatile, he can nest in the 125-140 bracket as a hurdler/chaser."**

The same maiden point has been won by Robin Roe (2015), Sir Gerhard (2019) and Found A Fifty (2021) and Real Quartz looks set for a productive career under Rules. Considered quick enough for two miles on slow ground, he could emerge as a live player in either the Grade 1 Formby Novices' Hurdle at Aintree (26th December) or Grade 1 Challow Novices' Hurdle at Newbury (29th December).

POINTS TO NOTE:

Probable Best Distance - 2m 4f

Preferred Going - Good/Soft

Connection's Comments: "He's a big, huge horse and Derek (O'Connor) was very impressed with him. He's a horse with loads of pace and Philip Enright has done a lot of work with him at home." Sam CURLING at Boulta (23/11/24)

GOING:	R	W	P	TRACK	R	W	P
Yielding	1	1	0	Left-Handed	1	1	0

TRIP:	R	W	P	JOCKEY:	R	W	P
3m	1	1	0	D.O'Connor	1	1	0

REGENT'S STROLL (IRE)

6 b g Walk In The Park (IRE) – Pretty Puttens (IRE) (Snurge (IRE))
OWNER: FERGUSON, MASON, HALES, HOGARTH & SMITH
TRAINER: Paul NICHOLLS OBE. Ditcheat, Somerset.
CAREER FORM FIGURES: 11 - 14212
CAREER WINS: 2023: Nov ASCOT Good NHF 2m: 2024: Mar NEWBURY Good/Soft NHF 2m; Nov NEWBURY Soft MH 2m: 2025: Mar WINCANTON Good/Soft NH 2m 4f

Paul Nicholls and Team Ditcheat were in terrific form at Aintree's Grand National meeting with three winners from 15 runners, including Grade 1 successes for Caldwell Potter (Mildmay Novices' Chase) and Kalif Du Berlais (Maghull Novices' Chase). The former was a high profile purchase out of Gordon Elliott's yard and the fourteen times champion trainer did a superb job improving the grey throughout the season culminating in big race glory at Cheltenham and Aintree in the spring.

The Martaline gelding was secured for a hefty sum and, similarly the dual bumper winner Regent's Stroll, was purchased for £660,000 for the same owners, including the late John Hales who sadly died in late January, as part of Chris Giles' dispersal sale in July last year. A £175,000 store, the son of Walk In The Park had looked above average at Ascot and Newbury, winning the Goffs UK Spring Sale bumper at the latter track. Having won readily on his hurdling bow at Newbury's Winter Festival in late November, he was sent off a warm favourite for the Grade 1 Challow Hurdle at the same venue over Christmas. However, Harry Cobden's mount got worked up beforehand and raced too freely. Fourth behind the unbeaten The New Lion, he was then runner-up in a Listed novice hurdle over an inadequate two miles at Exeter in February.

Connections elected to bypass the Cheltenham Festival and that decision was vindicated. Regent's Stroll barely came off the bridle when defeating four opponents under a penalty at Wincanton with Nicholls saying: **"In his bumpers last year, he never picked the bridle up, he was chilled and a completely different beast to deal with."** That patience was rewarded at Aintree in the Grade 1 Mersey Novices' Hurdle over two and a half miles. Fitted with a hood, he attempted to make all and was only headed late on by Honesty Policy (runner-up at the Punchestown Festival since). Half a length behind Gordon Elliott's winner, it was an excellent run with his trainer enthusing: **"That just shows Regent's Stroll is a real smart horse, and he's learning all the time. That's probably the best he's run. He jumped brilliant, and he's**

just chilled a bit more today. I thought better ground would help and I'm thrilled with him. It's a long-term project with a horse like him and, as I said to the lads, Rome wasn't built in a day. What a super chaser he's going to make."

Reported to have come back into work following his summer holiday 'a lot more chilled out,' he is set to go over fences and can develop into a top-class novice chaser. While three miles is likely to prove his optimum trip, Regent's Stroll is expected to begin his chasing career over two and a half miles. The £18,000 Stan Mellor Memorial Novices' Chase at Warwick (4th November) or two miles two novices' chase at Newbury (6th November) could be an ideal starting point before tackling the Grade 2 John Francome Novices' Chase at Newbury (28th November). The Irish challenge will doubtless be formidable, but the 50/1 (Paddy Power, *Sky Bet* & William Hill) for the Brown Advisory Novices' Chase at Cheltenham in March about Paul Nicholls' next future chasing star is too good to resist.

POINTS TO NOTE:
Probable Best Distance - 3 miles
Preferred Going - Good/Soft
Connection's Comments: "He's as good a young horse as we've had in a long time. We've seen what he can do at home and what he did in his bumpers. Regent's Stroll has lots of pace and I'd say he'll stay, too. I need to get some experience into him, but ultimately he'll make a lovely chaser one day. He's got loads of scope and he's a big unit." Paul NICHOLLS at Newbury (29/11/24)

GOING:	R	W	P
Soft	1	1	0
Good/Soft	4	2	1
Good	2	1	1

TRACK	R	W	P
Left-Handed	4	2	1
Right	3	2	1
Galloping	5	4	0
Stiff/Undul.	1	0	1
Tight	1	0	1

TRIP:	R	W	P
2m	4	3	1
2m 4f	3	1	1

JOCKEY:	R	W	P
H.Cobden	7	4	2

SALSINHA (FR)

4 gr f Montmartre (FR) – My Glitters (FR) (My Risk (FR))
OWNER: Dr S.P.FITZGERALD
TRAINER: Henry DE BROMHEAD. Knockeen, Co.Waterford.
CAREER FORM FIGURES: 1
CAREER WIN: 2025: July CORK Good NHF 2m 1f

Dr Peter FitzGerald, founder and managing director of Randox Health, who have sponsored the Grand National at Aintree since 2017, owned the 2021 Galway Plate winner Royal Rendezvous, who subsequently won the Grade 2 Champion Chase at Gowran Park a few months later. The same owner must be excited about the prospect of the unbeaten Salsinha running over hurdles this season having produced an explosive performance on her debut on a balmy summer evening at Cork in July.

A €9,000 foal, the daughter of Montmartre was heavily supported for a sixteen runner fillies' bumper at Mallow and ridden with supreme confidence by leading amateur and Cheltenham Festival winning jockey John Gleeson. Racing at the back of the field, Henry De Bromhead's charge scythed her way through the field in the homestraight before leading over a furlong out. Quickening away to win by nine lengths, the form is modest even though the fourth has won subsequently. However, it was a very taking performance and the clock suggested it was well above average. According to *Race Iq*, Salsinha hit a top speed of 38.71mph seconds inside the penultimate furlong and covered the final three furlongs in 11.79, 11.94 and 12.02 seconds.

Likely to go straight over obstacles, the four year old possesses a high cruising speed and a potent turn of foot. While testing ground is an unknown, her dam was placed on heavy at Auteuil and she appears to have the credentials to develop in a Graded mare over hurdles.

POINTS TO NOTE:
Probable Best Distance - 2 miles
Preferred Going - Good/Soft
Connection's Comments: "It was a nice performance. Henry and all the lads at home liked her and we were hopeful of a good run today. She's French bred and has loads of pace. She quickened up nicely on that ground." John GLEESON at Cork (11/7/25)

GOING:	R	W	P	TRACK	R	W	P
Good	1	1	0	Right	1	1	0
				Galloping	1	1	0

TRIP:	R	W	P	JOCKEY:	R	W	P
2m 1f	1	1	0	J.L.Gleeson	1	1	0

STARZAND (IRE)

5 b g Harzand (IRE) – Phoenix Twist (IRE) (Kalanisi (IRE))
OWNER: GWENT HOLDINGS Limited.
TRAINER: Philip HOBBS & Johnson WHITE. Minehead, Somerset.
CAREER FORM FIGURES: 2 - 11
CAREER WINS: 2024: Dec DROMAHANE Yielding/Soft PTP: 2025: Mar FFOS LAS Good NHF 2m

With 53 winners and a strike-rate of 19%, Philip Hobbs and Johnson White had an excellent 2024/2025. Progressive young chasers Imperial Saint (rated 144) and Lowry's Bar (148) spearheaded their challenge and Sandhill Farm Stables is also blessed with two hugely exciting bumper winners from last season, namely Listed winner Sober Glory and Starzand.

Declan Phelan discusses the latter: **"Attractive bay with white stripe on face: €21,000 store, dam won a Flat race, grand dam won a Listed hurdle in the UK. Two spins for the James Doyle stable in 2024 within the pointing discipline. Back in February 2024, he debuted over the 2m 4f distance at Knockanard: in a four-runner race, which culminated in a mini sprint, he held every chance at the final fence and was simply done for toe on the day by subsequent track winner Goraibhmaithagat: beaten a length. Connections parked him up and decided to wait for safe ground later in 2024 and he returned to action for the final**

point fixture of the year, at Dromahane in late December. Encountering twelve rivals, he lobbed along in front and once he cranked up the pace off the home bend with three to jump, his class shone through: leaving the remainder of the field in his wake, he asserted in some style to win by 25 lengths...different gravy to the rest. Sold to Philip Hobbs and Johnson White at a tariff of £230,000 in January, he continued his progression with a bloodless success in a bumper at Ffos Las (2m : Good) in March. Arguably, the long-term flagship horse for the stable, those associated with the animal in Ireland maintain he will be seen to maximum effect on soft terrain. Will win a maiden or novice hurdle (2m4f-3m) at his leisure and likely to be a contender in the Graded staying novice hurdles, and capable of winning at such a lofty level. An exciting recruit for team Hobbs/White."

Bought at the Cheltenham January Sale, Starzand was sent off 13/8 favourite on his Rules debut at Ffos Las in March – subsequent Grade 1 winners The Jukebox Man (2023) and Potters Charm (2024) won the previous two renewals. Sean Houlihan's mount moved smoothly throughout before breezing to the front three out. Pushed clear to score by seven and a half lengths, the five year old covered two of the last three furlongs in 12.67 and 12.91 seconds, according to *Race Iq*. Considered a stayer in the making, he could make up into a Grade 1 Challow Novices' Hurdle at Newbury type before tackling the Albert Bartlett Novices' Hurdle at Cheltenham in March – the Thyme Hill route.

POINTS TO NOTE:
Probable Best Distance - 2m 4f – 3 miles
Preferred Going - Good/Soft
Connection's Comments: "He stepped forwards from his summer break and we really fancied him coming here." Former trainer James DOYLE at Dromahane (30/12/24)

GOING:	R	W	P	TRACK	R	W	P
Heavy	1	0	1	Left-Handed	2	2	0
Yield/Soft	1	1	0	Right	1	0	1
Good	1	1	0	Galloping	1	1	0

TRIP:	R	W	P	JOCKEY:	R	W	P
2m	1	1	0	S.Houlihan	1	1	0
2m 4f	1	0	1	B.Dunleavy	2	1	1
3m	1	1	0				

THAT'S NICE (IRE)

5 b m Walk In The Park (IRE) – Bloody Mary (FR) (Fragrant Mix (IRE))
OWNER: J.P.McMANUS
TRAINER: Nicky HENDERSON. Lambourn, Berkshire.
CAREER FORM FIGURES: 1 - 141
CAREER WINS: 2024: Feb BELHARBOUR Yielding PTP 3m; Nov WARWICK Good/Soft NH 2m 3f: 2025: Jan WARWICK Good/Soft NH 2m 3f

The J.P.McManus owned and Nicky Henderson trained mare Joyeuse made a mockery of her rating of 123 when trouncing sixteen opponents by upwards of eight lengths in the William Hill Handicap Hurdle at Newbury in February. The same connections are responsible for another evidently well treated mare, namely That's Nice, who looks capable of winning a big handicap hurdle this winter off her mark of 126.

The daughter of Walk In The Park is out of Bloody Mary, who was placed in the Grade 2 Dawn Run Mares' Novices' Hurdle at the Cheltenham Festival in 2016 for McManus and Henderson. That's Nice began her career with Derek O'Connor in Ireland winning her point-to-point against geldings at Bellharbour in cosy fashion in February last year. Transferred to Seven Barrows, she won two out of three over hurdles with both victories being gained over the intermediate trip at Warwick. First time out, she beat subsequent 129 rated Listed winner Honky Tonk Highway by a length and a half under a confident ride by Nico De Boinville. It was a similar story at the Midlands track in January as she readily brushed aside Miss Cynthia by a length and a quarter. Lucy Wadham's runner-up won next time before being Listed placed at Doncaster. In between, she finished a disappointing last of four over two miles one against three geldings at Cheltenham's December meeting. Having travelled strongly into contention, her effort petered out tamely after the second last. Perhaps the race came too soon (22 days) after her reappearance or she didn't enjoy the uphill finish at Prestbury Park.

Parked up after her second win at Warwick, there is no doubt she is on an attractive mark. Best fresh, That's Nice looks tailormade for the 0-145 handicap hurdle over two and a half miles at Newbury's Winter Festival (29th November), an event Nicky Henderson has won three times in the last seven years - Champ (2018), The Cashel Man (2019) and Impose Toi (2024). Later on, the Walk In The Park mare could develop into a major player in a race such as the Lanzarote Hurdle at Kempton in January.

POINTS TO NOTE:
Probable Best Distance - 2m 4f
Preferred Going - Good/Soft
Connection's Comments: "That's Nice is absolutely gorgeous. She just travelled nicely and jumped. I liked the way she went about it, and it was the perfect introduction. The one in front was the form horse, so it was nice to see that she could track that and quicken up. I liked the way she quickened, it was fairly instant. There's a long way to go, but I think there's some nice days ahead of us." Nicky HENDERSON at Warwick (21/11/24)

GOING:	R	W	P
Yielding	1	1	0
Good/Soft	3	2	0

TRACK	R	W	P
Left-Handed	4	3	0
Stiff/Undul.	1	0	0
Tight/Undul.	2	2	0

TRIP:	R	W	P
2m 1f	1	0	0
2m 3f	2	2	0
3m	1	1	0

JOCKEY:	R	W	P
N.De Boinville	3	2	0
D.O'Connor	1	1	0

THE REVEREND

4 b g Lope De Vega (IRE) – Burning Rules (IRE) (Aussie Rules (USA))
OWNER: TONY BLOOM MBE & IAN McALEAVY
TRAINER: Willie MULLINS. Closutton, Co.Carlow.
CAREER FLAT FORM FIGURES: 1 – 22149 - 511
CAREER WINS: 2023: Nov NEWMARKET Heavy Mdn 7f: 2024: Sept ASCOT Soft Hcap 1m 4f: 2025: July RIPON Soft Hcap 1m 4f; Sept HAYDOCK PARK Good Hcap 1m 6f

In addition to Energumene winning the Queen Mother Champion Chase twice, owner Tony Bloom has tasted Cheltenham Festival success courtesy of ex-Flat racers Penhill (Albert Bartlett Novices' Hurdle & Stayers' Hurdle) and Poniros (100/1), who caused a huge shock when winning the Triumph Hurdle on his jumping debut last spring. The former was purchased for 230,000gns out of James Bethell's yard, while the latter cost 200,000gns having plied his trade on the level with Ralph Beckett.

The Reverend was a 150,000gns yearling and the four year old has developed into a high-class staying handicapper with William Haggas. The chairman of Brighton & Hove Albion Football Club owns the Lope De Vega gelding, along with Ian McAleavy, and he joined Willie Mullins in September with a view to going jumping. I spoke to William Haggas at York's Ebor Festival in August and this has always been the plan – in fact, the owners were keen for him to go hurdling last year but the head of Somerville Lodge wasn't convinced he was big enough for jumping. Maureen (Haggas) feels he is athletic and won't have a problem.

Successful in four of his nine races on the Flat and officially rated 102, he was an impressive winner of a three year old heritage handicap at Ascot last year. Having found the ground too lively in the *Sky Bet* Jorvik Handicap at York's Dante Festival in May (1m 4f : Good/Firm), he hasn't looked back since winning twice. Revelling in testing conditions at Ripon in July, Danny Tudhope's mount outclassed four opponents in the 0-105 Ripon Rowels Handicap winning by three and a quarter lengths under 10st 2lb. Raised four pounds to 98, The Reverend produced an even better display to win the Old Borough Cup at Haydock Park in early September. Tackling a mile and six for only the second time, he stayed on strongly to reel in stablemate Dramatic Star to prevail by a neck. The Somerville Lodge newsletter published on 12th September stated: **"He has been a very fun horse for the yard and has enjoyed some big handicap wins and Saturday's victory will represent his last start for Somerville Lodge as he transfers to Willie Mullins to embark on a jumping career and we wish him the best of luck in the future."**

Willie Mullins' new recruit possesses a good cruising speed, he stays well and handles soft ground. The four year old is tailormade for the *Sky Bet* Supreme Novices Hurdle next spring. He could be the best National Hunt horse to emerge from Somerville Lodge in Newmarket since the 2005 Arkle Trophy winner Contraband.

POINTS TO NOTE:
Probable Best Distance - 2 miles
Preferred Going - Soft
Connection's Comments: "I thought The Reverend wanted softer ground, but he was in really good form and went to post beautifully and was full of zest. We haven't run him over a mile-six much before and he came off the bit two out, but he ran right to the line." William HAGGAS at Haydock (6/9/25)

GOING:	R	W	P
Heavy	2	1	1
Soft	4	2	0
Good/Soft	1	0	1
Good	1	1	0
Good/Firm	1	0	0

TRACK	R	W	P
Left-Handed	5	1	1
Right	4	3	1
Galloping	8	4	1
Stiff/Undul.	1	0	1

TRIP:	R	W	P
7f	1	1	0
1m	1	0	1
1m 2f	1	0	0
1m 3f	1	0	1
1m 4f	3	2	0
1m 6f	2	1	0

JOCKEY:	R	W	P
T.Marquand	3	1	1
C.Fallon	2	1	1
D.Probert	1	1	0
D.Tudhope	1	1	0
R.L.Moore	1	0	0
C.Rodriguez	1	0	0

THEY'RE CHANCERS (IRE)

5 b g Milan – Valentines Lady (IRE) (Zaffaran (USA))
OWNER: PAUL & CLARE ROONEY
TRAINER: Nicky RICHARDS. Greystoke, Cumbria.
CAREER FORM FIGURES: 1
CAREER WIN: 2025: Jan AYR Soft NHF 2m

Nicky Richards and his team at Greystoke trained eight bumper winners during the last campaign and they featured some exciting youngsters for the future. The Cumbrian based handler invariably unleashes the pick of his bumper performers at Ayr (26 winners from 101 runners), Kelso (11 from 48) or Newcastle (16 from 48).

The once raced They're Chancers made his first public appearance at the first named track in January and vindicated the pre-race chat with a commanding performance. Bought for €70,000 at the Tattersalls Derby Sale in Ireland as a three year old on behalf of Paul & Clare Rooney, he was well prepared by Jason Maguire and had impressed in his homework since joining Richards. A half-brother to Grade 1 winning chaser Edwulf, he moved comfortably throughout before making good headway early in the homestraight. Despite showing signs of inexperience, he stayed on strongly under Danny McMenamin to account for the Lucinda Russell trained pair Triple Crown Ted and Caballo De Guerra. His fastest furlong was between three and two out covering it in 13.41 seconds, according to *Race Iq*.

Entered in the Grade 2 championship bumper at Aintree's Grand National meeting, the five year old is well schooled over timber and is set to go novice hurdling having spent the summer with the owner's racing manager. A three mile chaser in the making, he is expected to develop into a useful novice over two and a half miles plus.

POINTS TO NOTE:

Probable Best Distance	-	**2m 4f**
Preferred Going	-	**Soft**

GOING:	R	W	P	TRACK	R	W	P
Soft	1	1	0	Left-Handed	1	1	0
				Galloping	1	1	0

TRIP:	R	W	P	JOCKEY:	R	W	P
2m	1	1	0	D.McMenamin	1	1	0

UPON TWEED (IRE)

5 b g Berkshire (IRE) - Catchers Day (IRE) (Catcher In The Rye (IRE))
OWNER: EDWARD MELVILLE
TRAINER: Nicky RICHARDS. Greystoke, Cumbria.
CAREER FORM FIGURES: 1
CAREER WIN: 2025: Feb NEWCASTLE Good/Soft NHF 2m 1f

Eduard was a high-class chaser rated 151 winning 6 of his 16 career starts, including the Grade 2 Future Champions Novices' Chase at Ayr by 20 lengths in 2014. Runner-up in the Grade 2 Peterborough Chase at Huntingdon the following season, the Nicky Richards trained gelding sadly lost his life at Ascot two years later. The son of Morozov sported the familiar red and yellow silks of owner Eddie Melville, who has also enjoyed recent successes with the 137 rated chaser The Kalooki Kid.

The same patron has acquired impressive Newcastle bumper winner Upon Tweed, who is set to emerge as one of the north's brightest prospects this winter. The Greystoke team bought the Berkshire gelding for €60,000 as a three year old at the Goffs Arkle Sale. A half-brother to Great Yorkshire Chase winner If In Doubt, who was also placed in the Lanzarote Hurdle and Pertemps Final, he looked a smart type when defeating eight rivals by upwards of eight and a half lengths at Gosforth Park in mid February. Richards has sent out 16 bumper winners from only 48 runners at the track and racegoers were left in no doubt they had witnessed an above average victor. Partnered by Danny McMenamin, the five year old was held up towards the rear before swiftly moving into contention rounding the homebend. Leading two out, he lengthened away recording some impressive sectionals in the process - the winner covered the last three furlongs in 13.66, 13.84 and 13.63 seconds, according to *Race Iq*. Upon Tweed won by eight and a half lengths from the well regarded Conman Jack, who was bought for £170,000 having won an Irish point and subsequently finished fifth in a hotly contested bumper at the Punchestown Festival. The fourth has won since.

Upon Tweed will have no trouble staying two and a half miles plus on pedigree, but he didn't look slow on his debut and is likely to commence his hurdling career over the minimum trip. Expect him to reappear at either Ayr, Kelso or Newcastle before developing into a candidate for the Grade 2 Premier Novices' Hurdle at Kelso in early March, an event in which the aforementioned Eduard was narrowly defeated a dozen years ago. Eddie Melville may have another good 'un.

POINTS TO NOTE:

Probable Best Distance	-	**2m - 2m 4f**
Preferred Going	-	**Good/Soft**

GOING:	R	W	P	TRACK	R	W	P
Good/Soft	1	1	0	Left-Handed	1	1	0
				Galloping	1	1	0

TRIP:	R	W	P	JOCKEY:	R	W	P
2m 1f	1	1	0	D.McMenamin	1	1	0

WYOMING LINE (FR)

4 b g Doctor Dino (FR) – La Garde Royale (FR) (Kapgarde (FR))
OWNER: GIGGINSTOWN HOUSE STUD
TRAINER: Willie MULLINS. Closutton, Co.Carlow.
CAREER FORM FIGURES: 1
CAREER WIN: 2025: Apr DROMAHANE Yielding PTP 3m

Co.Wexford based Jonathan Fogarty trained 18 point-to-point winners during the 2024/2025 season, including the Walter Connors owned Wyoming Line, who cost €47,000 as a foal. A four lengths winner on his debut at Dromahane towards the end of April, the Doctor Dino gelding changed hands for €275,000 four days later at the Punchestown Festival Sale and is now owned by Gigginstown House Stud and trained by Willie Mullins.

Declan Phelan believes: **"Chunky bay: dam three-times winner in France, she already has three track winners amongst her offspring. Walter Connors sourced the horse as a foal in France and the gelding was the first horse the Waterford vet entrusted to the Fogarty's to educate for him. He arrived at Dromahane and was partnered by Finny Maguire. Setting out his stall early and assuming the lead, Finny varied the pace at different stages over the three miles journey. A few lengths to the good over the second last, he found sufficient reserves to resist the threat posed by The Burren Man and stretched out to win by four lengths, in the fastest time of the day (all his own work in essence). Joins Willie Mullins after selling for €275,000: now he did not impress as an instant superstar hit: however, he did precious little wrong at Dromahane and could be one of those horses who are easy to handle and not flashy on the eye. Willie has the foundation of a decent young prospect and he is one to pay a healthy respect to in any company."**

The four year old maiden at Dromahane has an envious roll of honour which includes Ask Tom (beat Suny Bay in 1993), Great Endeavour (2008), No More Heroes (2013), Black Hercules (2013), Appreciate It (2018) and Fury Road (2018). The trainer's brother Mikey, commented afterwards: **"We loved him when we saw him at the Derby Sale last year and Walter (Connors) then sent him to us. His homework has always been good."** Wyoming Line is expected to contest bumpers this season before hopefully developing into a household name over obstacles.

POINTS TO NOTE:

Probable Best Distance	-	**2 miles**
Preferred Going	-	**Good/Soft**

Connection's Comments: "I love the stallion, Doctor Dino, who has been very good for us, very successful for us. He is coming from a very good consignor in Walter Connors, who we have had huge success with. I loved him as a store at the Derby Sale, we very nearly

bought him as a store. I thought he was one of the top horses at this sale and I knew he'd be popular." Agent Harold KIRK at the Goffs Punchestown Festival Sale (1/5/25)

GOING:	R	W	P	TRACK	R	W	P
Yielding	1	1	0	Left-Handed	1	1	0

TRIP:	R	W	P	JOCKEY:	R	W	P
3m	1	1	0	F.Maguire	1	1	0

ONE JUMP AHEAD & AHEAD ON THE FLAT *UPDATES*

"ETHICAL DIAMOND (Willie Mullins)** is one of two leading contenders for Willie Mullins who is bidding to win the race for a third time (Sesenta (2009) & Absurde (2023)). Purchased for 320,000gns in July 2023, the five year old is rated 104 on the Flat and 143 over hurdles. A two lengths winner of the Duke of Edinburgh Stakes at Royal Ascot off 96, he finished fourth in the same event in 2024. Kept fresh since (64 days), he was fourth in the County Hurdle at the Cheltenham Festival in March and is accustomed to the hussle and bustle of large field handicaps. His record over twelve furlongs is 141 and handles any ground. If he stays, the Awtaad gelding looks set to play a leading role – he hasn't raced beyond a mile and a half on the Flat and is inclined to race keenly. With William Buick likely to be on board for the first time, the key to his chance could be how he settles early on. **Best Price: 8/1 (Bet365, William Hill).
Advised @ 8/1 WON the Sky Bet Ebor at York

BIG RACE SUCCESSES

GREATWOOD HURDLE – BURDETT ROAD Advised @ 5/1
KING GEORGE – BANBRIDGE @ 7/1
WILLIAM HILL HANDICAP HURDLE – JOYEUSE Advised @ 8/1
CORAL CUP – JIMMY DU SEUIL @ 16/1
GRAND NATIONAL – GRANGECLARE WEST (3rd) Advised @ 66/1
9 WINNERS @ ROYAL ASCOT 2025
***SKY BET* EBOR – 1st & 2nd ETHICAL DIAMOND Advised @ 8/1 & ASCENDING Advised @ 25/1**

For full details of the *One Jump Ahead Updates* see pages 191-197 and the *Ahead On The Flat Updates* pages 199

OWNERS' ENCLOSURE

RICH & SUSANNAH RICCI

GRADE 1 WINNERS: 104
CHELTENHAM FESTIVAL WINNERS: 23

Sixteen years after their first Grade 1 winner, Royale Pagaille provided Rich and Susannah Ricci with their 100th victory at the highest level when capturing the *Betfair* Chase at Haydock Park for a second consecutive year last winter. The eleven year old will bid to emulate Bristol De Mai and Cue Card and win it for a third time in November. Four more Grade 1 wins swiftly followed for the Ricci Family, including Lossiemouth's silky smooth success in the David Nicholson Mares' Hurdle in March. Their Cheltenham Festival tally is currently registering 23 and counting. The dashing grey mare, along with compatriot Gaelic Warrior, who landed big prizes at Aintree and Sandown during the spring, aided Willie Mullins' pursuit to retain the British trainers' title.

Never ones to rest of their laurels, whether its on the racecourse or the vineyard, the Ricci's have added to their equine portfolio during the spring and summer with acquisitions from France and Ireland. These include some exciting young hurdling prospects. Four times Grade 1 and Cheltenham Festival winner Gaelic Warrior remains one of the most talented horses in training and there is every chance the seven year old will line up in the King George Chase at Kempton on Boxing Day, while Lossiemouth is expected to follow a similar path culminating in Prestbury Park in March. As in previous years, Racing manager **Joe Chambers** has kindly passed on news of the pink and green 'superstars' and the other leading lights amongst the squad for 2025/2026.

DR EGGMAN (FR) 7 b g Saint Des Saints (FR) – Jahra (FR)
Bred to be a chaser, we are looking forward to him going over fences this year. Having missed the first half of the campaign, he got his act together during the second half of the season winning a maiden hurdle at Limerick before finishing runner-up at Cheltenham's April meeting. He had had enough by the time he ran at Sandown on the final day of the season. Yet to race beyond two and a half miles, we think he will get further and develop into a nice staying chaser over three miles.

GAELIC WARRIOR (GER) 7 b g Maxios – Game of Legs (FR)
A four times Grade 1 winner, he was placed in a couple of Grade 1 chases over two miles at Leopardstown at Christmas and the DRF in February. Unfortunately, he wasn't ready for Cheltenham in March and therefore missed the Festival. However, he made amends at Aintree and Sandown when stepped up in trip. Patrick (Mullins) was very good on him in the Bowl Chase at the former and, similarly, Paul (Townend) in the Oaksey Chase at the latter. He has come back in following his summer break and the King George VI Chase at Kempton on Boxing Day (26th December) would appear the logical mid season target.

JOYSTICK (FR) 6 gr g Coastal Path – Polka Valtat (FR)
Toughed it out in atrocious ground to beat subsequent Grade 1 winner Honesty Policy in a two miles maiden hurdle at Naas in January, he was runner-up in a Grade 3 novice at the same track the following month. Below par at Fairyhouse last time, he needs to learn to settle and finish off

his races better. A former pointer, the plan is for him to go novice chasing and we are hoping he will improve. He looked a stayer in his bumpers, but he needs to do things the right way around.

KARAK DE FAUST (FR) 3 b f Zarak (FR) – Katkobella (FR)
From the family of Grade 1 winner Kotkikova, Willie (Mullins) and Harold (Kirk) were keen on her at the Goffs Arkle Sale in June. She possesses a real National Hunt pedigree and, all being well, she will make her debut in a bumper in the spring.

KARA SACRE (FR) 5 b g Karaktar (IRE) – Divine Sacree (FR)
We bought him privately during the summer – Rich (Ricci) is very good friends with Paul Nolan, for whom he was placed in two of his three runs over hurdles during the spring. Runner-up at Naas and third at Down Royal, he had previously won a point-to-point for Sam Curling. He is rated 116 and we think the UK programme will suit him. One of four horses Rich and Susannah have in training with Venetia (Williams), who is planning to send him novice handicap chasing and we are hoping he will be progressive over fences.

KARPENN (FR) 4 ch g Goliath Du Berlais (FR) – Karpathina (FR)
Another new addition with Venetia (Williams), he was owned in France by Francois Nicolle who trained Royale Pagaille before we bought him. Handled by Jerome Delaunay, he has only raced five times. Placed twice over hurdles at Pau, including behind Lovely Guy (Listed winner since) in January, he was third on his chasing debut at Auteuil in March. Only four, he is the type of horse Venetia does very well with and is likely to run over hurdles this season.

KINGBEL DU LION (FR) 5 b g Non Rien De Rien (FR) – Tazabelle Du Lion (FR)
Only five, he is a horse we like a lot and feel is open to plenty of improvement. Placed over fences in France prior to joining us, we gave him plenty of time when he first arrived and he won in good style over hurdles at Bangor in February. We were keen to run him again during the spring but the ground dried up. We didn't want to risk him on fast ground. A work in progress, he is rated 123 and will go novice handicap chasing. Yet to race beyond two and a half miles, we think he will stay further and hopefully he will work his way through the ranks.

LAURETS D'ESTRUVAL (FR) 4 b g Saint Des Saints (FR) – Brise D'Estruval (FR)
A new recruit from France, he shaped well on his hurdles debut at Pau in December for Guillaume Macaire. We haven't bought many from the same source in recent seasons but have had plenty of success with ex-Macaire horses over the years, namely Burrows Saint, Let's Dance and Vautour. The form has worked out with the winner (Lovely Guy) following up twice more, including at Listed level. Willie (Mullins) hasn't done much with him yet and it is early days. He will start off in a maiden hurdle and we will see how far he can progress.

LOSSIEMOUTH (FR) 6 gr m Great Pretender (IRE) – Mariner's Light (FR)
She had another fantastic season winning three Grade 1 races, including the David Nicholson Mares' Hurdle at the Cheltenham Festival for a second time. She followed that up by winning the Aintree Hurdle. The plan was to run at the Punchestown Festival, but she came back jarred up from Aintree. The ground was quick enough for her. However, she has come back into work following her summer holiday and is fine now. In all likelihood, she will start off in the Grade 1 Hatton's Grace Hurdle at Fairyhouse (30th November), which she won last year. We haven't looked beyond that.

LOVE SIGN D'AUNOU (FR) 4 b g Goliath Du Berlais (FR) – Ossun (FR)
A strong looking individual, he won his only Irish point-to-point at Loughanmore on Easter Saturday. Trained by Ger Quinn, the runner-up was later sold for €120,000 and has joined Paul Nolan. Only four, he has settled in well at Willie's (Mullins) and will go down the bumper route.

MADNESS D'ELLE (FR) 3 b g Moises Has (FR) – Voulay (FR)
One of two three year olds we have acquired from France by Moises Has, he finished third on his hurdles debut at Auteuil in May when trained by Daniela Mele. Beaten around six lengths, the form looks solid with the winner (Shannon Maestro) finishing runner-up in a Listed event next time. I would imagine Willie (Mullins) will look to run him in a juvenile hurdle around Christmas time.

MANITA (FR) 3 gr f Moises Has (FR) – Mastermambo (IRE)
Another daughter of Moises Has, she is a fine looking filly. Previously trained by Yannick Fouin, who supplied us with Lossiemouth and Min, she finished runner-up in a conditions hurdle at Auteuil in March. It looked a strong contest with the winner (Manlaga) being subsequently bought by J.P.(McManus) and has joined Nicky Henderson. She is hopefully one to look forward to in juvenile hurdles.

MISTER POLICEMAN (FR) 7 ch g Triple Threat (FR) – Manhattan Princess
A horse we have always liked since coming over from France. However, he has proved frustrating on occasions because he possesses a lot of ability but hasn't always translated his homework to the track. We stepped him up to three miles for the first time in the Grade 3 Michael O'Sullivan Chase at Cork over Easter and he won impressively. He looked very good that day. Unfortunately, he incurred an injury afterwards and therefore won't be in action until the second half of the season. Rated 155, he looks a Grand National type and we are hoping he will be progressive in staying chases.

O'MOORE PARK (IRE) 8 b g Walk In The Park (IRE) – Glor Na Gaoithe (IRE)
Still a maiden over fences, he ran some good races in defeat, including when placed in the Jack Richards Novices' Handicap Chase at the Cheltenham Festival. He returned to the same track the following month and was narrowly beaten in the Grade 2 Silver Trophy Handicap Chase. I would put a line through his run in the Be365 Gold Cup at Sandown because he was over the top by then. Rated 141, he went back into training earlier with a view to getting him ready for the Coral Gold Cup Handicap Chase at Newbury (29th November).

PORT JOULAIN (FR) 6 b g Cokoriko (FR) – Apple's Noa (FR)
Won't be running until the second half of the season having injured himself in the Albert Bartlett Novices' Hurdle at the Festival. Despite not having the smoothest of campaigns last year, we still believe there is a good horse in there. Pulled up on his hurdles debut at Punchestown in December, Paul (Townend) thought he had gone wrong but was fine afterwards. He then ran well in a competitive maiden hurdle at Leopardstown over Christmas before winning at Punchestown towards the end of January. The intention is for him to go over fences in the New Year.

RISKABAHIA (FR) 5 b m No Risk At All (FR) – Bahia De Cerisy (FR)
Still yet to run for us, Anne-Sophie Pacault trained her to win a mile and seven fillies' maiden at Fontainebleau in September 2023. Bought privately soon afterwards, she was unable to run last

season, due to a setback, which was frustrating. By a top-class stallion, mares' novice hurdles will be her target and we are hoping she will make up for lost time and prove useful.

ROYALE PAGAILLE (FR) 11 b g Blue Bresil (FR) – Royale Cazoumaille (FR)
All roads lead to Haydock for the *Betfair* Chase once again (22nd November) in a bid to win it for a third time. He produced a very good performance last year and we will do what is right by the horse. He is ground dependent and found it too quick in the Grand National at Aintree.

SAINTE LUCIE (FR) 4 b f Great Pretender (IRE) – Sainte Folie (FR)
Placed on her hurdles debut at Auteuil when trained by Robert Collet, she looked very good when winning impressively at Punchestown on New Year's Eve. Her performance got both the trainer and jockey excited. Sent off favourite for the Grade 1 juvenile hurdle at the DRF at Leopardstown next time, she raced too keenly and was disappointing. We tried to teach her to settle in her subsequent races and came to the conclusion that she is a stayer in the making. With that in mind, she could be attractively treated off 127 when stepping up in trip.

SPARKLING WIT (IRE) 4 b g Maxios – Game of Legs (FR)
A full-brother to Gaelic Warrior, we acquired him last year and his debut is going to attract plenty of attention. It is early days, but he has done some nice pieces of work and will start off in a bumper.

RICH'S HORSE TO FOLLOW: RISKABAHIA
RACING MANAGER JOE CHAMBERS HORSE TO FOLLOW: LOVE SIGN D'AUNOU

Please see pages 191-197
for details of the

One Jump Ahead Updates

TALKING TRAINERS

Harry DERHAM

Stables: Upper Farm Stables, High Street, Boxford.
2024/2025: 57 Winners / 274 Runners 21% Prize-Money £647,865
www.harryderhamracing.com

ANNIE GLORY (IRE) 4 b f Blue Bresil (FR) – Glory O (IRE)
Owned by Highclere Thoroughbred Racing, she ran an eyecatching race on her debut in an Irish point-to-point in the spring. Subsequently bought privately, she is a nice filly to go novice hurdling with.

ASCENDING LARK 7 b m Great Pretender (IRE) – Miss Bailly (FR)
Unbeaten in six runs since joining us, she had an amazing season culminating in victory in a Listed handicap hurdle at the Punchestown Festival. She won mares' handicaps at Newcastle, Exeter and Ludlow en route and her work before Punchestown had been very good. She kept improving and is now rated 137. We aren't in a rush with her this winter because the better races for highly rated mares tend to come during the second half of the season and the spring. The Grade 2 Warfield Mares' Hurdle at Ascot in January is a likely starting point and that will hopefully tell us whether the Grade 1 David Nicholson Mares' Hurdle at the Cheltenham Festival is a realistic target.

AVIEMORE 4 b g Kodiac – Raincall
A useful horse on the Flat, Highclere Thoroughbred Racing kindly sent him to us and he took well to jumping winning twice at Warwick and Huntingdon. Over the top by the time he ran in the Grade 1 juvenile hurdle at Aintree's Grand National meeting, he had gone in his coat. It is not easy for second season four year olds but he looks well and we will give him a run on the Flat before going back over hurdles. His first target is the four year old hurdle at Chepstow (11th October). I think he will benefit from stepping up in trip later on because he looked a strong stayer when winning at Huntingdon in March. We will mix and match between the Flat and over hurdles.

BRENTFORD HOPE 8 b g Camelot – Miss Raven (IRE)
He has been a fantastic horse for us winning five times over hurdles and earning a lot of prize-money. Even though he didn't get his head in front last season, he ran some very good races in defeat. Runner-up in the Grade 2 Elite Hurdle at Wincanton and, most notably, behind Constitution Hill in the Grade 2 International Hurdle at Cheltenham, it paid for his season. The plan is to school him over fences in the Autumn with a view to going novice chasing. He possesses class and will be suited by the small fields and I hope he will develop into a useful novice.

CASUAL OBSERVER (IRE) 6 b g Pillar Coral – Oulart Star (IRE)
Only raced twice last winter, due to a minor issue, but he won over hurdles at Ffos Las on his final start. A former Irish pointer, he will go over fences and I think he will be progressive in novice handicap chases off his mark of 113. He loves soft ground and the switch to fences is likely to bring about further improvement. Quite a forward going type, he will stay well once relaxing in his races. It wouldn't surprise me if he ended up in the valuable staying novices' handicap at Uttoxeter's Midlands National meeting next March.

CLONDAW PARK (IRE) 4 b f Walk In The Park (IRE) – Zamani (IRE)
An exciting filly we bought at the Cheltenham Festival Sale in March having won her point-to-point in Ireland in impressive fashion. It was a steadily run race but she jumped brilliantly and quickened clear after the second last. Out of a Teofilo mare, there is speed in the pedigree and she doesn't look slow. Physically, she has made amazing progress during the summer and is a lovely horse for the future. We aren't going to rush her and haven't decided whether to run her in bumpers this season or go straight over hurdles. Either way, she will start off over two miles and it will be mid November onwards before she runs.

COURT IN THE ACT (IRE) 6 b g Court Cave (IRE) – Alexander Road (IRE)
Dual winner over hurdles at Market Rasen and Ascot last season, we have been minding him with a view to going chasing this Autumn. His jumping has improved and I hope he will develop into a nice chaser capable of competing in Saturday handicap chases over two and two and a half miles eventually. Still improving, he doesn't want the ground too soft.

CRISTAL D'ESTRUVAL (IRE) 4 b g Crystal Ocean – Aurore D'Estruval (FR)
He really took my eye at the Cheltenham Festival Sale in March – I loved him. Trained in Ireland by Colin Bowe, he won his only point-to-point in bottomless ground. Despite that, the time was very good and he jumped well bar the last. Well built, he was bought to be a high-class horse who will jump fences eventually. He is similar to Mossy Fen Road – a beautiful physical model and we start with a blank canvas. In all likelihood, he will go straight over hurdles and will start off over two and a half miles at a good track.

CRYSTELLO (IRE) 4 b g Crystal Ocean – Come Softly
By the same stallion as Cristal D'Estruval who we have invested in, he ran in two Irish points for Denis Hogan finishing runner-up last time. Purchased at the Goffs UK Spring Sale in May, it is difficult to gauge the strength of the form, but he has done well physically since arriving. He is likely to go novice hurdling.

DRAMATIC ENCORE (IRE) 5 b m Walk In The Park (IRE) – Lyrical Theatre (IRE)
Progressed over hurdles winning at Huntingdon in February before finishing a close second at Doncaster next time. She went over the top in the spring hence we didn't run her again. She has run two good races over hurdles and I would like to aim her at the Richard Barber Memorial Mares' Handicap Hurdle at Wincanton (8th November). Two miles five on a flat track is ideal and we will give her one run beforehand.

EMERALD LAD (FR) 6 gr g Diamond Boy (FR) – Attente De Sivola (FR)
Not the easiest horse to manage, he can be quite hot, like his dam, who I used to ride. However, he has ability and I thought he shaped nicely on his debut in a bumper at Plumpton on Easter Monday. He didn't get the clearest of runs before finishing fourth. It wasn't a bad race either. He will go novice hurdling over two miles in the Autumn.

ESCAPEANDEVADE (IRE) 9 b g Westerner – Sandrinechoix (FR)
Bought at the Goffs UK Spring Sale, he is a four times winner over fences and could be well treated in two mile handicap chases. He slightly lost his way last season and we have done well with that type of horse in the past. There is often good prize-money on offer in such races and they are usually contested by smallish fields.

FILIBUSTERING 4 b g Postponed (IRE) – Mystique

He spent the summer with Noel Fehily and we are hoping he could develop into a William Hill Hurdle type horse at Newbury in February. Bought at the Newmarket Autumn Horses in Training Sale last year, it wasn't a surprise when he won on his hurdles debut at Kelso in March. We then ran him in the Grade 1 4yo Anniversary Juvenile Hurdle at Aintree but found the ground too quick. Eligible for novice hurdles until the end of November, he has potential and we will aim him at the smart handicap hurdles later on.

FIRM BUT FAIR (IRE) 4 b g Yeats (IRE) – Cosmic Charm (IRE)

A chasing type, he is a beautiful horse we bought at the Goffs UK Spring Sale in May. Third in his Irish point for Sean Doyle, the winner (Grangeclare Park) was purchased privately afterwards for a lot of money and has joined Gordon Elliott. He will go novice hurdling over two and a half miles and I think he will be progressive. He reminds me of Storm Arising who was trained by Paul (Nicholls).

GALLIVANTED (FR) 3 b g Galiway – Fedya (IRE)

Lightly raced on the Flat for Tom Clover, he won over a mile and a half at Kempton in May. By a sire I like, we bought him at the Newmarket July Sales. His dam won over twelve furlongs on soft ground in France and he is a good model. Gelded since arriving, he will go juvenile hurdling.

JACKIE HOBBS 5 b m Jack Hobbs – Miss Milborne

We are looking forward to seeing her run in mares' novice hurdles this season. A winning pointer, she won in good style in bumpers at Ludlow and Ascot before stepping up in class at Aintree in the spring. Contesting a Grade 2 mares' bumper, she travelled well but Paul (O'Brien) felt she found the ground too quick. The experience won't be lost on her and we are hoping she will develop into a very nice mares novice hurdler. We will start her off over two miles, possibly at Newbury (6th November). It would be nice to think she will go back there for the Listed mares' novice hurdle at the Coral Gold Cup Festival (29th November).

JACKPOT CAUVELIERE (FR) 6 ch g Kamsin (GER) – Senanque (IRE)

A big strong horse who I really like, he was a wide margin winner of his Irish point for Stuart Crawford in November. Bought a week later, we decided there was no point running him in the spring and decided to give him more time. There is nothing flashy about him – he jumps and stays well and will be campaigned in novice hurdles over two and a half miles plus.

JASMINE BLISS 6 b m Blue Bresil (FR) – Burton Ash

She is a lovely mare who has size and scope and we are going to send her over fences this term. A dual bumper winner, she had a good season over hurdles winning at Ludlow and Southwell. We ran her in the mares' final at Newbury in March, but they went slow and then sprinted in the homestraight. We decided to leave her off after that and she has had a good break during the summer. An ex-point winner, she is a fantastic jumper and, while she stays well, I would be happy enough to run her over two miles on a stiff track. Very reliable, she has a good attitude and I think she will make a nice chaser.

JASMIN D'AIRY (FR) 6 b m Authorized (IRE) – Elna D'Airy (FR)

A bumper winner in Ireland, it took us a while to work her out last season. Runner-up a couple of times at Musselburgh and Ffos Las, we decided to make plenty of use of her at Plumpton over Easter and she won easily. Still a novice until the beginning of December, she will run in another mares' novice hurdle under a penalty and then she is likely to go mares novice chasing. She is effective over two and two and a half miles.

JOKER DE MAI (FR) 6 b g Balko (FR) – Divine De Stpierre (FR)
His owner David Maxwell was keen for him to go hunter chasing and his season revolved around the Foxhunters' Hunters' Chase at Aintree. Unfortunately, he fell at the third (The Chair) and it dented his confidence. Pulled up at Stratford last time, it was a non event. An easy winner over two miles at Leicester in March, it suited him being ridden aggressively. We have the option of campaigning him in handicap chases over two and two and a half miles.

JULIO COOLIO 4 ch f Crystal Ocean – Miss Bailly (FR)
She is a lovely filly who was in training with Aidan Fitzgerald last season but didn't run. A half-sister to Ascending Lark and Romeo Coolio, she will run in mares' bumpers.

JUS DE CITRON (FR) 6 b g Saint Des Saints (FR) – Rapide I (FR)
A proper chaser in the making, he won on his hurdles debut at Doncaster in December before finishing third under a penalty at Kempton when he found the ground too soft. He then fractured his fetlock on the gallops and therefore won't be running until around Christmas time onwards. Despite being a big horse, he wants top of the ground and I think he will develop into a nice chaser.

JUST ENNEMI (FR) 5 ch g Kamsin (GER) – Aubane (FR)
A smart horse who has yet to run for us having won twice over hurdles in France, including at Auteuil in September last year. Owned by David Maxwell, he arrived before Christmas and the time off won't have done him any harm. We nearly ran him in the Imperial Cup at Sandown but decided to leave him off. Officially rated 128, he will start off in a decent handicap hurdle and then we will decide whether to stay over hurdles or go chasing. There are plenty of options for him.

KARMA POLICE (FR) 5 br g It's Gino (GER) – Albain Champenoise (FR)
He won his Irish point-to-point for Michael Goff before being bought at the Cheltenham February Sale last year. Narrowly beaten in a bumper at Fontwell in January on his only start for us, he ran a nice race and is a horse I like. He has schooled well over hurdles and is a very good jumper. Two and a half miles novice hurdles will be on his agenda and he could emerge as an EBF Final contender at Sandown in the spring. He will find his level.

KATIE'S MELODY (IRE) 5 b m Flemensfirth (USA) – Little Dil (IRE)
Trained in Ireland by Jonathan Fogarty, she won a point-to-point on her debut before finishing runner-up in a bumper at Tipperary a couple of months later. She looks a nice mare and will go straight over hurdles.

KING WOODY 5 b g Getaway (GER) – Ms Parfois (IRE)
Unraced, he is hugely talented but was unable to run last season due to a small issue in the spring. Out of a very good mare who was Grade 1 placed, he has a staying pedigree and will go novice hurdling. A horse with a lot of ability, he looks well above average.

KIWI RUSH (IRE) 5 b g Mahler – Don't Forsit (IRE)
A very nice horse who I really like, he is one of the most eyecatching horses at home schooling

wise. He won a bumper at Kelso in February and was then narrowly beaten under a penalty at the same track. Patrick (Mullins) rode him and said he gave him a great feel but wishes he had made more use of him. A big long striding horse, we will start him off over two and a half miles and I think he will make a lovely staying novice hurdler.

KLUB DE REVE (FR) 5 b g Fly With Me (FR) – Silouette De Reve (FR)
Bought last year having won a point-to-point for Donnchadh Doyle, the Goffs Hundred Grand Bumper at Newbury in March was the plan. He finished third and I was thrilled with him. We have schooled him over hurdles and he jumps well. In all likelihood, he will start over two miles before stepping up in trip later on. He is another potential EBF Final type horse for the spring.

KORKORAN (FR) 5 b g No Risk At All (FR) – Kotkieglote (FR)
A big strong horse who won his point for Colin Bowe in Ireland. We thought he would run well in a bumper at Exeter in February but proved a bit disappointing. However, a couple of weeks later, we did a gastroscopy and found he was suffering from Grade 4 ulcers, which have been treated. Put away soon afterwards, he will go novice hurdling over two and a half miles on slow ground. I think he will want a trip.

LAKE TIBERIAS (IRE) 5 b g Diamond Boy (FR) – Sea of Galilee
Half-brother to Listed hurdle winner Ahorsewithnoname, he is a nice young unraced horse. He was due to run in a bumper at Newcastle last spring but coughed beforehand and we therefore left him off afterwards. We will give him a run in a bumper to gain some experience before going hurdling. He has schooled well.

LARIO (GER) 6 b g Nutan (IRE) – Larmina (FR)
Runner-up over hurdles at Haydock and Newbury, it was frustrating we weren't able to win with him last season. He works well at home and has plenty of ability. We may give him a run on the Flat before going over fences. He travels well and the fact there are more jumps over fences will suit him. We have high hopes for him in two mile novice chases.

LASKO DES OBEAUX (FR) 4 b g Bathyrhon (GER) – Shifra (FR)
Purchased at the Aintree Grand National Sale last spring, he is a lovely horse who ran very well in his point-to-point. Trained by Matty Flynn O'Connor, he finished second and, while he was quite lean at the sales, he has done really well physically during the summer. He will go novice hurdling and I like him a lot.

LE FRIMEUR (FR) 4 b g Gemix (FR) – Ty Perrine (FR)
Owned by Simon Munir and Isaac Souede, I am delighted to be training him. He only arrived in early August so we haven't done a lot with him yet but he won his point-to-point in Ireland for Pat Doyle in good style. We will decide whether he runs in a bumper or goes straight over hurdles. He is a lovely horse to have.

MAD MAXIOS (IRE) 4 b g Maxios – La Premiere Dame (IRE)
An interesting horse who was weak and backward last Autumn. However, he improved a lot from his debut to his second run being narrowly beaten at Market Rasen. A winner next time at Chepstow, he has done well during the summer and remains eligible for novice hurdling. I think he will come into his own in novice handicap hurdles.

MADAME LUNA 4 b f Sea The Moon (GER) – Madame (GER)
Unbeaten in two junior National Hunt hurdles, we still don't know how good she is. Not over big, she hadn't worked before going to Fakenham in November and won nicely. She then followed up at Wetherby in February making all and winning snugly. Officially rated 109, she is progressive and looks well treated.

MAITRE EN SCIENCE (FR) 4 gr g Master's Spirit (IRE) – Vassileva (FR)
Twice a winner over hurdles in France, he joined us halfway through last season but was disappointing in three runs. His work at home had been good and it is a case of back to the drawing board with him. We gave him a long break after his last run at Ascot in March and hopefully he will reproduce his homework on the track.

MILITARY ALLIANCE (IRE) 6 b g Churchill (IRE) – Dusty In Memphis (USA)
Placed on the Flat in Ireland, he did well to win on his hurdles debut at Hereford in the spring. He knocked himself afterwards hence he hasn't run since but remains unexposed. Still a novice until the end of November, we will aim him at another novice under a penalty and then go handicap hurdling.

MONDOUI'BOY (FR) 5 b g Castle Du Berlais (FR) – Mondovi (FR)
Runner-up in a point-to-point prior to joining us, he is a beautiful horse who I am very fond of. He ran two good races in bumpers at Sandown and Punchestown and has plenty of ability. He jumps well and will be suited by two and a half miles on soft ground over hurdles.

MOSSY FEN ROAD (IRE) 5 b g Flemensfirth (USA) – Molly Duffy (IRE)
Half-brother to Grade 1 winner Fury Road, he is a smart horse and one to look forward to over hurdles this season. A proper soft ground horse and a powerful galloper, he is a forward going type who won impressively in a bumper at Wetherby in February. We then ran him in the Grade 2 bumper at Aintree on Grand National day. He ran well for a long way but found the ground too quick. The experience he gained that day will stand him in good stead. We will start him off over two miles, although he will stay further.

NOAHSGREATRAINBOW (IRE) 6 b g Milan – Bowling Green (IRE)
He has a lot of natural talent and a horse I have always liked a lot. He had some very good bumper form winning at Wincanton before finishing runner-up in a Listed event at Newbury. Unfortunately, he bled both times he raced over hurdles last season at Sandown and Taunton. We left him alone after his run at the latter track and have hobdayed his soft palate during the summer. He looks stunning at the moment and hopefully he can recapture his best form in two and a half miles novice hurdles.

NORN IRON (IRE) 7 br g Soldier of Fortune (IRE) – Coco Des Champs (IRE)
Consistent, he finished second on three occasions before gaining a much deserved victory at Plumpton in April. The plan is for him to go over fences and I think he is nicely treated off a mark of 118. He could be ideal for some of those novice handicap chases at Newbury during the first half of the season.

ONE HORSE TOWN (IRE) 3 ch g Threat (IRE) – Almost Always (IRE)
Successful over twelve furlongs on the Flat at Kempton in the spring, he has taken well to hurdles during the summer. A convincing winner at Hexham and Stratford, he has had a break

since and will run next in either the Listed Wensleydale Juvenile Hurdle at Wetherby (31st October) or wait for the Grade 2 juvenile hurdle at Cheltenham's Paddy Power meeting (15th November). He doesn't want deep ground.

PARK TALK (IRE) 5 b g Walk In The Park (IRE) – Nova Cyngi (USA)
Half-brother to Dodging Bullets, he ran in four Irish points for Sean Doyle winning last time. Bought privately, he will go novice hurdling and we have been pleased with him since arriving.

PATRIMONIO (FR) 4 b g Barastraight – Primeiradama (FR)
Owned by The DTTW Partnership, he was kindly sent to us and we are delighted to be training for them. He is a big horse who ran well in his only point-to-point for Cormac Doyle in Ireland finishing second. Bought at the Cheltenham April Sale, he doesn't strike me as a bumper horse and is therefore likely to go novice hurdling over two and a half miles. I think he will stay well.

PYFFO (IRE) 7 b g Shantou (USA) – Maryota (FR)
Tough and genuine, he joined us last season and did well to win a Pertemps qualifier at Musselburgh in February. We were aiming him at the final at the Cheltenham Festival but he was ruled out due to a fetlock injury. He isn't a chasing type and will continue in staying handicap hurdles. He could be ideal for one of those three miles handicap hurdles at Cheltenham before Christmas and there is another suitable one at Newbury's William Hill Handicap Hurdle in February.

QUEENS GAMBLE (IRE) 7 ch m Getaway (GER) – Gambling Girl (IRE)
She has endured a tough spell during the summer suffering two bouts of colic. However, she is in good form now and the intention is for her to go novice chasing. A Listed novice hurdle winner the previous season, she finished runner-up in the Gerry Feilden Hurdle at Newbury on her reappearance. We then aimed her at a Listed mares' handicap hurdle at the DRF at Leopardstown in February and felt we had her at her best. Unfortunately, the ground went against her and she finished sixth. Found to have bled after running in the Grade 1 David Nicholson Mares' Hurdle at the Cheltenham Festival, we didn't see the best of her last season.

QUEENSBURY BOY (IRE) 6 br g Doyen (IRE) – Queens Wild (IRE)
A smart horse who underwent wind surgery last Autumn and then had a setback hence he didn't reappear until early March. Twice a winner over hurdles at Doncaster and Newbury, we let him take his chance in Grade 1 company at the Punchestown Festival. He ran OK but had probably had enough by that stage of the season. The experience of running in a race like that will stand him in good stead though. Still a novice until the end of November, his big target is the Grade 2 Persian War Novices' Hurdle at Chepstow (10th October). His performance there will decide whether he stays over hurdles and is aimed at something like the Coral Cup in the spring, or goes novice chasing. Two and a half miles is his trip at the moment but he ought to stay further later on.

RECITE A POEM (IRE) 4 b f Poet's Word (IRE) – Maldagora (IRE)
Raced in two Irish points winning nicely on the second occasion, Noel (Fehily) bought her soon afterwards. I am excited by her sire and she is likely to spend this season in mares' only bumpers. She looks a lovely filly.

SIORAI (IRE) 3 br f Masar (IRE) – Solas Na Greine (IRE)
Similar to Gallivanted, she was bought at the Newmarket July Sales with a view to going juvenile hurdling. Previously trained by Jim Bolger in Ireland, she only raced three times on the Flat. She has plenty of size and a staying pedigree and we were keen to buy a three year old filly to go jumping. The Listed fillies' juvenile hurdle at Newbury (28th November) is her target with one run beforehand.

SLUGGER 6 b g Ocovango – Dolly Boru
Joined us last season and did very well winning over hurdles at Carlisle, Doncaster and Musselburgh. Fourth in the Morebattle Hurdle at Kelso in March, he was then runner-up in the conditional jockeys' handicap hurdle at Aintree's Grand National meeting. He travelled strongly that day but came back lame afterwards. He underwent surgery the following day and won't be running until Christmas time onwards. His owner is keen for him to go over fences and I think he will make a nice chaser.

ST JUST IN TIME 5 b g Time Test – Porthledden Flight
Still a novice over hurdles, he has only raced once for us when unlucky not to win at Doncaster in early March. Beaten a short head, he is quite a nice horse who is capable of going one better.

TEDDY BLUE (GER) 7 b g Sea The Moon (GER) – Tickle Me Blue (GER)
He has his own ideas but is a capable horse who took well to fences last season. Twice a winner at Huntingdon and Kempton, he was also runner-up at Newbury. Rated 131, he is high enough in the weights but has the ability to win more races. Galloping tracks on decent ground suit him and he could be one for those two miles two handicap chases at Newbury in November.

TERRANO (FR) 4 bb g Triple Threat (FR) – Terravista (FR)
Placed in his point-to-point in Ireland for Jonathan Fogarty, he has settled in well and will go novice hurdling over two or two and a half miles.

THE BURREN MAN 4 b g Maxios – Ryme Bere (FR)
A beautiful horse who I loved at the Punchestown Festival Sale, he was second in a point-to-point a few days beforehand. The time was good and he was beaten by a very good horse (Wyoming Line). A fine big horse, he reminds me of Kiwi Rush and we are looking forward to sending him novice hurdling. He will find his level.

VIYANNI (IRE) 4 b g Almanzor (FR) – Viyana (IRE)
Won two of his three races over hurdles at Market Rasen and Ludlow, we were aiming him at the Fred Winter Juvenile Hurdle at the Cheltenham Festival. I thought he would have a live chance but, unfortunately, he suffered a setback and missed the remainder of the season. Long-term, I am expecting him to be a staying horse running over three miles. In the meantime, he is a possible for the Gerry Feilden Hurdle at Newbury (29th November), although he won't have a busy campaign because it can be tricky for four year olds during their second season. The Lanzarote Hurdle at Kempton in January is another possible target later on.

TRAINER'S HORSE TO FOLLOW: CLONDAW PARK

Oliver GREENALL & Josh GUERRIERO

Stables: Stockton Hall Farm, Oldcastle, Malpas, Cheshire.
2024/2025: 58 Winners / 454 Runners 13% Prize-Money £752,858
www.greenall-guerriero.com

A CHARA 4 b f Gentlewave (IRE) – Cara's Way (IRE)
It is early days, but she looks a useful mare who ran in two point-to-points for Pat Turley in Ireland. She ran against geldings on her debut finishing third before winning nicely next time. Dan Astbury was keen to buy her at the Cheltenham April Sale and we have the option of running her in either mares' bumpers or novice hurdles.

ABOUTDAMNTIME (IRE) 6 b g Flemensfirth (USA) – Give It Time
A former Irish pointer, he won on his hurdles debut at Carlisle in November. However, he struggled with his breathing thereafter and, even though he didn't run badly at Newcastle on his penultimate start, he rather lost his way. He has undergone wind surgery and the plan is for him to go novice handicap chasing over two and a half to three miles.

BACKWATERS (FR) 4 b g Doctor Dino (FR) – Frivolite (FR)
Unraced, he is a very nice horse who we really like. Bought at the Goffs Arkle Sale as a three year old, he was still weak last year. He has strengthened up during the summer though and works well at home. I think he will prefer better ground and we will start him off in a bumper.

BERKIE (IRE) 4 b g Berkshire (IRE) – Golded (IRE)
A lovely type, he is still a big weak horse who finished runner-up in his point-to-point in May for Michael Goff in Ireland. We aren't going to rush him and will probably start him off in a bumper in the New Year. He is very much one for the future.

CARRIG KATE (IRE) 7 b m Westerner – Carrig Millie (IRE)
Tough and consistent, I can't wait for her to go over fences. Placed four times over hurdles last season, she ran very well in a Listed mares' novice hurdle at Doncaster in March gaining some black type. A winning pointer, she jumps and stays well and handles soft ground. She is on a good mark and is one for novice handicap chases over two and a half miles plus.

CRYSTAL GLANCE 5 br m Passing Glance – Crystal Princess (IRE)
She prefers decent ground and is a nice mare who will be going over fences. A four times winner over hurdles, including at Warwick in May, she was suited by the step up to two and a half miles. She is learning to settle better and is a tough mare who is capable of making a nice chaser.

DALY BOY (FR) 5 b g Kamsin (GER) – Destinee Chalnetta (FR)
He is a lovely horse we acquired at the Cheltenham December Sale having finished second in his Irish point. We thought he would run well on his first start for us in a bumper at Ayr in the spring finishing third and the form looks sound. A bit keen last season, he will improve plenty for the switch to hurdling and is a horse we really like. He prefers some cut in the ground.

DAZZLELIKETHIS (IRE) 6 b m Mahler – Sister Bernadette (IRE)
Runner-up on her debut over hurdles at Carlisle, she struggled on soft ground in her subsequent runs because it was affecting her breathing. She was unlucky not to win her point-to-point and

the intention is to send her novice chasing. We will start her off over two and a half miles before stepping up to three miles later on. I hope she will improve over fences.

DIAMOND JIM (IRE) 3 b g Teofilo (IRE) – Lillian Russell (IRE)
One for the junior National Hunt hurdles, he is a nice horse we bought at the Tattersalls February Sale. A Godolphin cast-off, it is early days, but he looks a jumper and will be suited by a bit of cut in the ground. We like him.

FORCETORECKONWITH (IRE) 6 b m Workforce – Shining Beauty (IRE)
Acquired at the Cheltenham November Sale having won a point-to-point during the Autumn, she took a while to come right last season. Keen early on, we gave her three runs over hurdles during the spring and she is on a decent mark. Given a break since, she will stay further than two miles.

GABORIOT (FR) 9 ch g Muhtathir – Uddy (FR)
Placed in the Grand Sefton Chase at Aintree (8th November) last season, he is good fresh and will start off there once again. Then, all being well, we will aim him at the Becher Chase (6th December). He jumps and stays well and we have given him a long break since his last run in the Eider Chase at Newcastle.

GAMESTERS GUY 6 ch g Black Sam Bellamy (IRE) – Gamesters Lady
An exciting prospect for novice chases, he was still a shell of a horse last season. A winner over hurdles at Carlisle, he wasn't disgraced in Grade 2 company at Cheltenham's Trials meeting in January. I thought he ran a hell of a race under twelve stone on his final start at Newbury last time. He stays well and will improve again over fences. Very much at home on soft ground, he wants three miles plus and is one to look forward to.

GENTLEMAN BILL (IRE) 7 b g Rule of Law (USA) – Snow Water (IRE)
He had a good season over hurdles winning twice at Bangor and Doncaster. Runner-up at Carlisle, he went off the boil in the spring and we shouldn't have run him in the Morebattle Hurdle at Kelso because the track didn't suit him. We have been pleased with him during the summer and he is another one to look forward to over fences. He jumps and travels well and should make a very nice two mile novice chaser.

HALFTHEWORLDAWAY (IRE) 4 b m Jet Away – Ballela To Moscow (IRE)
Honest and straightforward, she looks an exciting filly who we bought at the Punchestown Festival Sale in the spring. Runner-up in her point-to-point in April, it was a good run and we have been pleased with her since arriving. We will probably give her a run in a mares' bumper before going over hurdles.

HOMME PUBLIC (FR) 8 b g Cokoriko (FR) – Uddy (FR)
He is in good form at home and will follow a similar programme. A winner over hurdles at Doncaster before Christmas, we switched him back over fences in the spring and he ran some good races. Runner-up in a valuable two miles handicap at Ayr's Scottish National meeting last time, we will probably start him off over hurdles once again. I think a strongly run two miles is his best trip.

IROKO (FR) 7 b g Cokoriko (FR) – Boscraie (FR)
The Grand National at Aintree is the plan once again having run well in the race last season finishing fourth. We are hoping for softer ground next spring. He was flat out at halfway before staying on in the straight. That effort early on took its toll and it left him with plenty to do. He has had a good summer break at Martinstown Stud in Ireland during the summer and he will follow a similar programme beforehand. He has only won one chase and therefore remains eligible for Graduation chases. He stays well and wants proper soft ground.

JACKS PARROT (FR) 6 b g Free Port Lux – Boscraie (FR)
A thorough stayer, he wants testing ground and only really got his conditions a couple of times last year. Runner-up in the Tommy Whittle Chase at Haydock and Devon National at Exeter, he is still a young horse and we will be aiming him at the decent long distance handicap chases. In all likelihood, he will be aimed at the Tommy Whittle Chase once again (20th December). He is capable of winning a good race.

JAGWAR (FR) 6 b g Karaktar (IRE) – Quizas Jolie (FR)
We went to see him at Martinstown Stud during the summer and he looked amazing. Still unfurnished last season, he has done particularly well physically and looks a monster. He has always had a massive engine and nothing can live with him at home. He improved with the switch to fences winning four of his five starts, including the Plate Handicap Chase at the Cheltenham Festival, and I think he will continue to progress. His jumping continued to improve throughout the campaign and, while we haven't discussed plans, the Paddy Power Gold Cup at Cheltenham (15th November) is a possibility. Longer-term, I think he will come into his own over three miles.

JOEYBOTTLES (IRE) 4 b g Harzand (IRE) – Feabhra (IRE)
A horse with a big engine, he is easy to deal with and an absolute star. Placed in a warm bumper at Perth on his debut in the spring, he has done well during the summer and is ready to go novice hurdling. He likes some cut in the ground and we will start him off over two miles. I love him.

KAHAVARI (FR) 5 gr g Tunis (POL) – Porte D'Auteuil (FR)
A winner over hurdles for Noel George & Amanda Zetterholm in France, he joined us halfway through last season. Despite finishing second a couple of times at Carlisle and Bangor, he took time to acclimatise and wasn't 100% ready. He has really benefited from his summer break and looks fantastic. A switch to fences will suit him and I think he could be well handicapped. He will begin over two miles before having the option of returning to longer trips later on.

KELYA WOOD (FR) 5 b m Al Namix (FR) – Du Tac Au Tac (FR)
A decent mare who won impressively on her hurdles debut at Uttoxeter before finishing runner-up in a Listed mares' novice hurdle at Haydock. She is quite hard on herself hence her form tailed off thereafter. We are going to send her novice chasing but she doesn't want over racing. She likes soft ground and it would be nice to think she will gain some more black type over fences. The Listed Yorton Mares' Novices' Chase at Bangor (12th November) should suit her.

KI WOO (FR) 5 b g Cokoriko (FR) – Calonge (FR)

Ex-French, he joined us last season and won twice over hurdles at Bangor in the spring. He stays well and improved for the better ground. The plan is for him to go novice handicap chasing in the Autumn and I think he will improve over fences. Three miles is his trip.

LAS CANALS (FR) 4 b g Cokoriko (FR) – Daviere (FR)

Only four and yet to run for us, I love him. Successful in an AQPS Flat race and placed over hurdles in France last Autumn, he joined us soon afterwards. We nearly ran him in the spring, but the ground dried up and we decided to put him away and look after him. A chaser in the making, he is a very nice horse who will go novice hurdling over two miles and is one to look forward to.

MASTERFIELD (FR) 3 b g Cokoriko (FR) – Toscane (FR)

A lovely big unraced three year old, he was in pre training in France prior to joining us. He has strengthened up during the summer and will be aimed at the junior National Hunt hurdles.

MELON (GER) 4 ch g Adlerflug (GER) – Mrs Miller (GER)

Progressive four year old who won over hurdles at Doncaster and Wetherby, he remains lightly raced. He likes soft ground and we will give him a run on the Flat before going back over hurdles. He is open to more improvement and I think he is on a fair mark. Two miles is his trip.

MOOSERWIRT (IRE) 5 ch g Sholokhov (IRE) – No More Storms (IRE)

An impressive winner of a maiden point-to-point for Jack Teal at Brocklesby Park in February, we bought him at the Cheltenham Sale later the same month. We haven't done a lot with him since, but he has strengthened up and looks tough. He will go novice hurdling and we like him.

MY NOBLE LORD (USA) 4 b g Noble Mission – Almashooqa (USA)

Joined us last season having shown progressive form on the Flat for Michael Bell. He won on his hurdles debut at Chepstow but was disappointing thereafter. He wasn't finishing off his races and we are hoping it was a case of him not being strong enough and he has needed time. Rated 116, he could be well handicapped because he has always gone well at home. A stayer on the Flat, I think he will benefit from stepping up to two and a half miles.

NEW INVENTION (IRE) 5 ch g Sholokhov (IRE) – Liss A Chroi (IRE)

Tough and genuine, he is capable of winning races. We gave him an educational run over two miles on his hurdles debut at Newcastle in February finishing fourth. We were pleased with him, and he will benefit from running over further. He jumps well and likes soft ground. Long-term, he is a chaser in the making.

PECKFORTON HILLS (IRE) 5 b g Youmzain (IRE) – Regal Force (IRE)

Half-brother to dual Grade 2 winning chaser Ballyoisin, he is a lovely horse who will go novice hurdling. A bumper winner at Carlisle in February, he found the ground too quick at Kelso last time. Effective on soft ground, he will be suited by two and a half miles over hurdles.

POKER WAY (FR) 3 ch c Galiway – Penjing (FR)

Bought as a two year old, he is a nice horse who will go three year old hurdling. He had a spell in France and we like him. I think he will be suited by better ground.

PORT GEORGE 3 b g Golden Horn – Harbour of Hope (GER)
He has raced four times on the Flat finishing second at Windsor in May. He has got plenty of size and the plan is for him to go juvenile hurdling in the Autumn. We like him and he could make a really nice hurdler.

ROSA DIAZ (IRE) 5 b m Pillar Coral – Quine De Sivola (FR)
Half-brother to six times winner Hidden Heroics, she is a lovely big mare who looks classy. She won her point-to-point for Pat Doyle in November before we purchased her a week later at the Goffs UK Coral Gold Cup Sale. She gives the impression she wants a trip and plenty of cut in the ground. Mares' novice hurdles will be her job this season.

SNOWY EVENING (IRE) 8 b g Snow Sky – Sherwolf (IRE)
Twice a winner over fences, he missed the whole of last season. However, the time off hasn't done him any harm and we are hoping he will continue to improve. Versatile in terms of trip, he stays well and even though he is a big horse, he prefers better ground. He should have more to offer over fences.

THEREYARE (IRE) 4 b g Jet Away – Letitbeso (IRE)
Runner-up in his point-to-point in Ireland in April when trained by Willie Codd, we bought him via an online sale the following month. A fine big horse who is very much a chaser in the making, he has done well during the summer. He will go novice hurdling in the Autumn.

TIMMYS JET AWAY (IRE) 4 b g Jet Away – Miss Cave (IRE)
A shell of a horse, he won a point-to-point on his debut for Cormac Doyle in May. One for the future, he was acquired at the Tattersalls Ireland PTP & HIT Sale later the same month but we won't be over racing him this season. We will give him a run in a bumper in the New Year and take our time. A big, raw horse, he is one to look forward to.

U S MARSHALL (IRE) 5 b g Jet Away – Monets Dream (IRE)
Similar to Timmys Jet Away, he ran in two Irish points winning on his latest start. Bought at the Cheltenham February Sale, we haven't rushed him because he was still quite raw to begin with. We will look after him and perhaps give him a couple of runs in two mile novice hurdles before stepping him up in trip.

WHITE RHINO (IRE) 9 b g Doyen (IRE) – Aventia (IRE)
Looked very good when winning his first two starts over fences at Ayr and Haydock. We then ran him in the Grade 1 Kauto Star Novices' Chase at Kempton on Boxing Day but he didn't get beyond the third fence. Unfortunately, he then bled at Doncaster in the spring and we left him off after that. Given a long break since, we won't over race him and something like the Becher Chase at Aintree (6th December) could suit him. He jumps well and has plenty of ability.

TRAINER'S HORSE TO FOLLOW: PECKFORTON HILLS

Philip HOBBS & Johnson WHITE

Stables: Sandhill Farm, Bilbrook, Minehead, Somerset.
2024/2025: 53 Winners / 274 Runners 19% Prize-Money £652,603
www.pjhobbs.com

AGUELLID (FR) 4 ch g Goliath Du Berlais (FR) – Green Hope (FR)
A big horse, he raced twice in France when trained by Daniela Mele finishing sixth in a bumper on his debut in August last year. Fourth on his hurdles bow at Auteuil the following month, he is owned by J.P.McManus and has been given time to mature. He will go novice hurdling.

BOBBY'S NELSON (IRE) 6 b g Mount Nelson – Bobby's Taken (IRE)
Missed the whole of last season due to injury but is back in work and ready to go novice hurdling. He finished runner-up in an Irish point-to-point for Sean Doyle before being narrowly beaten in a bumper at Chepstow in January last year. Lightly raced, he will be suited by two and a half miles plus over hurdles.

CALL ME LEGEND (IRE) 5 b g Milan – Morning Legend (IRE)
A half-brother to Orby Legend, who we trained to win four races including the Silver Trophy at Chepstow, he ran in three Irish points before we acquired him at the Cheltenham January Sales. Successful in a bumper at Newton Abbot during the spring on his only start for us, he will go hurdling and is capable of winning more races. He is likely to start off over two and a half miles.

CAN YOU HEAR ME (IRE) 4 b g Vadamos (FR) – Still Small Voice
Only four, he gained some experience in bumpers at Kempton and Chepstow last season. He improved from his first run finishing fourth last time. We are hoping he will progress again once switched to hurdling.

CAPTAIN HUGO (IRE) 5 ch g Soldier of Fortune (IRE) – Vic Chic (IRE)
One of our better young prospects, he was still very green on his debut when finishing runner-up in a bumper at Hereford in April. An impressive winner of a similar event at Worcester less than a month later, he is one to look forward to in novice hurdles this season. Not short of speed, he will start off over two miles.

DOCTORS HILL 5 ch g Doctor Dino (FR) – Countess Comet (IRE)
A nice horse we purchased at the Punchestown Festival Sale during the spring. He raced twice in point-to-points in Ireland before finishing second in a bumper at Bellewstown in April. Owned by Richard House, he is a five year old and will go straight over hurdles. We think he will be suited by two and a half miles plus.

DON'T WIND ME UP 6 b g Jack Hobbs – Kayf Willow
From the family of Tidal Flow, who we trained to win five races, he was progressive over hurdles last season. Placed on three occasions before winning at Taunton in March, we hope he will continue to improve. Still only five, he will jump fences in time but will continue over hurdles for the time being. He benefited from stepping up to two and a half miles last time.

FRENCH SHIP 5 b g French Navy – Starlit Cantata
Tough and likeable, he is not overbig but remains lightly raced and progressive. A bumper winner at Haydock last year, he did well over hurdles last season scoring twice at Chepstow

and Taunton. Officially rated 128, we will aim him at some of the better handicap hurdles over two and a half miles. The Silver Trophy Handicap Hurdle at Chepstow (11th October), a race we have won four times, is a possibility. Still improving, he is not slow.

GREY LAGOON (IRE) 5 gr g Sholokhov (IRE) – Quarry Endeavour (IRE)
He is a big strong horse who finished third in an Irish point before we bought him a few days later at the Goresbridge NH Sale in April. We haven't done a lot with him and it is early days but we like him and looking forward to sending him novice hurdling.

IMPERIAL SAINT (FR) 7 b g Saint Des Saints (FR) – Quinine De Mazille (FR)
Richard (Johnson) has been very successful buying ex-pointers and this horse has done amazingly well. Bought for £40,000 having won a point-to-point for Stuart Crawford, he has won five races, including three times over fences last season. Officially rated 144, all three of those victories came at Aintree, plus he was runner-up in a Grade 3 handicap chase on Grand National day. Even though he stays three miles, I don't think he necessarily needs those sort of trips because he isn't slow. The plan is to start him off in the Grade 2 Old Roan Chase at Aintree (26th October) and we hope he will continue to improve.

INTO THE PARK (IRE) 6 b g Walk In The Park (IRE) – La Sarrazine (FR)
Twice a winner over hurdles the previous season, he finished runner-up at Exeter in December. However, he was unhealthy for most of last term hence he only raced on three occasions. Given a good break since, he is capable of winning more races and will continue in handicap hurdles over trips around two and a half miles, although he could stay further.

KAP VERT (FR) 5 ch g Kapgarde (FR) – Tavera (FR)
Previously owned by Ronnie Bartlett, he will run under the Johnson White syndicate. Consistent over hurdles, he won at Exeter before being placed a couple of times. He ran creditably at the Punchestown Festival finishing seventh in a competitive big field handicap over two and a half miles. There is still room for improvement in the jumping department and he has only raced half a dozen times over hurdles. He should be open to further progress.

KAYF DANCER 7 b g Kayf Tara – Winning Counsel (IRE)
Full brother to the ill-fated Springwell Bay, he is a very talented horse who has had his share of issues, including with his bones. A wide margin winner of an ordinary race at Exeter in March, he is lightly raced and should have more improvement to come. Effective on most types of ground, he will be campaigned in two and a half miles handicap hurdles.

KIKIJO (FR) 5 b g Estejo (GER) – Crackboum (FR)
A winner over hurdles in France, he is still a young horse who only raced twice over fences last season. Successful on his chasing debut at Newbury in February, he was runner-up at the same track last time. Richard (Johnson) bought him at the Goffs Spring Sale in May to remain in the yard and we are hoping he will develop into a nice chaser over two and a half miles.

KILWAUGHTER (IRE) 5 b g Milan – Glory Days (GER)
Stuart Crawford trained him to win a bumper on his debut at Down Royal on Boxing Day, prior to him being bought at the Cheltenham January Sale. He was unlucky in the Grade 2 championship bumper at Aintree on his first run for us encountering trouble in running before finishing sixth. With a clearer run, I think he would have finished in the first four. He was then third in another

competitive bumper at the Punchestown Festival running very well. A nice young horse, he will go novice hurdling over two and a half miles.

KINGSTON GENT (IRE) 5 gr g Kingston Hill – Lady Kasora (IRE)
A UK point winner, he is a sound and genuine horse who was runner-up over hurdles at Fontwell in the spring. He struggled to hold condition last year and will hopefully improve having had a summer break. He should be capable of making an impact and winning handicap hurdles.

LIMIER D'ARTHEL (FR) 4 b g Cokoriko (FR) – Bellone D'Arthel (FR)
A promising youngster who we like a lot, he was due to run in juvenile hurdles last season but had an issue with a skin condition. He has therefore been given plenty of time and spent the summer at Martinstown Stud in Ireland. An easy winner of an AQPS Flat race in France prior to being bought by J.P.McManus, he is by a very good sire and is a lovely horse.

LIVIN ON LUCO (IRE) 7 ch g Malinas (GER) – Andrea's Answer (IRE)
A winner over hurdles and fences, he is genuine and has ability. Successful on his chasing debut at Newton Abbot in the Autumn, he was placed at Ffos Las over three miles last time. Effective on testing ground, he stays well and will be campaigned in handicap chases over three miles plus.

LOWRY'S BAR (IRE) 7 b g Malinas (GER) – Mac Idol (IRE)
He is a nice horse who developed into a useful novice chaser last season winning twice at Exeter and Chepstow before finishing runner-up in the Grade 2 Hampton Novices' Chase at Windsor in January. Pulled up in the Ladbrokes Trophy Handicap Chase at Kempton, he bled that day and it is the second time it has happened in February. His form prior to that was good and, with an official rating of 148, we will aim him at the good staying handicap chases. The Coral Gold Cup at Newbury (29th November) is a possibility.

MANUELITO 5 b g Cracksman – Navajo Charm
Joined us last season, he has a good attitude and is a horse we like. Flat bred and a half-brother to Grade 2 winning hurdler Navajo Pass, he won in good style at Newbury in March. Disappointing in a conditional jockeys' handicap hurdle at Aintree's Grand National meeting, we don't know why. Still relatively unexposed over hurdles, he will continue in handicaps over two miles.

MURPHY'S MILAN (IRE) 6 b g Milan – Vic Chic (IRE)
Half-brother to Captain Hugo, he was placed in a bumper before going hurdling last season. Fourth a couple of times at Chepstow, he wasn't beaten far at Newbury in the spring on his latest outing. He will hopefully improve this year and will be campaigned in novice handicap hurdles off his mark of 108.

NORTHANGER ABBEY (IRE) 5 ch g Casamento (IRE) – Didn't I Tell You (IRE)
Runner-up twice in his three point-to-points for Colin Bowe in Ireland, he was bought privately on behalf of his owner Nick Sutton for his son Ben to ride. Still cantering, we haven't done much with him but the plan is for him to start off in novice hurdles in the Autumn.

OH MY JOHNNY (IRE) 5 b g Soldier of Fortune (IRE) – Milan Dancer (IRE)
A former pointer, he is a nice horse who won twice over hurdles at Uttoxeter and Hereford last

season. Prior to that, he was unlucky at Bangor when falling at the last when still in front. Only five, he is open to more improvement and should be competitive in handicap hurdles over two and two and a half miles.

ROYAL JEWEL (IRE) 6 ch g Notnowcato – What A Jewel (IRE)
Consistent, he won over fences at Chepstow in January and also placed four times. He jumps well and handles testing ground. Even though he is effective over two miles on soft or heavy ground, he ideally wants further and is capable of winning more races over fences.

SAINT ANAPOLINO (FR) 6 b g Jeu St Eloi (FR) – Anamarina (FR)
Enjoyed a good season over hurdles winning at Exeter, Taunton and Kempton. Below par at Kempton on his final start, he is going the right way and we may school him over fences with a view to going novice chasing. Two and a half miles is his trip.

SOBER GLORY (IRE) 5 b g Mount Nelson – Milan's Fingal (IRE)
An exciting prospect who won all three of his runs in bumpers, including a Listed event at Newbury in February. A point-to-point winner, he is by Mount Nelson and has a very good temperament. He is a big strong horse who had worked well at home prior to winning on his first run for us at Chepstow in the Autumn. He is effective on soft ground and is crying out for further than two miles. Two and a half miles will be his trip to begin with, but I think he will be a three miler eventually. Depending on the ground, he could start off in the Grade 2 Persian War Novices' Hurdle at Chepstow (10th October), a race we have won on six occasions. Fingal Bay (2011) and Thyme Hill (2019) both won it on their hurdling debuts. This horse is bigger and stronger than that pair and more of a chasing type.

SOLAR SYSTEM (FR) 6 b g Pastorius (GER) – Solar Wind (FR)
He was progressive over hurdles last season winning on three occasions. Over the top by the time he ran at Bangor in March, he has had a good break since and we are hoping he will continue to improve. He is likely to continue over hurdles for the time being, although we have the option of switching to fences later on.

STARZAND (IRE) 5 b g Harzand (IRE) – Phoenix Twist (IRE)
An impressive winner of a point-to-point in late December, he was bought at the Cheltenham January Sale. He did what we hoped he would on his first run for us winning a bumper at Ffos Las in the spring. He looked smart and, similar to Sober Glory, has a very good temperament. The pair are staying types and will be suited by two and a half miles plus over hurdles. A big strong individual, we are hoping he will be running in the better novice hurdles this season.

THE HARDEST GEEZER (IRE) 6 br g Malinas (GER) – Lis Goold (IRE)
Successful over hurdles at Taunton in January, he was inclined to race keenly last season. Still lightly raced, he should stay further provided he learns to settle. We will start him off in a two miles handicap hurdle and hopefully he will progress.

TINY TETLEY 7 b g Passing Glance – Setter's Princess
Owned and bred by former trainer Ron Hodges, the progress he made last season was staggering. He won four times over hurdles and finished a good second at Haydock last time. Officially rated 136, he has provided Ron with a lot of pleasure. He is tough and stays well. We will continue to campaign him in the decent staying handicap hurdles. Three miles is his trip.

TOM DONIPHON (FR) 6 br g Great Pretender (IRE) – La Courtille (FR)
A dual winner over hurdles at Taunton, he was placed in his other three starts last season. Runner-up in one of his two point-to-points in Ireland for Colin Bowe prior to joining us, he ought to improve again once switched to fences. He is a nice horse to go novice chasing with two and a half miles being ideal.

TRAINER'S HORSE TO FOLLOW: SOBER GLORY

Gary & Josh MOORE

Stables: Cisswood Racing Stables, Sandygate Lane, Lower Beeding, Horsham, West Sussex.
2024/2025: 52 Winners / 407 Runners 13% Prize-Money £924,313
www.garymooreracing.com

AUTHENTIC LEGACY 5 bl g Authorized (IRE) – Forever Present (IRE)
It took him a while to get his head in front, but it was nice to see him win at Newbury in the spring. Runner-up at Fontwell last time, he was still quite weak last season and has benefited from his summer break. A chaser in the making, he will go over fences in the Autumn and I think he will improve. Two miles novices' handicap chases will be his target.

BOTOX HAS (FR) 9 b g Dream Well (FR) – Bournie (FR)
A triple Grade 2 winner, he has been a very good horse for us over the years. Third in the Grade 2 Cleeve and Rendlesham Hurdles at Cheltenham and Haydock respectively last season, he isn't getting any younger and probably needs to come down a few pounds in the weights. However, he has come back in following his summer holiday looking fresh and well and I am pleased with him. The Grade 3 *Betfair* Stayers' Handicap Hurdle at Haydock (22nd November), which he won in 2022, is a possible starting point.

CLOUD DANCER (IRE) 6 gr g Jukebox Jury (IRE) – Donna Graciosa (GER)
A winner over hurdles at Doncaster before Christmas, he finished third at the same track on his latest outing. Brian Hughes rode him that day and feels he will make a better chaser. Three miles is his trip, but he doesn't want the ground too soft. Officially rated 120, he will be aimed at staying novice handicap chases.

DISSIDENT 3 b g Frankel – Emulous
Very well bred, he is a half-brother to the Prix de L'Arc de Triomphe winner Bluestocking and also this year's Sussex Stakes winner Qirat. A 79 rated maiden on the Flat, Jamie (Moore) acquired him at the Newmarket July Sales. He belongs to Ben Haynes and Samantha Dunn and was bought with a dual purpose career in mind. Turned out since arriving, we haven't done anything with him yet, although juvenile hurdling is a possibility.

DOUBLE THE DANCE (IRE) 4 b g Maxios – Drive On Kate (IRE)
Owned by the Noel Fehily Racing Syndicate, he was bought at the Punchestown Festival Sale in the spring. Twice raced in Irish points, he fell on his debut before winning next time. He spent the summer with Noel and is well thought of. We are looking forward to seeing what he can do and, in all likelihood, he will start off in a bumper.

EL CAIROS (FR) 5 ch g No Risk At All (FR) - Linda Queen (FR)
A winning pointer, he is a very nice horse who had some smart form in bumpers last season. An impressive winner at Newbury on his first run for us in November, he was then fifth in the Grade 1 championship bumper at Cheltenham and was unlucky not to be placed. We then ran him at the Punchestown Festival and he was in front when hanging across the track in the homestraight. I think that was a one off and it wouldn't stop me from running him on a right-handed track in future. He is a lovely horse and I hope he will develop into a high-class novice hurdler. We will start him off over two miles because he possesses plenty of speed. I would expect him to handle most types of ground.

EMPIRE OF THE SEAS (IRE) 4 b g Sea The Stars (IRE) - Ambivalent (IRE)
Unraced, he is a fine big horse we bought at the Newmarket Autumn Sales last year. We gelded him straight away, which he badly needed, and have given him plenty of time. Well bred, he is a full-brother to Group 1 winner Teona, and we have the option of running him in bumpers.

FASHION HUNTER 4 b g Frontiersman - Scarlet Couture
A very nice unraced horse, he is by an under rated sire and I like him a lot. He nearly ran last season, but the ground dried up in the spring. He wants some cut in the ground and will start off in a bumper.

GALACTIC CHARM 4 b g Sea The Moon (GER) - Gold Charm (GER)
Purchased at the Newmarket Horses in Training Sale last Autumn, he is very genuine and was consistent over hurdles last winter. Successful at Fontwell on Boxing Day, he finished runner-up on four occasions. Rated 120, he could start off in the four year old hurdle at Chepstow (11th October). Later on, we might try him over further because I think he will stay beyond two miles.

GIVE IT TO ME OJ 4 b g Time Test - Matron of Honour (IRE)
A progressive horse, he took well to jumping winning three times including a valuable prize at Sandown on the final day of the season. Officially rated 143, it isn't going to be easy, but he is a horse I like a lot and I hope there is more to come from him. An impressive winner of the Jump Jockeys Derby Handicap at Epsom in September, we are going to aim him at the Masterson Holdings Hurdle for four year olds at Cheltenham (25th October). Later on, we will look at all the valuable two mile handicap hurdles.

GRIZZLED SQUIRREL 4 bb f Jack Hobbs - Lotties Lady
She is a lovely filly who raced twice in mares' bumpers during the spring and summer. Third at Uttoxeter in July, she unfortunately chipped a knee and therefore won't be running until the second half of the season. She is talented though and capable of winning a bumper. I like her.

HANSARD (IRE) 7 b g The Gurkha (IRE) - Quiet Down (USA)
Rated 138 over hurdles, he spent the summer with Noel (Fehily) and the plan is for him to go novice chasing. We haven't schooled him yet, but he is big enough to jump fences. A Grade 3 winning hurdler, he wasn't beaten far in the Grade 2 Kingwell Hurdle at Wincanton in February behind the subsequent Champion Hurdle winner (Golden Ace).

HURRICANE PAT (IRE) 5 b g Kalanisi (IRE) - Fedoria (IRE)
Runner-up in a couple of Irish points prior to joining us, he is a very nice horse who did nothing wrong in three bumpers last season. Twice a winner at Sandown and Chepstow, I was

impressed with him at the latter track in the spring. He showed a good turn of foot and looked above average. He has really grown up and we are looking forward to going novice hurdling over two miles. I think he will stay two and a half miles later on, too.

INVINCIBLE NAO (FR) 7 gr g Gris De Gris (IRE) – Quetzalya (FR)
A dual winner at Plumpton last season, including the Sussex National in February, his jumping improved and he should have more to offer. Officially rated 122, he is tough and genuine and remains fairly treated. We will be aiming him at the long distance handicap chases and as many regional Nationals as possible.

ISSAR D'AIRY (FR) 7 b g Sinndar (IRE) – Bassika D'Airy (FR)
Ran some good races in defeat last season, including when runner-up at Ascot and Cheltenham before Christmas. He is probably a few pounds too high, but he looks very well after his summer break. We will continue to target him at the decent two and two and a half miles handicap chases. He deserves to win one.

KING'S REIGN (FR) 4 b g Dubawi (IRE) – God Given
Well bred being a half-brother to four times Group 2 winner Silver Knott, he was an expensive yearling for Godolphin winning over a mile and a half on the Flat last year. Ted Durcan bought him during the winter and, following a couple of runs on the Flat at Goodwood, he won nicely on his hurdling debut at Fontwell in September. He jumped well and travelled strongly and I hope he will develop into a useful novice hurdler.

KOTMASK (FR) 7 ch g Masked Marvel – Kotkiline (FR)
He loves Ascot winning there in December and being placed on three other occasions last season. We have been pleased with him during the summer and he will follow a similar programme. He stays two and a half miles well but is equally effective over a strongly run two miles.

LAURIER DES OBEAUX (FR) 4 b g Bathyrhon (GER) – Ardeur Des Obeaux (FR)
Only four, he is a gorgeous horse who I like a lot. A fine big strapping individual, he has needed time and has schooled well over hurdles. Fourth on his debut in a bumper at Huntingdon in April, it was a good run considering the track wouldn't have suited him. He will be more at home on a big galloping track and we have the option of running him in another bumper before going novice hurdling. I think he is a very nice horse.

LE GALLI BIER (FR) 4 b g Clovis Du Berlais (FR) – La Loute (FR)
Half-brother to Le Patron, he was placed four times over hurdles in France prior to joining us earlier this year. He ran well twice at Fontwell and has thrived physically during the summer. He has grown an inch and should be capable of winning races off his mark of 112.

LE PATRON (FR) 7 b g Balko (FR) – La Loute (FR)
Won a decent handicap chase at Newbury's Winter Festival in November. He then found it tough in Graded events and is high enough in the weights off 150. He has been a very good horse for us though winning the Grade 1 Henry VIII Novices' Chase at Sandown a couple of years ago. Still only seven, he will continue in valuable handicaps and Graded races over two and a half miles. We may try him over three miles later on because I think he will stay.

LE TIEP'S SACRE (FR) 4 b g It's Gino (GER) – Sacree Tiepy (FR)
Runner-up in an AQPS Flat race and placed over hurdles in France, we bought him at the Arqana November Sale. I love him and think a hell of a lot of him. He is a gorgeous horse who finished third at Sandown on his first run for us before winning at Fontwell in March. Still lightly raced, he wants soft ground and will benefit from stepping up to two and a half miles. We will campaign him in two and a half miles handicap hurdles and I think he is fairly treated.

LUMI PLUGIN 6 b g Kayf Tara – Sudden Light (IRE)
A tough genuine horse who could be well handicapped, he won over hurdles at Plumpton in March. Runner-up at Leicester and Warwick, he is a big horse who should improve over fences. We will start him off in a two and a half miles novices' handicap chase and I think he will make a nice chaser.

LYLIAN (FR) 4 br g Tunis (POL) – Reine De Mai (FR)
Bought at the Arqana Summer Sale, he won over fences at Dieppe in June and remains a novice for this season. Turned out soon after arriving, we haven't done much with him, but he is a good looking horse who moves well. Still a maiden over hurdles, he is likely to be campaigned in novice handicap chases off a mark in the 120s.

MACKTOAD (FR) 3 gr g Beaumec De Houelle (FR) – Toady (FR)
Bought at the Arqana Summer Sale in July, he is a big horse who won an AQPS Flat race at Vichy during the spring. A racy type, we turned him out once he arrived and have given him plenty of time. He looks a very nice horse who will go juvenile hurdling.

MARK OF GOLD 8 b g Golden Horn – Polly's Mark (IRE)
He had an unbelievable season over fences winning three times, including the Grade 2 Noel Novices' Chase at Ascot before Christmas. Successful at Exeter in early March, he rounded off a memorable campaign by winning the Josh Gifford Novices' Handicap Chase at Sandown on the final day of the season. He kept surprising us and I hope he will continue to do so. It won't be easy for him off his mark of 146 and we will look at Graded chases over two and a half miles. The Grade 2 Copybet 1965 Chase at Ascot (22nd November) is a likely starting point.

MILLER SPIRIT (IRE) 5 b g Australia – Esprit De Tauber (IRE)
Ran twice over hurdles winning at Lingfield on his debut before finishing second at the same track before Christmas. He has been running well on the Flat during the summer finishing fourth at Ascot in July. Unlucky next time at Yarmouth, he stays well and, while he is likely to start off in a two miles handicap hurdle, I think he will benefit from stepping up to two and a half miles. He is on a good mark over hurdles.

MONDO MAN 4 ch g Mondialiste (IRE) – Moghrama (IRE)
A high-class horse on the Flat in France, we bought him at the Arqana Arc Sale last Autumn with a view to him being a Triumph Hurdle and Royal Ascot horse. Runner-up behind Lulamba on his hurdles debut at Ascot in January, he wasn't beaten far in the Grade 2 Adonis Juvenile Hurdle at Kempton next time. Fourth in the Group 3 Ormonde Stakes at Chester in the spring, we were aiming him at Royal Ascot but he suffered a fracture which ruled him out for the summer. The plan is for him to run in novice hurdles before Christmas and it wouldn't surprise me if he developed into a William Hill Handicap Hurdle type horse at Newbury in February. It is possible he will stay further than two miles.

NASSALAM (FR) 8 ch g Dream Well (FR) – Ramina (GER)

A former Welsh National winner, that is his main target once again with the likelihood of two runs beforehand. The handicapper raised him sixteen pounds for winning it a couple of years ago and he has struggled ever since. We ran him too early last season and he got jarred up on quick ground at Cheltenham in November. Off since, he has had a long break and we purposely brought him back in after his summer holiday a bit earlier to prepare him for Chepstow (27th December).

NELSON GATE (IRE) 3 b g Australia – Star of Spring (IRE)

Runner-up over a mile and a half at Windsor in May and Kempton in August, he is very much ground dependent because he prefers plenty of cut. He may have another run on the Flat before going juvenile hurdling.

NUNC EST BIDENDUM (IRE) 4 b f Masar (IRE) – Selfara

She is a nice filly who was placed on the Flat in Ireland last year. We have schooled her over hurdles and the plan was to go juvenile hurdling last season but she went wrong. Disappointing on the Flat at Sandown during the summer, she will start off in a mares' novice hurdle over two miles.

OLD COWBOY 5 b g Blue Bresil (FR) – Tara View

Ran in a couple of UK point-to-points prior to joining us last season. A wide margin winner over hurdles at Plumpton in March, he was also placed a couple of times at Newbury. A chaser in the making, I think he will improve over fences and we will aim him at novice handicap chases over two and a half miles. Rated 122 over hurdles, I would expect him to make a better chaser.

RISK IT ALL (FR) 4 b g No Risk At All (FR) – Popin's Du Berlais (FR)

An easy winner on the Flat in France last summer, we thought he was a Triumph Hurdle prospect when we bought him. He raced three times over hurdles but struggled with his breathing. We have therefore operated on his wind and hopefully that will make a difference because he has plenty of ability. Quite keen, if he learns to relax, he is on a good mark.

ROYAL WAY (FR) 5 b g Galiway – Belle Et Royale (FR)

Looked very good as a juvenile hurdler winning three times. However, he struggled last season although he ran better at Kempton last time. Well handicapped on his best form, he is another who is going to have wind surgery before continuing over hurdles.

SALVER (FR) 5 b g Motivator – Salve Evita

A Grade 2 winning hurdler, we are very much looking forward to him going novice chasing. We are hoping he will be mixing it with the big boys over fences and contesting Graded events. Narrowly beaten in a valuable event at Windsor in January, it was a similar story in a Grade 2 hurdle at Sandown on the final day of the season. He has done well during the summer and looks great. Trips around two and a half miles are ideal and I hope he will develop into a very good chaser.

SHUTFRONTDOOR 4 b f Frontiersman – Sudden Light

Half-sister to Lumi Plugin, she is a nice filly who won on her debut in a mares' bumper at Fontwell. Runner-up under a penalty at Market Rasen, she has had a break since. She is one for mares' novice hurdles and is a filly I like.

THE BELLHOP (IRE) 3 ch g Belardo (IRE) – Royal Free Hotel (IRE)
He has been running on the Flat during the summer finishing third at Lingfield. Ground dependent, he wants some cut underfoot and we are going to school him over jumps with a view to going juvenile hurdling. Rated 72, he has got ability.

THE BOSS BEAR (IRE) 5 br g Doyen (IRE) – Tipp On Air (IRE)
A nice young horse, he ran in bumpers at Huntingdon and Fontwell during the spring winning well last time. He has improved during the summer and we are very pleased with him. We have the option of running him in an bumper before going novice hurdling. I like him.

THE RON DO RON 5 b g Golden Horn – Rewaaya (IRE)
I love him. He showed promise in bumpers the previous season but then I made the mistake of running him on fast ground over hurdles at Ascot last Autumn where he incurred an injury. Off since, we have given him plenty of time and the plan is for him to resume in novice hurdles later in the season. I haven't lost faith in him.

TRAINER'S HORSE TO FOLLOW: FASHION HUNTER

Olly MURPHY

Stables: Warren Chase Stables, Wilmcote, Stratford Upon Avon.
2024/2025: 141 Winners / 570 Runners 25% Prize-Money £1,709,800
www.ollymurphyracing.com

ACT OF AUTHORITY (FR) 7 b g Authorized (IRE) – Leah Claire (IRE)
Still unexposed, he had a good season winning twice at Sandown and Wetherby before finishing runner-up in the Martin Pipe Conditional Jockeys' Handicap Hurdle at the Cheltenham Festival. We stepped him up to three miles for the first time at Aintree on his latest start but they went steady and it didn't suit him. The plan is for him to remain over hurdles and aim him at the good staying handicaps. Provided the ground isn't too soft, the *Betfair* Stayers' Handicap Hurdle at Haydock (22nd November) is a possible target. Longer term, the Pertemps Final at the Cheltenham Festival could be his aim. Despite not being over big, he is an accurate jumper and I think he will jump fences one day. I hope there is more improvement to come.

ADONEDEAL (IRE) 5 b g Califet (FR) – Shokalocka Baby (IRE)
The first horse we have trained for the Noel Fehily Racing Syndicate and I am delighted to be doing so. Bought at the Goffs UK Spring Sale in May, he was a wide margin winner of his Irish point-to-point for Sean Doyle on good ground. He travelled well that day and looks a sharp sort. He will start off in a bumper.

ALNILAM (FR) 6 bb g Sea The Stars (IRE) – Awareness (USA)
Won a valuable handicap hurdle at Southwell on New Year's Day before finishing an excellent second in the Morebattle Hurdle at Kelso. Below par at Aintree last time, he had had enough by that stage. He will go over fences and I think he will make a nice two mile chaser. Versatile in terms of ground, he handles most surfaces.

AMERICAN MIKE (IRE) 8 b g Mahler - American Jennie (IRE)
A Grade 2 winner and high-class horse on his day, we are delighted to be training him having been kindly sent him during the summer. We haven't made any definite plans but have the option of running him in intermediate chases.

BALLYCOMMON BOY (IRE) 4 b g Harzand (IRE) - Atasha (GER)
An exciting young horse who won his only Irish point-to-point for Tom Keating. Highly regarded, he is one for the future and will start off in a bumper.

BARLOVENTO (IRE) 6 b g Soldier of Fortune (IRE) - Playhara (IRE)
Successful on his hurdles debut at Carlisle last Autumn, he finished runner-up in his two subsequent starts but is better than he showed at Warwick and Leicester. Found to have choked at the latter venue, we have operated on his wind since. He will go novice handicap chasing over middle distances and there should be plenty more to come.

BOOSTER BOB (IRE) 7 b g Malinas (GER) - Ceka Dawn (IRE)
Sean (Bowen) gave him a fantastic ride to win the Greatwood Gold Cup Handicap Chase at Newbury in March. Earlier in the season, he won on his chasing debut at Ffos Las and tended to be hot and cold through the campaign. On his day, he is a useful horse and is crying out for a step up to three miles. His first target is likely to be the Listed Colin Parker Memorial Chase at Carlisle (2nd November).

BURNCOURT BOY (IRE) 5 b g Shirocco (GER) - Present Gesture (IRE)
Bought at the Cheltenham April Sale, he is a nice horse who ran in three Irish points for Tom Keating, for whom we have done well over the years. A winner last time, he could have a run in a bumper before going novice hurdling.

BUTCH 8 b g Kayf Tara - Leading On
He has a massive engine winning four times over hurdles and successful on his chasing debut at Leicester in late December. Unfortunately, he bled next time at Carlisle and has undergone wind surgery since. He lacks experience over fences and will be aimed at intermediate chases over two and a half miles plus.

CARISMATIC SOLDIER (IRE) 6 b g Soldier of Fortune (IRE) - Lady Charisma
Despite winning over hurdles at Chepstow and finishing runner-up at Leicester prior to that, he was still raw last season. He is a nice horse who needs racing to gain more experience. Rated 113, he will continue over hurdles and has the ability to win more races.

CASTLE IVERS (IRE) 6 b g Malinas (GER) - Made Easy (IRE)
A talented horse with a big engine, he won on his hurdles debut at Warwick in November. Unfortunately, he suffered a slight injury afterwards, which forced him to miss the remainder of the season. He won't be the easiest to place but will remain over hurdles before going chasing next year. Even though he will stay further, he possesses plenty of speed and is quick enough for two miles.

COASTAL ROCK (FR) 6 ch g Coastal Path - Adamantina (FR)
Joined us last season and was progressive winning at Uttoxeter, Bangor and Southwell. The ground was quick enough for him at the last named track in late March. He is very effective on soft ground and appreciated stepping up in trip. We are going to send him novice chasing.

DAMBUSTER 4 b g Kingman – Wall of Sound

A dual winner on the Flat for Andrew Balding, we bought him at the Newmarket Autumn Horses in Training Sale last year. He is a grand horse who finished runner-up over hurdles at Stratford and Fakenham in the spring. Unlucky not to win at the latter venue, he made a mistake at the last. Sidelined with a pelvic injury since, he will continue in novice hurdles in the Autumn and has the ability to win races.

DAYLATEDOLLARSHORT (IRE) 4 br g Wings of Eagles (FR) – Hannah Mori (IRE)

Won his point-to-point for Colin Bowe in Ireland producing a tough performance. We bought him at the Goffs UK Spring Sale and he looks good value. The plan is for him to run in a bumper in the Autumn.

DIAMONDS FOR LUCK (IRE) 6 ch g Diamond Boy (FR) – Alice Pink (IRE)

Progressive over hurdles, he won three times and we were going to run him in the conditional jockeys' handicap hurdle at Aintree's Grand National meeting. However, we pulled him out because the ground was too quick. A horse with a lot of ability, he will make a nice chaser eventually but we feel he has unfinished business over hurdles. Well treated off 122, he stays two and a half miles but isn't slow.

FINGLE BRIDGE (IRE) 7 b g Flemensfirth (USA) – Royale Video (FR)

Unbeaten in three runs over hurdles last season, including a Listed novice at Exeter in February, he is fragile but very talented. He loves soft ground and we feel he has the ability to develop into a Graded horse. Sean (Bowen) is keen to stay over hurdles with him, but I would prefer to go chasing. Quick enough for two miles, I think he will improve again over two and a half miles and could be a prime candidate for the Grade 1 Scilly Isles Novices' Chase at Sandown in February, if we decide to go over fences.

FORWARD THINKING (IRE) 5 br g Elusive Pimpernel (USA) – Def It Vic (IRE)

A lovely horse who ran well on his debut in a bumper at Warwick in December. I thought he would win next time at Market Rasen, but the track didn't suit him, plus he was beaten by a potentially very good horse (Un Sens A La Vie). He jumps well and I think he will develop into a nice novice hurdler.

GEE FORCE FLYER (IRE) 5 b g Jet Away – Forge Field (IRE)

Yet to run for us, he does everything nicely at home. A comfortable winner of his point-to-point in Ireland in December, we nearly ran him in the spring. He will go novice hurdling over two miles and looks a lovely horse.

GO DANTE 9 b g Kayf Tara – Whoops A Daisy

It was fantastic to win the Imperial Cup at Sandown for a second consecutive year. He loves soft ground and, even though he is effective over two miles, I think he will benefit from stepping up in trip this season. In the meantime, he could start off in the Welsh Champion Hurdle once again, which has been transferred to Chepstow (12th October).

HARBOUR ISLAND (FR) 6 b g Ultra (IRE) – Saraoushka (FR)

A nice horse who possesses a lot of ability, he won both his starts in bumpers at Wetherby and Ffos Las. He jumps well and will start off in a two miles maiden hurdle. He is one of our nicer novices for this season.

HOLD THE SERVE (IRE) 5 gr g Jukebox Jury (IRE) – Bisoguet (IRE)
Half-brother to Pleasington, he looked very good when winning a point-to-point in Ireland in December when trained by Sean Doyle. Given time since joining us, he will go novice hurdling and looks well above average.

HOMEGROWN HERO (IRE) 4 b g Jukebox Jury (IRE) – Shesafoxylady (IRE)
Similar to Ballycommon Boy, he won his point-to-point for Tom Keating in Ireland. Bought privately since, he is a very nice horse who may have a run in a bumper before going novice hurdling.

INDEEVAR BLEU (FR) 7 b g Blue Bresil (FR) – Ardissone (FR)
Looks great following his summer break, he has been doing some roadwork and I am very pleased with him. He isn't the easiest to train but has plenty of ability. Twice a winner over hurdles at Leicester and Ffos Las, we haven't decided whether to go handicap hurdling off his mark of 126 or send him over fences. There are more races to be won with him and even though he will stay beyond two miles, he isn't slow either.

INVECTO (FR) 4 ch g Doctor Dino (FR) – La Islaminima (FR)
A lovely unraced horse we bought at the Tattersalls Derby Sale in Ireland last year, I am delighted to be training for Andrew Brooks once again – we have had a lot of success together. He wants a bit of time but has been in pre training in Ireland and does everything nicely.

JACCOURS (FR) 6 b g Gris De Gris (IRE) – Ty Perrine (FR)
Placed in two of his three starts over hurdles at Ffos Las and Warwick, he incurred a minor injury to his pedal bone hence he missed the second half of the season. Back in work, he will contest another maiden hurdle and is capable of winning races off his mark of 115.

JACKPOT D'AINAY (FR) 6 ch g No Risk At All (FR) – Vanille D'Ainay (FR)
Lightly raced, he won a novice hurdle at Market Rasen on Boxing Day. Third next time on his handicap debut at Sandown, I was pleased with him that day and I think he will improve a lot this year. Nicely treated off 110, he is one for middle distance handicap hurdles.

JAMADA (IRE) 5 b g Affinisea (IRE) – Sounds of Thunder
A nice horse who ran in three bumpers in Ireland for John Queally, he won at Naas in early April. Bought privately since, he will start off in a two miles maiden hurdle and will stay further later on.

JUNKER D'ALLIER (FR) 6 b g Kapgarde (FR) – Star Flight (FR)
Enjoyed a good season in novice hurdles winning at Carlisle, Bangor and Perth. We ran him in a couple of Pattern novice hurdles, including the Grade 1 Formby Novices' Hurdle at Aintree on Boxing Day, but he came up short in those. I thought he would achieve more than he did. We have operated on his wind and looking forward to running him over fences. I think he will make a nice two mile novice chaser.

KAPAL LAYAR (IRE) 6 b g Milan – Shees A Dante (IRE)
Improved when stepped up to two and a half miles during the second half of the season, he won at Chepstow and Perth. I think he will progress still further when tackling three miles this season and could develop into a Pertemps Final type horse at the Cheltenham Festival.

KARTON PLEIN (FR) 5 b g Karaktar (IRE) – Porta Romana (FR)
A former pointer, he raced twice over hurdles winning comfortably at Southwell last time. Officially rated 110, I hope he will improve and make his mark in two and a half miles handicap hurdles.

KAYDENCE 5 b m Kayf Tara – Susie Sheep
She ran well on her debut finishing fourth in a bumper at Uttoxeter in the spring. The ground was quick enough that day and I think she will improve on a softer surface. We will aim her at a mares' bumper in the Autumn.

KEFIR D'OUDAIRIES (FR) 5 b g Seahenge (USA) – Dame D'Oudairies (FR)
Ran twice in bumpers finishing second on his debut at Hereford in November. He then won at Fakenham in February, despite the track, and will go hurdling this season. We will start him off in a maiden hurdle over two miles but he will benefit from racing over further. He should win more races.

KINGS CHAMPION (FR) 5 bl g Jeu St Eloi (FR) – Joly Nelsa (FR)
Owners Neil Smith & Alfie Smith have kindly sent us a few horses during the summer. A promising third on his only start in a bumper at Ffos Las last spring, he was behind The Blue Room who we like a lot. He will start off in a two miles maiden hurdle in the Autumn.

KINGSTON PRIDE (IRE) 6 gr g Kingston Hill – Milans Pride (IRE)
Bought on behalf of Mrs Barbara Hester and Mrs Diana Whateley at the Goffs UK Spring Sale, we are looking forward to running him over fences. Dual winner over hurdles last season, he appears to prefer better ground. With that in mind, we will start him off in a two and a half miles beginners chase or novices' handicap chase in the Autumn and then keep him going until the ground changes. Following a mid winter break, we will bring him back in the spring.

LARAKTAR (FR) 4 b g Karaktar (IRE) – Arcafet (FR)
Purchased at the Goffs Arkle Sale as a three year old, the reports about him from Ireland were encouraging. He is a very nice horse who will run in a bumper during the Autumn.

LIRION (FR) 4 b g Voiladenuo (FR) – Rirta (FR)
A fine big horse who finished runner-up in a bumper at Huntingdon in early March for Tom Weston. The winner (Mydaddypaddy) is highly regarded by Dan Skelton. We bought him later the same month and he is likely to have another run in a bumper before going novice hurdling.

LITTLE LEDGEND (IRE) 5 b g Yeats (IRE) – Nicat's Benefit (IRE)
Ran well in bumpers at Ascot and Wetherby before making his hurdles debut over two miles at Ffos Las in the spring. He found the trip sharp enough and will improve when stepped up to two and a half miles. He has the ability to win races.

LON CHANEY (IRE) 5 b g Walk In The Park (IRE) – Oscar Ladensa (IRE)
He is a nice big horse we acquired at the Cheltenham November Sale last year. Twice raced in Irish points for Denis Hogan, he was narrowly beaten last time. We have given him plenty of time and he looks a staying type who will be suited by soft ground. He will go novice hurdling in the Autumn.

LONG DRAW (IRE) 6 br g Affinisea (IRE) – Honey Away (IRE)

Progressive, he had a very good season winning twice at Cheltenham and was placed on five other occasions. Narrowly beaten at Haydock last time, he stays three miles well and prefers better ground. We are going to try and accumulate as much prize-money with him during the Autumn before having a winter break. He loves Cheltenham (211) and could be a Pertemps Final contender in the spring.

MISTER ST ELOI (FR) 4 b g Jeu St Eloi (FR) – Miss Frog (FR)

Bought at the Cheltenham Festival Sale in March, word was out about him after running in two Irish point-to-points for Alan Ahern. Unlucky on both starts, including when narrowly beaten last time, he is a nice big horse who will have a run in a bumper in the Autumn.

MISTER URSUS (IRE) 4 ch g Raven's Pass (USA) – Diamond (IRE)

A three times winner on the Flat in Poland and France, including over twelve furlongs at Nantes in March, he handles soft ground. He seems straightforward and will go novice hurdling over two miles.

MOYGANNY PHIL (IRE) 5 b g Califet (FR) – Moyganny Lass (IRE)

Runner-up in both starts in Irish points for Tom Keating, we bought him at the Cheltenham November Sale. Yet to run for us, his work in the spring was good and we will start him off in a two miles maiden hurdle. He shows plenty at home.

NEXT TWIST (FR) 5 ch g Muhtathir – Poprock Du Berlais (FR)

Raced twice in bumpers at Sandown and Ffos Las and, while he performed creditably, we ran him at the wrong tracks. He is a strong traveller and speed horse and will be suited by two mile novice hurdles on sharper tracks. He is capable of winning races.

NO TRICKS AT ALL (FR) 4 b f No Risk At All (FR) – Pearl Sky (FR)

An expensive store, she finished fourth on her debut in a bumper at Southwell in the spring. Still quite weak last year, she has done well during the summer and will improve once sent hurdling. We will aim her at mares' novice hurdles over two miles.

NOBLE CHARGE (IRE) 4 b g Order of St George (IRE) – Crafted Mastery (IRE)

A lovely big type, we bought him as a store at the Tattersalls Derby Sale last year. He had an educational run in a point-to-point for Michael Kennedy in Ireland during the spring. I think he will enjoy soft ground and will run in a bumper in the Autumn / early winter.

ORDEROFTHEDAY (IRE) 5 b g Order of St George (IRE) – Jolie Landaise (FR)

A point winner, he ran well in both his starts in bumpers finishing second at Market Rasen and Wetherby. He is a horse I have always liked and he jumps well. Two mile novice hurdles will be on his agenda.

PERTEMPS (IRE) 5 br g Milan – Britway Lady (IRE)

He is a big strong horse who wasn't beaten far in bumpers at Market Rasen and Chepstow finishing third on each occasion. Likely to start off in a two miles maiden hurdle, he will be suited by two and a half miles later on.

PIERROT JAGUEN (FR) 6 b g Saint Des Saints (FR) – Soif D'Aimer (FR)
An ex-winning pointer, he is a nice horse who is crying out for fences. Having run well on his first start for us at Cheltenham on New Year's Day, he confirmed the promise by winning at Lingfield next time. Third at Newbury on his last time, he is a staying chaser in the making. We may give him another run over hurdles before going novice handicap chasing over three miles.

PLEASINGTON (IRE) 7 br g Shantou (USA) – Bisoguet (IRE)
Dual winner over hurdles at Leicester and Lingfield, he loves soft ground. He disappointed in a Grade 3 novice hurdle at Naas in March and never ran his race. Given a break since, he will go novice chasing over two and two and a half miles.

RESPLENDENT GREY (IRE) 7 gr g Walk In The Park (IRE) – Caltra Princess (IRE)
Enjoyed a very good season over fences culminating in victory in the Bet365 Gold Cup at Sandown. Sean (Bowen) gave him a fantastic ride and it capped a tremendous season for us. The plan is for him to start off in the Listed Colin Parker Memorial Chase at Carlisle (2nd November) before being aimed at the Coral Gold Cup at Newbury (29th November). I have been pleased with him during the summer and it wouldn't surprise me if we entered him in the Grand National later on.

ROARING CONQUEST (IRE) 6 b g Doyen (IRE) – Bealath Champ (IRE)
Won his maiden hurdle at Lingfield before Christmas before finishing third in a Grade 2 novice hurdle at Haydock. The softer the ground the better and he is likely to stay over hurdles for the time being. Chasing will be his job one day.

SCORPIO RISING (IRE) 5 b g Jukebox Jury (IRE) – Sixofone (IRE)
A chaser in the making, he will spend this season in novice and handicap hurdles over two and a half miles. Third in a bumper at Exeter on his debut, I thought he ran well over hurdles at Ffos Las in the spring finishing third once again.

SIR GALAHAD (IRE) 4 b g Churchill (IRE) – Katiyra (IRE)
A cheap buy off the Flat last year, he has taken very well to jumping winning four of his five starts. Fourth in the Summer Handicap Hurdle at Market Rasen in July, he could go back to the same track for the Prelude Handicap Hurdle (27th September). Others options in the Autumn include either the Grade 2 Persian War Novices' Hurdle (10th October) or the Silver Trophy (11th October) at Chepstow. He likes decent ground.

SNUFFLEPOT 4 b g Maxios – Via Delle Volte
Unraced, he arrived during the summer and is a nice horse with a good pedigree. Owned by Gordon & Su Hall, he will run in a bumper during the Autumn.

STICKTOTHEPLAN (FR) 5 gr g Great Pretender (IRE) – Fulleren (FR)
Twice a winner over hurdles, including a Listed novice at the Galway Festival in late July, he was subsequently bought by some new owners (Not One But Two) to the yard. Rated 133, he remains a novice until the end of November and the plan is for him to run in the Grade 2 Persian War Novices' Hurdle at Chepstow (10th October). Hopefully, he can take high rank in some of the early season novice hurdles.

STRONG LEADER 8 b g Passing Glance – Strong Westerner (IRE)
Despite not winning a Grade 1 hurdle, he had another very good season. He won the Grade 2 Long Distance Hurdle at Newbury and was runner-up in the Grade 1 Liverpool Hurdle. Very much at home on flat tracks, he is likely to follow a similar programme, although he could reappear in the Grade 2 West Yorkshire Hurdle at Wetherby (1st November). Then, all being well, he will bid to defend his crown at Newbury (28th November). Later on, we may consider taking him to Leopardstown over Christmas and then the Grade 2 Rendlesham Hurdle at Haydock in February. His end of season target will once again be the Grade 1 Liverpool Hurdle, which he won in 2024.

THE BLUE ROOM (IRE) 5 br g Order of St George (IRE) – Saintly Lady (IRE)
I think he will develop into a very nice novice hurdler. Runner-up in his Irish point, he ran well in three bumpers last season winning at Ffos Las on his final start. A staying type, he will reappear over two miles but will come into his own over two and a half miles.

THE BLUESMAN (FR) 6 b g Crillon (FR) – Firmini (FR)
Arrived during the summer, he looked a nice horse when winning over hurdles at Chepstow last season. We are hoping a switch to fences will bring about further improvement and he could be nicely treated in novice handicaps chases.

THE FOUR SIXES (IRE) 7 b g Westerner – Lemon Cello (IRE)
Things didn't go to plan early on last season when we tried him over fences. We will give it another go one day but he came good back over hurdles in the spring winning at Bangor and Ayr. Rated 144, he stays well and we may try him in a Graded hurdle over three miles. He copes well with soft ground.

THERE RUNS MARY (IRE) 5 b m Flemensfirth (USA) – Morning Run (IRE)
A good mare who was an impressive winner on her debut in a bumper at Wincanton in late January. Runner-up next time at Newbury, the ground wasn't soft enough for her. She will be campaigned in mares' novice hurdles and we are hoping she will gain some black type at some stage.

THUNDER ROCK (IRE) 9 b g Shirocco (GER) – La Belle Sauvage
Back over hurdles last season, we discovered he had a fibrillating heart at Ascot on his reappearance. He is rated 155 over fences and there is every chance we will go down that route this winter. We have the option of running in veterans chases in the New Year, which is something we may exploit. A dual Listed winner, he has been a good horse over the years and still retains plenty of ability.

WADE OUT (IRE) 6 b g Shantou (USA) – Whats Up Britta (IRE)
A three times winner over hurdles, he benefited from stepping up in trip last season. His future lies over fences, but we are going to give him another run over hurdles. The Silver Trophy at Chepstow (11th October) is an option in the Autumn and he remains attractively treated off a mark of 127. I think he will make a very nice chaser.

WANDERING EGO (IRE) 5 b g Order of St George (IRE) – All The Queens (IRE)
Progressive in bumpers, he was placed at Newbury and Huntingdon before winning in good style at Wetherby. Sean (Bowen) likes him a lot and he ought to develop into a nice novice hurdler over two miles. He isn't short of speed.

WESTERNINTHEPARK (IRE) 7 b g Walk In The Park (IRE) - Western Skylark (IRE)
Took well to fences winning impressively on his chasing debut at Stratford last Autumn. Runner-up a couple of times since, including at Cheltenham's Paddy Power meeting, he disappointed in the Kim Muir at the Festival. He stays well and handles soft ground. We will be aiming him at some of the decent three mile handicap chases.

WILSTAR (IRE) 5 b g Doctor Dino (FR) - Star Face (FR)
A well bred youngster being a half-brother to Douvan and Jonbon, I like him a lot. He took time to come to himself but ran two good races in bumpers last spring. Third on his debut at Warwick, I think he would have won if he had relaxed early on. He made no mistake next time at Perth winning in good style and is one to look forward to in novice hurdling. Likely to reappear over two miles, he will want two and a half miles later on.

WOODIE FLASH (IRE) 7 b g Leading Light (IRE) - Lady Em (IRE)
I was delighted with him winning three out of four last season and his official rating climbing from 117 to 139. It is going to be tougher this time around, but he stays well and handles most types of ground. We will aim him at the good staying handicap hurdles.

WOODLAND PARK (IRE) 6 b g Walk In The Park (IRE) - Lonesome Dove (IRE)
A very nice horse who has only raced twice over hurdles. Runner-up at Carlisle, he won easily next time at Leicester. Absent since, he needs more experience but is well handicapped and will be aimed at two and a half miles handicap hurdles.

ZAMEK (FR) 5 gr g Beaumec De Houelle (FR) - Zanatiya (FR)
Placed in a bumper at Chepstow on his only start last spring, he joined us during the summer and looks a nice prospect. Only five, he is a very attractive horse who will run in a maiden hurdle in the Autumn.

TRAINER'S HORSE TO FOLLOW: HOMEGROWN HERO

14 times Champion Trainer

Paul NICHOLLS OBE

Stables: Manor Farm Stables, Ditcheat, Somerset.
2024/2025: 99 Winners / 550 Runners 18% Prize-Money £2,541,051
www.paulnichollsracing.com

ABSOLUTELY DOYEN (IRE) 5 b g Doyen (IRE) – Duffys Present (IRE)
Cantering at the moment, he joined us during the summer having been placed in two of his three runs over hurdles for Fergal O'Brien last season. A former point-to pointer, he is rated 113 and looks capable of winning novice handicap hurdles off his mark.

AFADIL (FR) 6 b g Camelot – Afsheen (FR)
Has dropped to a decent mark and is capable of winning off his rating of 122. He ran some good races in defeat last season, most notably when narrowly beaten in the Imperial Cup at Sandown. Runner-up in the Scottish County Hurdle at Musselburgh, he could have another run over hurdles before going chasing. We might run him in the two miles handicap hurdle at Cheltenham's first meeting (24th October).

A KING OF MAGIC (FR) 4 b g Desinvolte (FR) – Kisis De La Pree (FR)
Owned by the Paddy Brennan Racing Syndicate, he finished third in a bumper at Kempton on his debut when trained by Tom Weston. Bought privately since, he arrived in the spring and we are still learning about him. He looks great following his summer break and could have another run in a bumper before going novice hurdling.

BABYKEN (FR) 3 ch g Goken (FR) – Maybe (GER)
A nice recruit from France, he raced twice on the Flat winning on his debut at Le Mans in May. Runner-up next time, he is by a speedy sire but stays well. We turned him out soon after arriving and he will go novice hurdling over two miles.

BEAUTY IN THE PARK (IRE) 5 b m Walk In The Park (IRE) – Blue Berlais (IRE)
Big, strong mare who had a couple of runs in bumpers at Warwick and Wincanton. She ran well on both occasions but isn't a bumper horse. She wants a trip and will run in mares' novice hurdles over two and a half miles plus.

BELLIANO 6 b g Black Sam Bellamy (IRE) – Miliana (IRE)
A very nice horse who will go novice chasing. Runner-up behind The New Lion on his hurdles debut at Chepstow, he won twice at Ascot and Market Rasen. We thought he would run well in the EBF Final at Sandown in March but he wasn't at his best. Given a break since, he is a former winning Irish pointer and very much a chaser in the making. Two and a half to three miles is his trip.

BELOW THE RADAR (IRE) 7 b g Getaway (GER) – Benfaithful (IRE)
It was frustrating that he didn't manage to get his head in front last season having won three times the previous year. However, he ran a good race when narrowly beaten in a two and a half miles handicap hurdle at Ayr's Scottish National meeting. Rated 118, he will go novice handicap chasing.

BLUEKING D'OROUX (FR) 6 b g Jeu St Eloi (FR) – Belle Du Bresil (FR)
A high-class hurdler, I think he will make a very nice chaser. He won the Grade 2 Select Hurdle at Sandown on the final day of the season. The key to him is the ground – he doesn't want it soft. He disappointed twice at Windsor and Fontwell, due to the ground. Trips around two and a half to two miles six are ideal, having failed to stay three miles in the Grade 1 Long Walk Hurdle at Ascot before Christmas. He is ready to go over fences and the Grade 2 Rising Stars Novices' Chase at Wincanton (8th November), which we have won eleven times, looks a suitable target.

BOND BROKER (IRE) 6 b g Doyen (IRE) – Indian Love (FR)
Consistent, he is a good fun horse who won twice over hurdles at Southwell and Sedgefield. Runner-up on his chasing debut at Ffos Las in May, he wants an easy two miles and prefers decent ground. He will be running in two mile novice handicap chases in the Autumn.

BYZANTIUM (FR) 5 gr g Magneticjim (IRE) – Ticket Holder (FR)
A winner on the Flat in France, he was very keen in his races to begin with. However, he came good during the summer winning twice over hurdles at Warwick and Newton Abbot. Still a novice for the whole season, he stays two and a half miles and I think he will keep improving.

CALDWELL POTTER (FR) 7 gr g Martaline – Matnie (FR)
Looks fantastic following his summer holiday having developed into a top-class novice chaser last season. John Hales was convinced he was a two miler but he really improved once we stepped him up in trip. He was labelled a soft ground horse having won a Grade 1 novice hurdle in Ireland in testing conditions before he joined us. However, he loved the better ground in the spring winning the Jack Richards Novices' Handicap Chase at the Cheltenham Festival before following up in the Grade 1 Mildmay Novices' Chase at Aintree over three miles one. Even though he won at Aintree, I think he was over the top and it was his class which got him home. He hasn't been the easiest horse to train but we have done a lot of work on his feet and have learned to manage him. His form is very good and we are excited about the season ahead. If the ground is suitable, he could reappear in the Weatherbys Intermediate Chase at Newton Abbot (18th October), which we have won with Bravemansgame (2021), Pic D'Orhy (2022) and Complete Unknown (2023). We will then consider either the Paddy Power Gold Cup at Cheltenham (15th November) or *Betfair* Chase at Haydock (22nd November).

CALVINO (IRE) 5 b g Walk In The Park (IRE) – Antartica De Thaix (FR)
Out of a useful mare we trained, he ran three times in bumpers winning nicely at Taunton in the spring. He appreciates better ground and will be ready to go novice hurdling in the Autumn.

CAPTAIN BELLAMY 6 b g Black Sam Bellamy (IRE) – Himitas (FR)
We have not seen the best of him yet and I think he is attractively treated off 120. Still a maiden over hurdles having been disqualified at Newbury before Christmas, he was second at the same track in March. A winning Irish pointer, he will go over fences and is better suited racing left-handed. Two and a half miles is his trip.

CAPTAIN TEAGUE (IRE) 7 ch g Doyen (IRE) – Dancingwithbubbles (IRE)
A Grade 1 winning novice hurdler, he came back into work at the beginning of September with a view to resuming over fences after Christmas. He walked over on his chasing debut at Exeter in November before finishing fourth in the Grade 2 John Francome Novices' Chase at Newbury. Unfortunately, he sustained an injury and came back lame. Off since, he has had a long break and remains eligible for novice chases.

CLOTILDA (FR) 4 gr f Clovis Du Berlais (FR) – Goldflake (FR)
Joined us last Autumn having been placed over hurdles and fences in France. Despite winning on her first run for us at Huntingdon in December, she took a while to acclimatise. She ended the season well though with a very good run at Cheltenham in April finishing a close second in a Grade 3 mares' juvenile handicap hurdle. We will probably give her another run over hurdles before going novice handicap chasing. She has got experience of running over fences in France and her age and sex allowance will be handy.

COURAGEOUS STRIKE 4 ch g National Defense – Mademoiselle Marie (FR)
Bought at the Newmarket Autumn Sale last year, he did nothing wrong in three runs over hurdles during the spring. Twice a winner at Chepstow and Newton Abbot, he is on a nice mark and remains a novice until the end of November. A stayer on the Flat, he is quick enough for two miles and will reappear in the Autumn.

DOCTOR ON CALL (FR) 5 ch g Doctor Dino (FR) – Tornada (FR)
Half-brother to Grade 3 winning chaser Martator, he is a nice horse who won a bumper at Hereford on his debut. The ground dried up in the spring and we therefore gave him a break. He is ready to go novice hurdling and we will start him off over two miles. He will benefit from stepping up to two and a half miles later on.

ELLIE MARIE (IRE) 4 b m Walk In The Park (IRE) – Tarantella Lady
Purchased at the Tattersalls Ireland PTP & HIT Sale in May, she was runner-up in her only point-to-point for Andrew Slattery. Only four, she will run in mares' bumpers and looks a nice type.

EMAILANDY (IRE) 7 b g Mount Nelson – Eoz (IRE)
A decent novice hurdler a couple of seasons ago, he was never right last year, including on his chasing debut at Newbury. We have given him a long break since and hopefully he will make his mark in novice handicap chases over two and a half miles plus.

FASOL 6 b g Galileo (IRE) – Silasol (IRE)
He has done well during the summer and I think he is on a nice mark. A winner over hurdles at Taunton in March, he ran a good race at Sandown on the final day of the season. Third in a valuable novices' handicap hurdle, he is a novice until the end of November. He doesn't want to hit the front too soon and likes good ground. There is a good race to be won with him.

GILLESPIE (IRE) 5 br g Getaway (GER) – Princess Mairead (IRE)
Successful on his debut in a bumper at Ffos Las before Christmas, we nearly ran him again in the spring but the ground wasn't suitable. Still very green, he is a well bred horse who should to improve. He is a nice prospect for novice hurdles.

GO WEST (IRE) 7 b g Westerner – Topathistle (IRE)
Enjoyed a good season over hurdles winning at Fakenham, Taunton and Kempton. We then stepped him up to three miles in a Listed novice hurdle at Perth last time but he raced too freely. I think he will stay three miles eventually and we will send him novice chasing.

GOLD CAST (FR) 3 b f Telecaster – Shannon Marigold (FR)
She is a very nice filly we bought at the Arqana Summer Sale in France. She raced three times over hurdles, winning a valuable conditions event at Auteuil in late May. Bryony (Frost) rode her twice and liked her. We will be aiming her at the good mares' novice hurdles and she could be one for the Listed Byerley Stud Mares' Novices' Hurdle at Taunton (30th December).

GRAND GARCON 5 b g Kapgarde (FR) - Urticaire (FR)
Stayed on well in second on his debut at Chepstow in March, he could have another run in a bumper. He is a nice horse who will stay two and a half miles over hurdles.

HENRI THE SECOND (FR) 8 b g Saddler Maker (IRE) - Rock Treasure (FR)
Fourth on his chasing debut at Sandown, we decided to go back over hurdles and he won well at the same track in December. Runner-up in a Grade 3 handicap hurdle at Sandown once again in February, we will give him another go over fences. If he gets his act together, he could develop into a Welsh National type horse one day because he stays well and handles testing ground.

HISTRIONIC (IRE) 6 b g Walk In The Park (IRE) - Flemensbay
A winning pointer who stays well, he won over hurdles at Chepstow in the spring. Rated 121, he will go novice handicap chasing and should improve over fences.

HYDATION STATION (IRE) 5 b g Idaho (IRE) - Good Looking Woman (IRE)
Ran in two Irish points for Sean Doyle winning last time, he will go novice hurdling. We haven't done much with him yet, but we have been pleased with him.

IDAHO FIRE (IRE) 4 b g Idaho (IRE) - Thisgirlisonfire (IRE)
Owned by Million In Mind Partnership, he was bought after finishing second in a UK point-to-point. Only four, he will probably start off in a bumper before going novice hurdling.

IL RIDOTO (FR) 8 b g Kapgarde (FR) - L'Exploratrice (FR)
We were delighted with his victory in the Paddy Power Gold Cup at Cheltenham. He tends to show his best form before Christmas and will therefore follow a similar route. Once again, he will reappear in the £40,000 John Ayres Memorial Handicap Chase at Chepstow (12th October) before attempting to defend his crown in the Paddy Power Gold Cup (15th November).

INCH HOUSE (IRE) 8 b g Ocovango - Ask Hazel (IRE)
He endured a frustrating campaign having joined us last season. We think he may have been still feeling the effects of a fall at Ayr the previous year. He disappointed in both runs at Newbury. We have given him a long break since and he is beginning to show more in his work at home.

INSURRECTION (IRE) 8 b g Getaway (GER) - Rock In The Park (IRE)
Runner-up in the Listed Robert Mottram Memorial Trophy at Chepstow on his chasing debut, he won a novices' handicap at Musselburgh in February. Two and a half miles on decent ground suits and he is another who could reappear at Chepstow (12th October) in the Autumn.

INTHEWATERSIDE (FR) 7 b g Jeu St Eloi (FR) - Vared (FR)
Back cantering having missed the second half of last season, he is fine now. He ran well in a decent handicap hurdle at Newbury's Winter Festival in November before winning in good style on his chasing debut at the same track over Christmas. Rated 140 over fences, he lacks experience and we will aim him at a Graduation chase. Effective over two and a half miles, he will stay three miles eventually.

ISAAC DES OBEAUX (FR) 7 b g Kapgarde (FR) - Varda Des Obeaux (FR)
Still a novice over fences, he was placed a couple of times including in a valuable novices' handicap at Uttoxeter in March. He stays well and wants cut in the ground and will continue in novice handicap chases. He jumps well and is capable of winning more races.

JACKPOT DES BORDES (FR) 6 b g Vision D'Etat (FR) – Carmen Des Bordes (FR)
Despite winning over hurdles at Taunton, he was a bit disappointing last season. Still green, he didn't jump as well as we hoped. Runner-up at Taunton last time, he looks well following his summer break. If he can get his act together, he is on a fair mark. He could have another run over hurdles before going chasing.

JAKAR DU MOULIN (FR) 6 b g Kapgarde (FR) – Maguy Des Plages (FR)
A winning pointer, he is an attractive horse who was still backward last year. Runner-up over hurdles at Leicester, he was in front when unseating his jockey at Chepstow last time. He is on a good mark and will be aimed at novice handicap hurdles.

JENA D'OUDAIRIES (FR) 6 b m Buck's Boum (FR) – Une D'Oudairies (FR)
She won over hurdles at Chepstow in March and will continue in mares' handicap hurdles. Rated 111, her first target is the Paul & Richard Barber Memorial Mares' Handicap Hurdle at Wincanton (8th November).

JOYAU ALLEN (FR) 6 ch g Muhtathir – Reaction (FR)
A full brother to Envoi Allen, he missed the whole of last season due to injury. Back cantering, he ran twice for us in bumpers the previous year winning at Exeter before finishing second under a penalty at the same track. He will go novice hurdling.

JUBILEE ALPHA (IRE) 6 b m Flemensfirth (USA) – Queen Alphabet (IRE)
She is a smart mare who had a very good season over hurdles. A three times winner, including Listed events at Taunton and Cheltenham, she won over two and a half miles at the latter in the spring. That gives us more options this season. The Listed mares' hurdle at Wetherby (1st November) or the Paul & Richard Barber Memorial Mares' Handicap Hurdle at Wincanton (8th November) are a possible starting points with the Grade 1 David Nicholson Mares' Hurdle at the Cheltenham Festival her ultimate target.

JUST A ROSE (FR) 6 b m Saint Des Saints (FR) – Daring Rose (FR)
She hasn't been easy to train but is a good mare who won very easily on her hurdles debut at Taunton. We then ran her in the Grade 2 Dawn Run Mares' Novices' Hurdle at the Cheltenham Festival where she lacked experience. She hasn't got a mark yet but is another possible for the Paul & Richard Barber Memorial Mares' Handicap Hurdle at Wincanton (8th November).

KAJIKIA (FR) 5 b g It's Gino (GER) – Kilfenora (FR)
Ran in three bumpers including when winning on his debut at Ascot. I thought he ran OK on his final start at Plumpton over Easter under a penalty finishing third. He will go novice hurdling and will stay two and a half miles.

KALIF DU BERLAIS (FR) 5 b g Masked Marvel – Kadika (FR)
The apple of my eye, he is a very smart horse who developed into a top-class two mile novice chaser. Unlucky on his chasing debut at Carlisle, he won well at Newbury and Cheltenham on his next two starts. We then ran him on heavy ground in the Grade 1 Scilly Isles Novices' Chase over two and a half miles at Sandown, which was a mistake. We wanted to run him in the Kingmaker Novices' Chase at Warwick the following weekend instead, but the same owners had L'Eau Du Sud for that. We missed Cheltenham and kept him fresh for Aintree and I thought he was very good in the Grade 1 Maghull Novices' Chase jumping well and making all. Rated

156, we are going to train him for the Queen Mother Champion Chase in March. He will start off in either the Grade 2 Haldon Gold Cup at Exeter (7th November) or the Grade 2 Shloer Chase at Cheltenham (14th November). We have had plenty of top-class two mile chasers and I think he is up there with them.

KANDOO KID (FR) 9 gr g Kapgarde (FR) – Scarlett Du Mesnil (IRE)
It was great to win the Coral Gold Cup at Newbury once again. His whole season was then geared towards the Grand National at Aintree. He was travelling well in behind the leaders when falling on the second circuit. Unfortunately, he picked up an injury which means he won't be running until the New Year. Likely to be entered in the Grand National once again, he is rated 151 and something like the Cotswold Chase at Cheltenham in January might suit him.

KILNEW SUPREME (IRE) 4 b g Harzand (IRE) – Littlemissfit (IRE)
A nice young horse who I like, he finished runner-up in his point-to-point for Denis Murphy in Ireland. We bought him at the Cheltenham April Sale and have given him time. He is only four and will therefore start off in a bumper.

KNAPPERS HILL (IRE) 9 b g Valirann (FR) – Brogella (IRE)
Off the track since winning the Grade 2 Rising Stars Novices' Chase at Wincanton nearly two years ago, he was jarred up afterwards and missed the whole of last season. Back cantering, we brought him back in early. Not easy to place off 152, we will aim him at Graduation chases. He likes decent ground but doesn't want it too quick.

LANCELOT D'ALENE (FR) 4 ch g Jeu St Eloi (FR) – Serbanne (FR)
We bought him as a store as a three year old and he ran in a UK point-to-point for Will Biddick. Narrowly beaten in a maiden at Charlton Horethorne in March, he could start off in a bumper at Chepstow (12th October).

LANCELOT DU LARGE (FR) 4 b g Kapgarde (FR) – Garline Du Large (FR)
Another nice youngster who was acquired at the Aintree Sale in April. Cormac Doyle trained him to win his point-to-point in Ireland and he is one for the future. Only four, he will run in a bumper in the Autumn.

LARGY POET (IRE) 6 ch g Malinas (GER) – Our Soiree (IRE)
He wasn't right for most of last year before winning on his chasing debut at Exeter in February. Rated 137, we have the option of Graduation chases. Alternatively, we might give him one more run and then aim him at the Badger Beer Handicap Chase at Wincanton (8th November). I think he is better going right-handed.

LEN (IRE) 5 b g Wings of Eagles (FR) – Lenora (IRE)
Ran in two point-to-points for Stuart Crawford and was unlucky on the second occasion when leading and unseating his rider at the last. It is early days because we haven't done a lot with him but the plan is for him to go straight over hurdles.

MAKIN'YOURMINDUP 8 b g Kayf Tara – Subtilty
Back in training having been sidelined for the whole of last season, he remains lightly raced over fences. Rated 142, he stays well and wants soft ground. With that in mind, we are going to aim him at the Welsh National at Chepstow (27th December) with two runs beforehand.

MALDINI MILANO (IRE) 5 b g Milan – Tellthemnuttin (IRE)
An easy winner on his debut at Exeter, he then got bogged down in soft ground in a Listed bumper at Newbury in February. Runner-up under a penalty at Wincanton last time, he prefers better ground and will go novice hurdling in the Autumn.

MATTERHORN (FR) 7 b g Martaline – Sacarine (FR)
A five times winner over fences, he is rated 147 and keeps improving. Runner-up behind Sans Bruit in the Sussex Champion Chase at Plumpton, he then stepped up to two and a half miles for the first time and won the Clarke Chase at Uttoxeter in May. We might aim him at the John Ayres Memorial Chase at Chepstow (12th October) or wait for the Intermediate Chase at Newton Abbot (18th October) the following week. He likes good ground.

MISS ALTEA BLUE (FR) 4 b f Great Pretender (IRE) – Miss Salsa Blue (FR)
Arrived from France last Autumn with a lofty rating having finished second twice at Auteuil and took a while to acclimatise. She won a mares' novice hurdle at Wincanton in March before falling at Kempton next time. I thought she ran respectably on her final outing in a Grade 3 mares' handicap hurdle at Cheltenham in April. She has benefited from a break during the summer and ought to improve.

MON CHAMPION (FR) 5 b g Bathyrhon (GER) – Promets Moi (FR)
An interesting recruit from France, he gained plenty of experience winning over hurdles at Auteuil and finishing second three times over fences. He is a fun horse to go novice chasing.

MONMIRAL (FR) 8 bl g Saint Des Saints (FR) – Achere (FR)
A former Grade 1 and Cheltenham Festival winner, he had another good season finishing runner-up in the Grade 2 Long Distance and Cleeve Hurdles at Newbury and Cheltenham respectively. Not easy to place, he will remain over hurdles with the Grade 2 West Yorkshire Hurdle at Wetherby (1st November) a likely starting point.

MULINAS 6 b g Malinas (GER) – Multisphere
I like him and we are looking forward to seeing him over hurdles having missed last season due to a minor injury. A winning pointer, he ran well in bumpers at Chepstow and Ffos Las.

NARDARAN (FR) 4 b g Waldgeist – Narniyn (IRE)
Placed on the Flat in France, we bought him at the Arqana Summer Sale last year. Despite winning over hurdles at Taunton in April, he struggled with his wind last season. He has therefore undergone surgery and I am hoping he will improve. Eligible for novice hurdles until the end of November, he is on a workable mark.

NECRONAUT 5 b g Blue Bresil (FR) – Potters Den (IRE)
From the family of Denman, I like him a lot. He ran twice in bumpers finishing second on his debut at Wincanton. We have been pleased with him during the summer, he has strengthened up and will go novice hurdling over two and a half and two miles six. He is a lovely prospect.

NO DRAMA THIS END (IRE) 5 gr g Walk In The Park (IRE) – La Segnora (FR)
An exciting horse who looked very good when winning a bumper at Warwick on New Year's Eve. We thought he would run well beforehand, although he doesn't show much at home. We then ran him in the Cheltenham Festival bumper and, while he ran OK, he would have preferred

slower ground. From a good family, he won a point-to-point for Will Biddick and jumps well. He will start off in a two and a half miles maiden hurdle on soft ground. A big horse, he will hopefully develop into a Grade 1 Challow Novice Hurdle contender at Newbury (29th December).

ONE ISLAND (FR) 3 b g Romanised (IRE) – Mira Star (IRE)
He won on his debut over a mile and a half on the Flat in France in May. Bought privately afterwards, we gave him a break during the summer with a view to going juvenile hurdling in the Autumn.

OUTMASTER 4 b g Masterstroke (USA) – She's Dylan (IRE)
A nice horse who won a point-to-point at Edgcote in April for Gina Andrews, we bought him soon afterwards at the Cheltenham April Sale. He jumped and travelled well and we will probably run him in a bumper before going hurdling.

OUTLAW PETER (IRE) 9 b g Mustameet (USA) – My Katie (IRE)
A three times winner over fences, we couldn't get him right last season hence he only raced twice. However, he has come back in looking much better and I think he could win a nice race this year. Two and a half to three miles is ideal.

PARK BLUE (IRE) 5 b g Walk In The Park (IRE) – Blue Maxi (IRE)
Well bred, he ran in three Irish points for Sean Doyle winning on his second start before finishing runner-up last time. He looks a nice horse for novice hurdles.

PIC D'ORHY (FR) 10 b g Turgeon (USA) – Rose Candy (FR)
A wonderful horse who gained his third Grade 1 win in the *Betfair* Ascot Chase in February. It was as good a performance as he has produced throughout his career. We didn't over race him and kept him for the Grade 2 Oaksey Chase at Sandown at the end of the season, but he made a mistake early on. He looks great following his summer break and will start off in the Grade 2 Copybet1965 Chase at Ascot (22nd November), a race he has won for the last two years. The Grade 2 Peterborough Chase at Huntingdon (7th December) is another option and we might enter him in the King George at Kempton (26th December).

POURQUOI PAS PAPA (FR) 3 b g Manatee – Pourquoi Pas Elle (FR)
Runner-up on his only start over hurdles at Clairefontaine in June, Anthony Bromley liked him and we bought him at the Arqana Summer Sale a few weeks later. He looks a very nice horse to go juvenile hurdling.

QUEBECOIS (FR) 6 ch g No Risk At All (FR) – Miss Poutine (FR)
An exciting prospect for novice chases, he has had a wind operation during the summer having struggled with his breathing last season. Twice a winner over hurdles, including over three miles at Ayr's Scottish National meeting. He stays well and should improve again over fences. We are hoping he will develop into a Graded novice chaser over three miles. He doesn't want the ground too soft.

REGENT'S STROLL (IRE) 6 b g Walk In The Park (IRE) – Pretty Puttens (IRE)
He has done very well during the summer and is in awesome form at home. Last year, he was boisterous and lit up before his races, but he is a lot more chilled out now and we are very pleased with him. He came good in the spring when we fitted him with a hood and encountering

better ground at Aintree. Narrowly beaten in the Grade 1 Mersey Novices' Hurdle over two and a half miles, we have always felt he was very smart and anything he achieved over hurdles was a bonus. We will start him over fences at somewhere like Exeter and get him to enjoy it. Ultimately, I think he will develop into a three miler. The good horses need minding and given time as youngsters. He is a very nice horse.

RUBAUD (FR) 7 b g Air Chief Marshal (IRE) – Fulgence (FR)
He has been a great horse and enjoyed another good season winning the Grade 2 Elite Hurdle at Wincanton for a second consecutive year before switching to fences and winning the Grade 2 Pendil Novices' Chase at Kempton. We will probably switch between hurdles and fences once again and he could start off in the Listed hurdle at Kempton (19th October), which he has won for the last two years. The £100,000 Byrne Group Handicap Chase at Ascot (1st November) or the Grade 2 Haldon Gold Cup (7th November) are other options we will consider. A fun horse who has earned a lot of prize-money, he prefers racing right-handed.

SANS BRUIT (FR) 7 b g Triple Treat (FR) – Swedish Dancer (IRE)
Similar to the previous year, he came good in the spring winning the Red Rum Chase at Aintree for a second time before following up in the Sussex Champion Chase at Plumpton. It won't be easy off 144 but there are plenty of options for him, including the Haldon Gold Cup at Exeter (7th November) and those valuable two mile handicap chases at Ascot. Jay (Tidball) got on well with him at Plumpton and his claim will be useful in those type of races.

SAUVIGNON (FR) 4 b g Inns of Court (IRE) – Salicorne (USA)
A Listed winner over hurdles at Auteuil in France, it took him a long time to acclimatise and things didn't really work out last season. However, he has come back in looking very well following his summer break. The handicapper has dropped him a few pounds and might start him off in the four year old hurdle at Chepstow (11th October).

STAGE STAR (IRE) 9 b g Fame And Glory – Sparky May
We will be aiming him at the good staying chases with the Charlie Hall Chase at Wetherby (1st November) his first target. We will also enter him in the Grade 1 *Betfair* Chase (22nd November). He stays well and must go left-handed. Despite the fact he didn't win last season, he ran some good races in defeat, most notably when a close second behind L'Homme Presse in the Grade 2 Cotswold Chase at Cheltenham conceding weight. We have the option of running him in the Grade 1 Savills Chase at Leopardstown (28th December) and the Cotswold Chase in January once again.

SUBURBAN LEGEND (IRE) 5 b g Harzand (IRE) – Donnelly's Hollow (IRE)
Purchased at the Goffs UK Coral Gold Cup Sale last November, he won the second of his two Irish points for Colin Bowe. We have given him plenty of time and he will be going novice hurdling after Christmas. Long-term, he is a chaser in the making.

SWINGIN SAFARI (IRE) 5 bb g Walk In The Park (IRE) – Sara's Smile
We are hoping he will make a very nice novice hurdler having done well in bumpers last season. Ex-Irish, he was quite keen to start with but is learning to settle now. A winner at Wincanton on his first run for us, I thought he ran well in the Grade 2 bumper at Aintree finishing fourth. He will be suited by stepping up to two and a half miles over hurdles.

TAKEONEDAYATATIME 5 b m Time Test – Sea Pride (IRE)
She ran in a couple of bumpers being placed on her debut at Wincanton in October before winning nicely at Newton Abbot in the spring. We have schooled her and she will be campaigned in mares' novice hurdles.

TALK TO THE MAN (IRE) 5 b g Walk In The Park (IRE) – Windermere Sky (IRE)
A winning pointer, he ran twice in bumpers last season and is a horse I like a lot. He didn't enjoy the testing ground on his first run at Exeter and then I thought he ran OK in the Goffs Hundred Grand Bumper at Newbury in March finishing fourth. He will go novice hurdling and will be suited by two and a half miles on decent ground. There is a lot more to come from him.

TEESHAN (IRE) 6 b g Westerner – Miss Pepperpot (IRE)
Missed last season due to a tiny fracture, the time off hasn't done him any harm. Back cantering, we aren't going to rush him because he is a horse with plenty of ability. A point-to-point and bumper winner, we could start him off in a maiden hurdle over two and a half miles.

TREASURE PLANET (IRE) 3 b g Footstepsinthesand – Beach of Falesa (IRE)
A nice prospect for juvenile hurdles, my daughter Megan (Nicholls) bought him privately. Twice raced on the Flat during April for Donnacha O'Brien in Ireland, he was fourth on his debut over ten furlongs at Navan before finishing second at Tipperary over a mile and a half.

THREEUNDERTHRUFIVE (IRE) 10 b g Shantou (USA) – Didinas (FR)
Placed in a couple of valuable handicaps at Ascot last season, he isn't the easiest to place off his rating of 152. He will follow a similar programme and be aimed at those good staying handicaps at Ascot and is more likely to run in the Scottish National at Ayr rather than Aintree, which we tried last term.

TUTTI QUANTI (FR) 5 b g Chanducoq (FR) – Terebella (FR)
A very smart horse, he has summered well and I love him. Twice a winner over hurdles at Ffos Las last season, we have looked after him and he is a very nice horse. He ran OK in the *Sky Bet* Supreme Novices' Hurdle at Cheltenham in March before bolting up at Ffos Las next time. Rated 132, his first target is the Welsh Champion Hurdle at Chepstow (12th October). We will then decide whether to stay over hurdles or go novice chasing. He jumps well and will make a lovely two mile chaser.

VIROFLAY (FR) 8 b g Air Chief Marshal (IRE) – Red Vixen (IRE)
Joined us during the summer having done very well in point-to-points and hunter chases for my daughter Olive (Nicholls). He was a wide margin winner at Kempton in April before finishing second in the Champion Hunter Chase at the Punchestown Festival. Eligible for novice chases until the end of November, he is better going right-handed and the Grade 2 Rising Stars Novices' Chase at Wincanton (8th November) is a possible target.

WELCOM TO CARTRIES (FR) 7 b g No Risk At All (FR) – Nasou (FR)
A nice horse who ran twice over fences finishing fourth in the Grade 2 Esher Novices' Chase at Sandown and Grade 1 Kauto Star Novices' Chase at Kempton on Boxing Day. Runner-up over hurdles at Newbury in the spring, he is on a fair mark over fences and we will campaign him in the decent staying handicap chases. The experience he gained last season will stand him in good stead.

WICKED THOUGHTS (IRE) 6 ch g Mahler – Emily's Princess (IRE)
A winner over hurdles at Ascot in the spring, he was runner-up a couple of times at Southwell and Hereford. He is rated 118 and will go over fences and we will aim him at novice handicap chases over two and a half miles.

ZAOCHEN ENKI (FR) 4 b g Barastraight – Lady Needles (IRE)
Runner-up over hurdles in France, he was quite lean and light when first arriving last Autumn. We gave him some time and he won nicely at Wincanton in the spring. Placed at Chepstow under a penalty last time, he remains a novice over hurdles until the end of November. He will benefit from stepping up to two and a half miles and is a nice young horse.

In addition, Manor Farm Stables is also responsible for a strong team of **hunter chasers** for later in the campaign. Paul's daughter Olive (Nicholls) will be partnering **GOLDEN SON, MR GLASS, QUEL DESTIN** & **SHEARER**.

UNRACED BUMPER HORSES

In last year's edition of *One Jump Ahead*, the 14 times champion trainer handpicked 8 unraced bumper horses, including **CALVINO (5/6), KAJIKIA (17/2)** and **SINNATRA (5/4)**. Once again, Paul has kindly selected the following 8 unraced horses to keep an eye on this Autumn and beyond from the yard's new crop of bumper performers for 2025/2026.

ARTABAN DE MAINE (FR) 4 ch g Motivator – Day Lily (FR)
He was purchased for **€60,000** at the Goffs Arkle Sale as a three year old.

BEAU SPEED (FR) 4 b g Beaumec De Houelle (FR) – Tangaspeed (FR)
Owned by **Kate & Andrew Brooks**, he is out of a dual Listed winner in France and a half-brother to the useful Authorised Speed. He was acquired for **£110,000** at the Goffs UK Spring Sale as a three year old.

JPR TWO (IRE) 4 br g Poet's Word (IRE) – Lady Knightess (IRE)
Half-brother to dual Grade 2 winning chaser JPR One, he is owned by **Mr J.P.Romans** and was bought for **€120,000** as a three year old at the Tattersalls Ireland Derby Sale.

KALI SANA (IRE) 4 b g Walk In The Park (IRE) – Lourdes (FR)
Owned by **Mrs Helen Moger**, he is another who was recruited from the Tattersalls Ireland Derby Sale last year for **€110,000**.

LE COLD GREY (FR) 4 gr g Cokoriko (FR) – Athena Du Mesnil (FR)
Owned by **The Brooks & Stewart Families**, he is a half-brother to triple Grade 1 winner and Grand National placed Gaillard Du Mesnil. He cost **€95,000** at the Goffs Arkle Sale as a three year old.

RIVER KWAI (FR) 4 b g No Risk At All (FR) – Princess Kap (FR)
Out of a high-class Grade 2 winning mare in France, he was bought for **€130,000** at the Tattersalls Ireland Derby Sale as a three year old. He is owned by **Mrs Kathy Stuart**.

ROXIMAN (FR) 3 ch g Kapgarde (FR) – Roxinela (FR)
Only three, the dam was a dual Grade 2 winner in France and he is owned by **John White & Anne Underhill**.

SAPPINGIRL (IRE) 4 b g Blue Bresil (FR) – Blath Beag
Owned by **Kate & Andrew Brooks**, he was bought for **€88,000** at the Goffs Arkle Sale last year.

TRAINER'S HORSE TO FOLLOW: KALIF DU BERLAIS

Jonjo & A.J. O'NEILL

Stables: Jackdaws Castle, Temple Guiting, Cheltenham, Gloucestershire.
2024/2025: 72 Winners / 565 Runners 13% Prize-Money £1,223,059
www.jonjooneillracing.com

ALL FOR GLORY 8 b m Fame And Glory – Glorybe (GER)
Twice a winner over hurdles at Musselburgh and Southwell, she was also placed in the Scottish County Handicap Hurdle at the former track in February and enjoyed a good season. Rated 132 over hurdles, the plan is for her to go over fences and aim her at mares' novice chases. That will give us more options.

ASSERTIVE WALK (IRE) 5 b g Walk In The Park (IRE) – Assertive Lady (IRE)
A fine big horse who was very green on his debut in a bumper at Chepstow last November. He still ran well considering how inexperienced he was finishing third and we have given him plenty of time since. He has filled out and is ready to go novice hurdling over two and a half miles.

BATHARA (FR) 4 b g Bathyrhon (GER) – Zamhara
Only four, he was still quite weak last year and ought to improve. He was fourth in a bumper at Bangor during the spring and we may give him another run in a similar event before going novice hurdling.

BEACHCOMBER (FR) 7 b g Bathyrhon (GER) – Alpes Du Sud (FR)
Produced a good performance to win a decent handicap chase at Kempton over Christmas. We fitted him with blinkers and it sharpened him up. Suited by racing right-handed, he wants good ground and I thought he ran well when finishing third in a Listed handicap chase at the Punchestown Festival. Rated 135 over fences, we will be looking at those valuable three miles handicap chases at tracks such as Ascot and Kempton. The Sodexo Gold Cup Handicap Chase at the former track (1st November) could be a suitable target.

BEST TRUMP (IRE) 4 b g Walk In The Park (IRE) – Samsha (IRE)
Half-brother to Gwennie May Boy, who we previously trained, he looked good when winning his only point-to-point for Derek O'Connor in Ireland. We have followed him since he was a store horse and we are delighted to have been sent him by Mr (J.P.) McManus. We haven't had him long but we like what we have seen. No decision has been made over whether he will have a run in a bumper or go straight over hurdles.

BILL JOYCE (IRE) 6 b g Mahler – Bettys Delight (IRE)

We are excited about the prospect of him going over fences this season. He enjoyed a good season over hurdles winning twice, including the Grade 2 Winter Novices' Hurdle at Sandown in early December. He then produced a career best finishing third in the Grade 1 Challow Novices' Hurdle at Newbury over Christmas on ground which arguably wasn't soft enough for him. Not the same horse when third in another Grade 2 novice at Cheltenham's Trials meeting in January, we decided to skip the Festival and freshen him up for Aintree. Stepped up to three miles for the first time in a valuable handicap hurdle on Grand National day, I think he would have gone close that day but unfortunately fell when travelling well. He had had enough by the time the Punchestown Festival came around. He overachieved as a hurdler because we have always felt he will make a better chaser. A winning point-to-pointer, he will stay three miles, but we will start him off over two and a half miles.

BOSTON BOY 6 b g Black Sam Bellamy (IRE) – Samrana (FR)

A horse with ability, he proved frustrating during the first half of last season running out twice at Leicester and Windsor. However, he showed what he is capable of later on finishing third at Doncaster before winning at Fontwell. He also ran creditably at the Punchestown Festival last time. Runner-up in an Irish point, we are going to send him novice chasing and it could be the making of him. We will start him off over two miles.

COLLECTORS ITEM (IRE) 8 b g Flemensfirth (USA) – Leading Lady

We were pleased with him last season winning the Somerset National at Wincanton in January on a track which wouldn't have been ideal. He conceded nearly a stone to Katate Dori, who subsequently won the Grade 3 Ladbrokes Trophy Handicap Chase at Kempton by fifteen lengths. Prior to that, the London National at Sandown had been one of his main targets and he ran well finishing second. He wasn't at his best in the Eider Chase at Newcastle before running respectably in the Bet365 Gold Cup at Sandown. A strong stayer, we will be aiming him at the likes of the London National at Sandown (6th December), Welsh National at Chepstow (27th December) and the Midlands National at Uttoxeter in March.

COUNTRY PARK (IRE) 6 b g Walk In The Park (IRE) – Glacial Drift

Still a maiden over hurdles, he was unlucky not to win last season. He made a mistake at the last at Cheltenham's November meeting and was cantering when falling at the penultimate flight at Ascot next time. Fourth in a valuable handicap hurdle at the latter track in February, he is rated 120 and has plenty of experience. With that in mind, we are going to aim him at some of the better races with the Grade 2 Persian War Novices' Hurdle at Chepstow (10th October) a possible target. Versatile in terms of trip, we have the option of going novice chasing later on.

CREBILLY (IRE) 8 b g Soldier of Fortune (IRE) – Blueberry Bramble (IRE)

A bit disappointing last season having done well the previous one, we didn't get the smoothest of runs with him last winter. He came back sore after his reappearance at Chepstow and didn't return until mid January when finishing a good third at Windsor. We struggled with him thereafter but he has come back in looking well and I think it is a case of the further the better for him having learned to settle.

DIAMOND WHITE (IRE) 4 ch f Berkshire (IRE) – Wilde Ruby (IRE)

A lovely filly who came from the same source in Ireland as Bill Joyce. She was well recommended having won her point-to-point in March and we bought her a few days later at the Cheltenham

Festival Sale. We have been very pleased with her during the summer, she has strengthened and could have a run in a bumper before going mares' novice hurdling. We like her a lot.

FORTUNATE MAN (IRE) 6 b g Soldier of Fortune (IRE) – Lady Azamour (IRE)
We thought he would go close on his second run over fences at Carlisle at the beginning of December. He was beaten a short head by O'Connell who subsequently won twice more, including the Lincolnshire National, before finishing runner-up in the Eider Chase. Thankfully, he went one better at Aintree on Boxing Day. Runner-up once again at Windsor's Winter Million Festival in January, he stays well and handles slow ground. Officially rated 125, he remains lightly raced and I don't think we have got to the bottom of him yet. We are hoping he will develop into a regional National type horse. More immediately, the Cumberland Handicap Chase at Carlisle (2nd November) is a possible early season target.

HASTHING (FR) 8 b g Konig Turf (GER) – Trendy (FR)
Did well over fences winning twice at Windsor before finishing fourth in a valuable handicap chase at Ascot. A faller at the last in the National Hunt Chase at the Cheltenham Festival, I think he would have been placed. We thought he would run well in the Scottish National at Ayr, but he got brought down and it was a very heavy fall. If he can brush up his jumping and put it all together, he is capable of further improvement and we will be aiming him at the nice staying handicap chases. Similar to Fortunate Man, he is another possible for the Cumberland Handicap Chase at Carlisle (2nd November).

IRON BRIDGE (IRE) 9 b g Milan – Chit Chat
Placed in the Cumberland Handicap Chase at Carlisle on his reappearance, he failed to back that up in his subsequent runs. He struggled with a few minor issues thereafter and hopefully they have been sorted out. A horse with plenty of ability, he stays well and handles testing ground. He will follow a similar programme and has the option of veterans chases in the New Year.

JACK TO BAT 6 ch g Jack Hobbs – Sherry Darling (IRE)
Runner-up in an Irish point, we liked him in the Autumn last year but he failed to translate his homework to the track. Placed over hurdles at Ffos Las, he needs to show more but we are hoping he will improve with the switch to fences. We will start him off in a two and a half miles novices' handicap chase, although he will stay further later on. He could be on a workable mark.

JIPCOT (FR) 6 b g Choeur Du Nord (FR) – Blinngaroe (FR)
Useful on his day, he won over hurdles at Newbury over Christmas before being placed at the Winter Million Festival at Windsor in January. He is suited by a well run race on soft ground. He was tried over fences prior to joining us and that is an option because he remains a novice.

JOHNNYWHO (IRE) 8 br g Califet (FR) – Howaya Pet (IRE)
Successful on his chasing debut at Carlisle last Autumn, he looked good that day. He ran some very good races in defeat thereafter, including when unlucky not to win the Kim Muir Handicap Chase at the Cheltenham Festival. Beaten narrowly, he also ran well in the Irish National at Fairyhouse over Easter finishing fifth. Effective on most types of ground, especially soft, he needs to improve again off his mark of 146 but we are hoping he will make an impact in the good staying handicap chases.

KAKA'S COUSIN (IRE) 5 b g Mahler – Dancing Baloo (IRE)
Purchased at the Cheltenham December Sale, Sean Doyle trained him in his two point-to-points in Ireland and he was recommended to us. Narrowly touched off on the second occasion, the winner followed up in a bumper at Cork over Easter. We considered running him in the spring but the ground dried out. A typical Mahler, he looks as though he wants a trip and is a nice horse to go novice hurdling.

LARGY GO (IRE) 4 b g Poet's Word (IRE) – Jo Go (IRE)
A fine big horse who won a point-to-point for Stuart Crawford in late March. Acquired less than a week later at the Aintree Sale by Mr McManus, he was kindly sent to us in August. He did well to win as a four year old and has really filled his frame during the summer. We have the option of running him in a bumper or going straight over hurdles. It is early days because we haven't done much with him, but he looks a very nice horse.

LION ROSE SIVOLA (FR) 4 gr g Victory Song (IRE) – Wild Rose Bloom (FR)
A nice horse to have in the yard, he won the first four year old maiden point-to-point of the year in February and we bought him a few weeks later at the Cheltenham February Sale. A tall horse, he could run in a bumper before going over hurdles. We like him.

MISTER MEGGIT (IRE) 7 b g Shantou (USA) – Miss Garbo (IRE)
He is a very nice horse who unfortunately had a curtailed first season over hurdles last year. An impressive winner on his hurdles debut at Aintree in November, he then suffered a setback and didn't return until the spring. Fourth in the Grade 1 Sefton Novices' Hurdle at Aintree's Grand National meeting, it was a very good effort considering it was only his second run over hurdles. He lacked match practice but still ran well. I would put a line through his final run at Perth. Provided he stays sound, he is a horse with plenty of ability. Quick enough for shorter trips on slow ground, he has plenty of stamina, too, and stays three miles. It is possible he will have another run over hurdles, although he has been schooled over fences and jumps well.

MONBEG GENIUS (IRE) 9 b g Shantou (USA) – Ella Watson (IRE)
We were delighted to see him win at Uttoxeter in February having run well at Haydock and finished fourth in the Welsh National at Chepstow. We are keen to have another crack at the Grand National at Aintree provided it is soft ground and, in all likelihood, we will aim him at the Becher Chase at Aintree (6th December). Nick (Scholfield) did a great job and I am looking forward to being reunited with him this season.

MOSSY FEN COOLIO 5 b g Kayf Tara – Little Acorn
A big tall horse, he looked very good when winning his point-to-point in Ireland in February. We bought him privately and have given him plenty of time since. He couldn't have won any easier and is a chaser in the making. He will go novice hurdling over two and a half miles and is one to look forward to.

MT FUGI PARK 7 b g Walk In The Park (IRE) – The Real Athlete (IRE)
Twice a winner over hurdles the previous season, he was a bit disappointing to start with over fences last winter. However, he produced a better performance to win at Carlisle in the spring before finishing fourth in the Highland National Handicap Chase at Perth. We have sorted a few things out since, which will hopefully make a difference. He wants extreme distances and will be running in handicap chases over three miles plus.

OH CLARE (IRE) 5 b m Walk In The Park (IRE) - Kilcoleman Lady (IRE)
A nice mare who ran in a couple of bumpers at Carlisle last season. Fourth on her debut, she gave me a good feel that day but ran no race next time. However, she came back sick and we purposely gave her time off. She will go mares' novice hurdling.

ONEFOURNINE (IRE) 5 b m Kalanisi (IRE) - Smart Talk (IRE)
Out of a Grade 2 winning mare, she is a lovely mare who was recommended to us. She won her Irish point-to-point for Colin Bowe last Autumn and we acquired her at the Cheltenham November Sale. Her owner Martin Tedham is very patient and wasn't in a rush to run her, so we have given her plenty of time. She has pleased us during the summer and is one for mares' novice hurdles. There is stamina in her pedigree but we will start her off over two miles.

PEAKY BOY (IRE) 7 b g Kayf Tara - Joanne One (IRE)
He came back poorly after running in the Grade 2 Reynoldstown Novices' Chase at Ascot in February on his first start for us. Lightly raced, we have given him a long break since and look forward to aiming him at some decent handicap chases. A three times winner at Cheltenham, he prefers nice ground and could start off in a £100,000 handicap chase at Cheltenham (25th October) over three miles one.

PESO (IRE) 6 gr g Shirocco (GER) - Flaming Poncho (IRE)
Lightly raced, he won an Introductory hurdle at Newbury over Christmas before running well under a penalty at Wetherby. Runner-up behind Chart Topper of Willie Mullins', the winner was subsequently second in a Grade 2 novice hurdle at Kelso. We thought he would run well in the EBF Final at Sandown, but he was forced to miss that. Given time since, he will go novice handicap chasing off his mark of 125. He should continue to improve and is a nice horse. We will start him over two miles before stepping up in distance later on.

PETIT TONNERRE (FR) 7 b g Waldpark (GER) - Perpette (FR)
A horse with plenty of ability, Richie (McLernon) gave him two very good rides when winning £50,000 handicap chases at Doncaster and the Punchestown Festival last season. Runner-up at Aintree last Autumn, too, he enjoys nice ground and will continue in valuable two mile handicap chases. He could start off in the £100,000 Byrne Group Handicap Chase at Ascot (1st November).

PIONEER PETE 5 b g Frontiersman - Premier Blanc
Owned and bred by Anthea Leigh, he has a great attitude and ran well in both starts in bumpers at Warwick last spring. Placed on each occasion, he has done well during the summer and will provide his owner with a lot of fun over hurdles this season. Capable of winning a maiden hurdle, he will start over two miles before staying further in time.

RED DIRT ROAD (IRE) 8 b g Fame And Glory - Miss Otis Regrets (IRE)
Having missed the whole of the previous season, he enjoyed a very good campaign last winter winning two decent handicap hurdles, including a Grade 3 event at Sandown in February. Life will be tougher now off his mark of 142, although we have the option of going novice chasing. He needs soft ground and stays three miles well.

RIVIERA WALK (IRE) 5 gr m Walk In The Park (IRE) – Brave De Comptoir (FR)
A winner on her debut in a bumper at Sedgefield last Autumn, she was too keen next time in a Listed event at Cheltenham's November meeting. Given a break, she ran better at the same track in the spring. She will go mares' novice hurdling and ought to settle better over jumps. There is more improvement to come.

ROADLESSTRAVELLED (IRE) 6 b g Lauro (GER) – Liz's D'Estruval (IRE)
A nice horse who did well as a novice hurdler winning three times, including the Grade 2 Newton Novices' Hurdle at Haydock. He prefers better ground but got away with a slower surface on that occasion. We then ran him in the Grade 1 Formby Novices' Hurdle at Aintree on Boxing Day but it was sticky ground and he didn't enjoy it. Pulled up again in the Grade 2 Premier Novices' Hurdle at Kelso in early March, all of our horses under performed that day and we don't know why. Nothing came to light afterwards. Off since, he will go novice chasing and could be an interesting horse over two miles. I think he is at his best in a strongly run race over two miles, although my dad (Jonjo snr) thinks he will stay further.

RULA BULA (IRE) 6 b m Mount Nelson – Kopitar (IRE)
Runner-up in a Listed bumper at Sandown the previous season, she won nicely on her hurdles debut at Market Rasen last winter. She was then second in a Listed novice hurdle at Newbury with Jubilee Alpha behind her. Not at her best in three subsequent runs, she is a decent mare capable of winning more races off her mark of 118. She will continue in handicap hurdles.

SAINT DAVY (FR) 8 b g Balko (FR) – Saintejoie (FR)
Still a maiden over fences, he ran very well on his chasing debut when finishing third behind Handstands (Grade 1 winner) and Resplendent Grey (won the Bet365 Gold Cup) in the Grade 2 Esher Novices' Chase at Sandown in December. He then suffered a heavy fall at the third last in the rescheduled Grade 2 Towton Novices' Chase at Ffos Las and was never the same afterwards. Given a long break since running in the Midlands National at Uttoxeter, he will continue over fences and could run in the Esher Novices' Chase once again (5th December).

SAYVA (IRE) 5 br g Harzand (IRE) – Mae's Choice (IRE)
Dual winner over hurdles at Newcastle and Hereford, he has schooled over fences with a view to going novice chasing. He jumps well and the plan is for him to run during the Autumn because he prefers better ground. Two and two and a half miles suits him.

SO PROUD (IRE) 4 b g Shirocco (GER) – Rosa Danica (IRE)
Bought at the Goffs UK Spring Sale at Doncaster, he is a nice forward going type who won a bumper at Haydock in May. It looked a decent race, too, and he has settled in well. He will go novice hurdling.

TELLHERTHENAME (IRE) 6 b g Malinas (GER) – Whos To Know (IRE)
On his day, he is a useful horse. He joined us last season and ran well in the Grade 1 Fighting Fifth Hurdle. He failed to reproduce that level of form in his two subsequent starts. The plan is for him to go over fences and we are hoping he will do well as a novice chaser.

VANDERFLIER (IRE) 5 b g Milan – Maiden City (IRE)
A nice horse who ran in two Irish point-to-points for Sam Curling winning last time. Derek O'Connor rode him on each occasion and we bought him at the Cheltenham February Sale having been recommended to us. A chaser in the making, he is a fine big horse who should make his mark in novice hurdlers this season.

WALK OF FAITH (IRE) 5 b g Walk In The Park (IRE) – Askanna (IRE)
Half-brother to Grade 1 winner Minella Cocooner, I really liked him last year. He made his debut in a bumper at Carlisle last Autumn, but he did too much and is better than he showed that day. He wasn't beaten far though in a race which contained subsequent Grade 2 winner Jet To Vegas. He hasn't shown what he is capable of yet but I haven't lost faith in him. The time off won't have done him any harm and he is ready to go novice hurdling.

WE'RE RED AND BLUE 5 b g Blue Bresil (FR) – Samarayia
Twice a winner over hurdles at Carlisle and Kelso, he beat Grade 2 winner Jet To Vegas at the former track. He also ran some good races in defeat, including in the Imperial Cup at Sandown. Only five, he will continue over hurdles and I think there is still some mileage in his rating.

WELLINGTON ARCH 6 b g Blue Bresil (FR) – Moyliscar
A model of consistency, he had a very good season over hurdles winning three times, including a valuable Grade 3 handicap at Aintree's Grand National meeting. Stepping up to two and a half miles in the spring suited him and I thought he was better than his mark heading to Aintree. Rated 133, I still don't think we have seen the best of him and, in all likelihood, he will go novice chasing. I suspect he will show more respect to his obstacles over fences than he did over hurdles.

WILFUL (IRE) 6 br g Westerner – Shuil Milan (IRE)
Four times winner over hurdles, including at Ayr's Scottish National meeting, he is another of ours who disappointed at Kelso the previous month. Rated 134, it didn't surprise us when he bounced back at Ayr. His first target is the Welsh Champion Hurdle at Chepstow (12th October) and then, all being well, the Greatwood Hurdle at Cheltenham (16th November).

WRECKLESS ERIC 5 ch g Masterstroke (USA) – Santa Diana (FR)
Consistent, he had a good first season for us winning over hurdles at Cheltenham's November meeting. Unlucky not to win the Imperial Cup at Sandown, he was only beaten half a length having met trouble in running before the last hurdle. I would forgive his last run at Aintree because he had had enough by then. Still only five, we are hoping he has further improvement to come. Likely to remain over hurdles for the time being, he could go chasing later on.

TRAINER'S HORSE TO FOLLOW: BILL JOYCE

Ben PAULING

Stables: Naunton Downs Estate, Naunton, Cheltenham, Gloucestershire.
2024/2025: 66 Winners / 401 Runners 16% Prize-Money £1,067,387
www.benpaulingracing.com

AFANCY GETAWAY (IRE) 5 b m Getaway (GER) – Noras Fancy (IRE)
A lovely mare with loads of ability, she was an easy winner of her point-to-point in Ireland over Christmas. Bought privately for the Embiricos family in the hope she will develop into a top class mare, Valda sadly passed away during the summer. We were hoping to run her in a bumper during the spring, but the ground dried out. She came well recommended and, while she is quite a headstrong mare, we are teaching her to relax and looking forward to running her over hurdles in the Autumn. We will start her off in a two miles mares' novice hurdle but she will stay further in time.

AS LEGENDS HAVE IT 6 b g Jack Hobbs – Easter Legend
Placed in all three of his runs over hurdles, we were aiming him at the EBF Final at Sandown in March, but he missed out by one. I thought he would run well, too. Stamina is his strong suit and we are going to send him over fences. I envisage him developing into a solid 125 – 130 staying chaser who could tackle marathon trips eventually.

BAD (FR) 6 gr g Morandi (FR) – Love Over Gold (FR)
Took well to fences winning two good prizes at Kempton during the second half of the season. We fitted him with blinkers and they made a difference. A strong traveller who jumps well, we are going to operate on his wind once again in the Autumn and that will hopefully bring about more improvement. He has plenty of ability and is suited by big handicaps. The Paddy Power Chase at Cheltenham (15th November) is a possibility.

BALLYNORTH (FR) 5 br m Saint Des Saints (FR) – Oekaki (FR)
Bought at the Goffs UK Spring Sale, she is a nice mare who came highly recommended by Aidan Fitzgerald. She ran in three Irish points and will be suited by soft ground. She looks capable of winning a maiden hurdle.

BETTY'S DAISY 5 b m Jack Hobbs – Burgundy Betty (IRE)
We have trained the whole family and they were all good fresh. An impressive winner on her debut in a bumper at Warwick in February, we then ran her in the Grade 2 mares' bumper at Aintree in the spring. I thought she ran OK but never got into a rhythm. She possesses size and scope and jumps well. Mares' novice hurdles will be her job this season.

CHAMPAGNE TWIST (IRE) 7 b g Shantou (USA) – Aunt Nora (IRE)
Progressive over hurdles the previous year, nothing went right for him last season. Still travelling well when unseating his rider at the third last at Cheltenham's November meeting, he bled next time at Ascot. We then ran him at Huntingdon hoping to give him a confidence booster but then he had an issue with his knee. We have given him a long break and he has come back in looking better and I hope he will be competitive in two and a half to three miles novice handicap chases. Not over big, he puts everything into his races.

COLLANISI (IRE) 5 br g Kalanisi (IRE) - Colla Pier (IRE)
A nice horse who was placed in a decent bumper at Ffos Las on his debut. He hung left in the homestraight and it transpired he had suffered a hairline fracture in his hind pastern. Back in action following his summer break, he has matured physically and his work has always been good. He has plenty of speed and is an exciting type for two mile novice hurdles.

DIG DEEP (IRE) 4 b g Poet's Word (IRE) - Theatre View (IRE)
A big rangy horse measuring 16.2 / 16.3hh, I love him. By a popular sire, I think he is a very nice horse with loads of scope. Runner-up in his Irish point-to-point in March, the form is strong with the winner (Green Hint) subsequently finishing second in a bumper at the Punchestown Festival. He will go novice hurdling over two and two and a half miles and, all being well, we will aim him at a decent target over Christmas, if he is good enough. I am very keen on him.

DIVA LUNA (IRE) 6 b m Diamond Boy (FR) - Longhouse Presents
A high-class bumper mare and, while she had a good season over hurdles last term, it wasn't what we had hoped. She got a nasty bug in the Autumn and it took her a long time to get over it and things never really flowed for her. She was never the same mare compared to the previous season in bumpers. Runner-up on her hurdles debut at Lingfield, she ran well but wasn't straight enough that day and needed it. I thought we were back on track when she won at Cheltenham on New Year's Day, but I made a mistake running her on bottomless ground at Sandown. We nursed her back and she ran a blinder in the Grade 2 Dawn Run Mares' Novices' Hurdle at the Cheltenham Festival finishing third. She has done incredibly well during the summer and we are very much looking forward to running her over fences and taking on the geldings with her mares' allowance at some stage. We will start her off over two miles, but we know she stays further.

DROPEMATTHESTATION 5 b g Frontiersman - La Creole (FR)
Purchased at the Cheltenham November Sale, he ran twice in point-to-points for Georgina Ellis. A three lengths winner at Knightwick six days before the sale, the form is very good with the runner-up winning his subsequent six starts. He was ready to run in the spring, but he is a big horse and we didn't want to take any chances on drying ground. He has come back in looking a million dollars and we may give him a run in a bumper before going novice hurdling. Owned by Old Gold Technologies Limited, he is a very nice horse.

DUNSKAY (FR) 6 gr g Night Wish (GER) - Ardissone (FR)
A horse with huge ability, he had some smart form in bumpers winning twice including when beating Jax Junior at Huntingdon. Things didn't go to plan over hurdles last season though with him struggling with his wind. Hopefully those issues have been resolved and he is potentially well handicapped off 105.

ECLAT DE MARVEL (FR) 5 b g Masked Marvel - Eclatante (FR)
A tall, rangy horse who finished a close second in his point-to-point for Denis Murphy in Ireland in March. We bought him at the Aintree Sale the following month. Still weak when he arrived, I am amazed he ran so well in his point. A very good mover, he is agile and has plenty of size and scope. We will probably run him in a bumper before going novice hurdling.

FIERCELY PROUD (IRE) 6 b g Iffraaj – Estiqaama (USA)
We were delighted with his win in the Ladbrokes Handicap Hurdle at Ascot before Christmas. He tends to show his best form during the first half of the season and then tail off a bit. We are going to send him novice chasing and, with that in mind, aim him at the Grade 2 Noel Novices' Chase at Ascot (19th December) with a couple of runs beforehand. He was inclined to be brave at his hurdles and hopefully he will make a nice chaser. If not, we have the option of going back over hurdles and aiming him at the valuable handicaps or conditions events.

GET ON EARLY (IRE) 4 b g Getaway (GER) – L'Unique (FR)
Out of a Grade 1 winning mare, he has a good pedigree and is a nice horse. He didn't have much luck in his Irish points and is better than he showed. He moves well at home and will start off in bumpers.

HANDSTANDS (IRE) 6 br g Getaway (GER) – Wattle Bridge (IRE)
He looks a million dollars following his summer break and I can't wait to run him again. He enjoyed a phenomenal first season over fences winning the Grade 1 Scilly Isles Novices' Chase at Sandown and Grade 2 events at Sandown and Ffos Las. Prior to that, even though he was taken off his feet on quick ground in the Grade 2 Rising Stars Novices' Chase at Wincanton on his chasing debut, I think he would have won before falling at the third last. He had a busy campaign mid season. With hindsight, I wish we had aimed him at the Brown Advisory Novices' Chase at Cheltenham in March after The Jukebox Man picked up his injury. I am aware that he has disappointed twice now at the spring Festivals, but our horses weren't at their best towards the end of last season. The plan is for him to reappear in the Listed Colin Parker Memorial Chase at Carlisle (2nd November). I don't view him as a King George horse, so we will likely aim him at either the Peterborough Chase at Huntingdon (7th December) or the Cotswold Chase at Cheltenham in January. Then, all being well, he will go straight to the Festival for the Cheltenham Gold Cup in March. He demonstrated that he stays very well when beating Jango Baie at Sandown in February. That form is strong and he is a horse I adore. We purposely won't give him a hard time before the spring.

HENRY'S FRIEND (IRE) 8 b g Shirocco (GER) – Easter Bonnie (IRE)
A Grade 2 winning novice chaser the previous season, he played the bridesmaid's role last term. His main target was the Coral Gold Cup at Newbury and, while he ran well in fifth, he made a mistake down the backstraight which knocked him out of his rhythm. Back on track next time, he won the Mandarin Handicap Chase at Newbury, which could be his target once again this time around (29th December). Rated 143, I think he has a bit in hand and has more to offer. He could be a National type horse.

HORNICA (IRE) 5 br m Affinisea (IRE) – Manuels Sister (IRE)
Not the easiest to train last year, she was inclined to be fizzy at home. We sent her to Cheltenham in April for a mares' bumper only 75% fit and she ran a mighty race finishing fourth. An exceptional jumper, she is a proper one for mares' novice hurdles being dropped out and ridden patiently.

IT'S HARD TO KNOW (IRE) 6 ch g Malinas (GER) – Sean's Oscar (IRE)
Best fresh, he won his first two races over hurdles at Lingfield and Market Rasen before taking his chance in the Grade 1 Challow Novices' Hurdle at Newbury. Below par in the EBF Final at Sandown in March, he has plenty of ability and will go over fences. We will run him in the early

part of the season before having a break and bringing him back in the spring. Effective on any ground, he will contest two and a half miles novice handicap chases.

JIG'S FORGE (IRE) 6 b g Westerner – Tisonlyme (IRE)

I think he will be one of our better novice chasers this season. A former point winner, he produced a good performance to win on his hurdles debut at Ffos Las in November. He had an interrupted preparation prior to the Grade 2 River Don Novices' Hurdle at Doncaster, plus he was too keen during the race. We then ran him in the Grade 1 Albert Bartlett Novices' Hurdle at the Cheltenham Festival and he performed very well for a long way before finishing sixth. I am not sure he quite stayed three miles at Perth last time and may be better over shorter trips. A lovely horse, he has a very good mind and loads of ability. He jumps well and we will start him off in a two and a half miles beginners / novice chase and hope he develops into a proper Grade 2 novice around Christmas / early January.

JIMBO SPORT (FR) 6 b g No Risk At All (FR) – Bahia De Cerisy (FR)

Placed in two of his three Irish points for Pat Turley, from whom we have bought the likes of Handstands and It's Hard To Know, we purchased him at the Cheltenham December Sale and he looks a good buy. Improving all the time, he went quick in his bumper at Hereford in the spring and still managed to win. He has a lot of speed and jumps very well. He belongs to some great owners (Transatlantic Thoroughbreds) and is a decent type for two and two and a half miles novice hurdles.

KALKBRENNER (IRE) 5 b g Getaway (GER) – Coillte Alainn (IRE)

One of our better novice hurdlers, I am very sweet on him. He is a gorgeous horse with a great mind and I could envisage him starting off over two miles three at Warwick in the Autumn. He won his point-to-point for Jonathan Fogarty in December before being bought less than a week later at the Cheltenham Sales. I thought he ran well in a bumper at Ayr's Scottish National meeting considering our horses weren't at their best by that stage of the season. He is one to look forward to.

KICOUR LA (FR) 5 b g Nom De D'La (FR) – Paquerette Des Champs (FR)

Purchased at the Cheltenham April Sale, he is a great big individual who loves the mud. A proper chaser in the making, he finished second on his debut in a point in Ireland for Rob James. He jumps well and is capable of winning races over hurdles before going chasing in twelve months time.

KILGAD (IRE) 5 br g Affinisea (IRE) – Luck Or Logic (IRE)

Half-brother to Grade 2 winning hurdler Sixmilebridge, he ran in two Irish points before joining us last season. He is a nice horse but won't be running until after Christmas having tweaked a leg. He will go novice hurdling.

LANESBOROUGH (IRE) 6 b g Diamond Boy (FR) – Castlevennon (IRE)

A solid handicapper with a good attitude, he won over hurdles at Warwick in February and we were aiming him at the Punchestown Festival. Unfortunately, he incurred a knock which ruled him out. Back in work, he has unfinished business over hurdles and I think he is well treated and view him as a 125 - 130 horse in the making. Trips around two and a half miles suit him.

LEADER IN THE PARK (IRE) 7 b g Walk In The Park (IRE) – Supreme Breda (IRE)
Took well to fences winning novice handicap chases at Kempton and Warwick. Flat tracks suit him. Undulations find him out – he didn't finish off his races at either Cheltenham or Kelso last season. Rated 128, he is a big strong horse who should improve again. He is one for those good two and a half miles handicap chases at Newbury.

LEGAL WEAPON (GER) 5 b g Al Wukair (IRE) – Lucretia (GER)
A winner on his debut at Warwick, he was disappointing on his two subsequent outings. He will have learned plenty and ought to improve over hurdles. He jumps well and isn't short of ability. Novice hurdles over two or two and a half miles will be his target. He isn't slow.

LOCK STOCK 5 b g Jack Hobbs – Two Smokin Barrels
Not the biggest, he was runner-up in a couple of bumpers at Wincanton and Huntingdon. Over the top last time, he has the ability to make his mark in novice hurdles and win races.

MAMBONUMBERFIVE (FR) 4 b g Born To Sea (IRE) – Sweet Mambo (FR)
Only four, I am a big fan of his and very much looking forward to him going novice chasing. I think he is made for fences and we will try and make the most of his four year old allowance. Placed twice over hurdles in France before joining us, he has a Flat pedigree but is a big horse. Everything that could go wrong on his first run for us at Cheltenham in January did so, racing too keenly, before making amends at Kempton next time. I thought it was a very good performance to win the Grade 2 Adonis Juvenile Hurdle. Not right in Grade 1 company at Aintree in the spring, he possesses a lot of speed and will start off over two miles. He looks great following his summer holiday.

MEETMEBYTHESEA (IRE) 5 b g Watar (IRE) – Lake Wakatipu
Unbeaten in his first three runs over hurdles at Ludlow twice and Doncaster, everything went to plan before his main target the EBF Final at Sandown in March. Despite running well finishing a close third, he scoped dirty afterwards. Rated 133, I view him as a Graded horse in the making and we are expecting him to improve over fences. Runner-up in an Irish point, he is built for chasing and, even though he was winning over two miles over hurdles, he stays well over two and a half miles. He is classy and I can't wait for him to go chasing.

MOJITO DES MOTTES (FR) 3 b g Clovis Du Berlais (FR) – Magie Des Landes (FR)
Not the biggest, he is strong and has a good attitude. Successful on his only start over hurdles at Moulins in France during the spring, J.P. (McManus) kindly sent him to us and we had him for three or four weeks before going to Ireland for his summer break. He has had time to acclimatise and has improved and will go juvenile hurdling in the Autumn.

NICE ONE ERIC 4 b g Harzand (IRE) – One Gulp
Out of a dual Listed winning mare, he was very straightforward during the Autumn and I thought he was an ideal candidate for the Listed four year old bumper at Cheltenham on New Year's Day. Unfortunately, he got loose at home and incurred a nasty cut to his coronet band. It took six to eight weeks for the wound to heal and he wasn't the same horse afterwards. We have given him a long break and he is starting to go the right way. All being well, he will run in a bumper before Christmas.

NO QUESTIONS ASKED (IRE) 7 ch g Ask – Fancy Fashion (IRE)

A three times winner over hurdles, he was a close second in the Listed Sidney Banks Memorial Novices' Hurdle at Huntingdon. That form looks strong. Disappointing in the Martin Pipe Conditional Jockeys' Handicap Hurdle at the Cheltenham Festival, he scoped badly afterwards. Active earlier on in his career, he is a different horse nowadays and has plenty of scope. Bigger and stronger, I think he will make an even better chaser and we are hoping he will develop into a Graded novice this season. Trips around two and two and a half miles are ideal.

OCTO GANE (FR) 5 b g Muhtathir – Polie Gane (FR)

Fourth on his debut in a bumper at Huntingdon in May, he was too keen that day. Given a break, he is back in work and looks very well. He will go straight over hurdles and is a horse I like a lot.

OUR BOY STAN 4 b g Kapgarde (FR) – Whoops A Daisy

Half-brother to dual Imperial Cup winner Go Dante, he is a very promising young horse. Owned by Forty Winks Racing, who also have Nice One Eric in training with us, he was the polar opposite last year. Still quite weak, he did well in bumpers finishing runner-up in the Listed four year old event at Cheltenham on New Year's Day before winning at Kempton next time. A strong traveller, there is still more work to be done with his jumping, but he can only improve. Two miles will be his trip over jumps because he isn't slow.

PERFECT PACKAGE (FR) 4 b f Muhtathir – Goldie Jolie (FR)

A lovely filly who ran in an Irish point-to-point for Aidan Fitzgerald, who adored her. Owned by Lynne and Angus MacLennan's Mal Bloodstock Ltd, she is very highly regarded and I hope she will climb through the ranks. Physically, she has improved during the summer and we will aim her at mares' novice hurdles.

PERSONAL AMBITION (IRE) 6 br g Sandmason – Saoirse's Sister (IRE)

A Grade 2 winning novice hurdler, he didn't help himself on occasions over fences last season. He should have won the Grade 2 Noel Novices' Chase at Ascot before Christmas and wasn't brave enough in the Plate Handicap Chase at the Cheltenham Festival. Small fields suit him better and he remains a novice over fences. That is the route he will continue down over two and two and a half miles, although we have the option of going back over hurdles.

PIC ROC (IRE) 7 ch g Mount Nelson – South Africa (FR)

Still a novice over fences, he has a lot of unfinished business as far as chasing is concerned. Runner-up twice at Exeter and Newbury, it was a rush to get him qualified for the novices' handicap chase at the Festival. Then he wasn't right in the spring and things didn't go to plan at Ayr. He has a lot of ability and stays well. Despite the fact he is a novice, it is possible we will enter him in the Coral Gold Cup at Newbury (29th November).

QUEENS ABBEY (IRE) 5 b m Elusive Pimpernel (USA) – Wild Spell (IRE)

Half-sister to Grade 1 winner Sporting John, she ran in two Irish points for Aidan Fitzgerald before we bought her at the Goffs UK Coral Gold Cup Sale in late November. A brilliant jumper and a straightforward mare, we ran her twice in bumpers at Newbury and Cheltenham and she was unlucky to bump into a very good mare at the former. She will run in mares' novice hurdles.

ROCK SENSATION (IRE) 5 b m Elusive Pimpernel (USA) – Far Away Rock (IRE)
Runner-up in her only point-to-point for Warren Ewing in Ireland, she did too much early on in a mares' bumper at Uttoxeter on New Year's Eve. Returning in the spring, we held her up at Southwell and she did it nicely winning in good style. Easy to train, she has strengthened up since and is another who will be campaigned in mares' novice hurdles over two miles.

ROYSSE 6 b g Kayf Tara – Rattlin
A very talented horse, he has been his own worst enemy racing too freely. He has no respect for himself and didn't find a lot off the bridle last season. Twice at Newbury, he looked sure to win before getting very tired. He managed to get his head in front at Uttoxeter and, on his final start, we decided to drop him in and ride him more patiently. He needs to relax and allow himself the opportunity to keep going in his races. We are going to send him novice chasing over two miles and hope he settles better over fences.

STARMOUNT (IRE) 5 b g Mount Nelson – Sparky May
Half-brother to Grade 1 winner Stage Star, he won the second of his two Irish points for Jonathan Fogarty before we bought him in December. A forward going type, his homework has been impressive and we fancied him to go close in a bumper at Wetherby in March. The ground was too quick though, so we pulled him out. Ready to go novice hurdling over two miles, he will stay further later on and is an exciting prospect.

TAURUS BAY (IRE) 4 b g Poet's Word (IRE) – Tea Time Tilly (IRE)
A very nice horse who has a lovely way of going. He won his point-to-point for Denis Murphy in convincing fashion before we purchased him at the Cheltenham February Sale. Bought on behalf of Harry Redknapp and Geoff Hill, he is a very good jumper and will be running in novice hurdles over two miles. All being well, he will be contesting one of the better novice events at Christmas. He did a piece of work during the spring and came alive.

THE JUKEBOX KID (IRE) 6 b g Jukebox Jury (IRE) – Baraza (IRE)
Bred to stay well being a half-brother to the Grand National Trial winner Yeah Man, he was an easy winner of his Irish point before we bought him. I was pleased with his win on his hurdles debut at Uttoxeter in March. Below par at Ayr next time, he didn't travel on that occasion. A good jumper who handles soft ground, he will go novice chasing over three miles. The Grade 2 Hampton Novices' Chase at Warwick in January could be an ideal mid season target.

THE JUKEBOX MAN (IRE) 7 b g Ask – My Twist (IRE)
A beautiful horse with a sprinkling of stardust about him, he has got it all. Placed three times at Grade 1 level over hurdles, including an agonising defeat in the Albert Bartlett Novices' Hurdle the previous season, he took very well to fences last term. He was unbelievable on his chasing debut at Newbury winning the Grade 2 John Francome Novices' Chase before producing a very professional performance in the Grade 1 Kauto Star at Kempton on Boxing Day. Unfortunately, while being prepared for the Brown Advisory Novices' Chase at the Cheltenham Festival, he incurred a leg injury and missed the remainder of the season. Still unexposed, he never got the opportunity to run at the big spring Festivals. Given plenty of time, he looks great and, while we know he stays three miles, I am not convinced he is an out and out stayer. Officially rated 151, the Paddy Power Gold Cup at Cheltenham (15th November) is a possible target, although he needs to have a third run over fences in order to qualify. That would mean a prep run. Alternatively, he could start in the Grade 2 Copybet 1965 Chase at Ascot (22nd November).

The King George at Kempton (26th December) is his main target before Christmas and then his season will be geared towards the Cheltenham Festival. It is possible he is a Ryanair Chase horse in the making because he doesn't lack speed.

TWIG 10 b g Sulamani (IRE) – Southern Exit
Runner-up in the Grade 2 West Yorkshire Hurdle at Wetherby on his reappearance, his season revolved around the Grand National at Aintree. I thought he ran a great race finishing tenth, especially after missing the start and getting too far back. We haven't made any plans but he enjoyed jumping those fences and it is possible he will go back there for the Becher Chase (6th December). We also have the option of running him in veterans' chases, which will suit him.

UPTOWN DANDY (IRE) 5 b g Milan – Bettys Delight (IRE)
A half-brother to Grade 2 winner Bill Joyce, I couldn't believe he ran so well in his three bumpers. He doesn't show much at home but was placed twice at Exeter and ran creditably at Market Rasen last time. I have been pleased with him during the summer, he has grown a lot and will hopefully develop into a nice novice hurdler. He jumps well.

VANDERPOEL (IRE) 6 b g Sholokhov (IRE) – Dear Songbird (IRE)
I like him a lot and we are looking forward to him going novice chasing. An easy winner of an Irish point, we bought him a week later and he won over hurdles at Huntingdon and Ludlow in the New Year. The form of his victory at the former has worked out well and he followed up under a penalty at the latter. Stepped up in class at Kelso last time, he bled and has been given a long break since. A chaser in the making, he has bags of ability and possesses a lot of speed. We will start him off over two miles before running over two and a half miles later on. I think he will be a smart novice chaser.

WOLF MOON 5 b g Pether's Moon (IRE) – Cutielilou (FR)
Half-brother to Grade 1 bumper winner Redemption Day, he slightly surprised us last season winning twice over hurdles. A winner at Southwell and Huntingdon, he wants cut in the ground having suffered with sore shins. We ran him on quick ground at Sandown on the final day of the season and he barely raised a gallop. Rated 121, he will go novice handicap chasing and I hope he will continue to improve.

WONDERING WHY (IRE) 4 b g Sea Moon – Margarita (GER)
Bought at the Goffs UK Spring Sale, we are delighted to be training him. Very straightforward with a great mind, he ran in two bumpers for Richard Bandey last season. Fifth in the Goffs Hundred Grand Bumper at Newbury in March on his debut, he won next time at Huntingdon. He jumps well and will go novice hurdling over two miles.

TRAINER'S HORSE TO FOLLOW: VANDERPOEL

Nicky RICHARDS

Stables: Rectory Farm, Greystoke, Penrith, Cumbria.
2024/2025: 36 Winners / 208 Runners 17% Prize-Money £517,541
www.nickyrichardsracing.com

ABBEY SCOPE 5 b g Telescope (IRE) – Brockwell Abbey
From the family of Scottish National winner and high-class chaser Grey Abbey, he won well on his debut in a bumper at Kelso in April. The runner-up (Jimmy Hurdstrom) was strongly fancied on the day, and our lad beat him comfortably. Six weeks earlier, it would have been a surprise if he had won a bumper, but he kept on improving at home and his work really picked up. Physically, he has progressed during the summer and is a big strong horse who is ready to go hurdling. We will probably start him off in a National Hunt novice hurdle over two miles, but he is going to stay well and will have no trouble going further.

ATTIN (FR) 4 b g No Risk At All (FR) – Apokalypse (GER)
Purchased at the Goffs Arkle Sale as a three year old, he was broken in by Brian Harding. He is a lovely horse who is owned by Mrs & Miss Sellars. He looks sharp and is one to look forward to in a bumper before Christmas.

BALLYNOE BOY (IRE) 5 br g Affinisea (IRE) – Ballerina Queen (IRE)
A fun horse who ran in a couple of bumpers last season. Not beaten far on his debut at Catterick in December, he was then third at Wetherby in the spring. Back cantering after his summer break, he has schooled nicely and will be ready to run early Autumn. I think he will come into his own once running in handicaps.

BARATABLET (IRE) 5 b g Wings of Eagles (FR) – Perfect Woman (IRE)
Owned by Jimmy Fyffe, who is a great supporter of National Hunt racing, he had a good year winning twice over hurdles. Still green, he took his races very well during the spring and is improving all the time. A winner at Hexham and Perth, he ran well at Ayr in between. A big strong horse, he will continue over hurdles and we will aim him at staying handicaps over two and a half and three miles. He enjoys a dig in the ground and remains on a good mark.

BIG ZOUK (IRE) 6 gr g Milan – Miss Zouk (FR)
James Ewart kindly recommended us following his retirement in the spring and WRR UK Ltd have sent us three horses, including this former point-to-point winner. Denis Murphy trained him in Ireland before running twice over hurdles last season. Fourth at Wetherby in December, Brian (Hughes) has told us all three horses will win races. He will continue in novice hurdles.

CAYENNE 3 ch g Ghaiyyath (IRE) – Spice Trail
Out of a ten furlongs winner in France, we bought him at the Tattersalls Horses in Training Sale in May. Ex-Juddmonte, he is bred to win the Derby and is a lovely young horse belonging to Mrs Sloan. We gelded him straight away and left him off for the summer. He has done well and the plan is to run him in a junior bumper before Christmas.

CENTURION'S SISTER (IRE) 5 ch m Getaway (GER) – Ain't Misbehavin (IRE)
A half-sister to Caius Marcius, who won 17 races for us and was a marvellous horse, she ran three nice races in bumpers last season. She nearly got knocked over on her debut at Carlisle before finishing runner-up at Newcastle and Musselburgh. Like her brother, I think she prefers

decent ground and will be running in mares' novice hurdles in the Autumn. Her schooling has gone well and I hope she will develop into a nice mare.

DILRISK (FR) 4 b g No Risk At All (FR) – Perdicilla (FR)
Similar to Attin, he was acquired at the Goffs Arkle Sale last year and spent some time pre training in Ireland. He is a grand horse who we like a lot. He will start off in a bumper around November / December time.

FAMOUS BRIDGE (IRE) 9 b g Fame And Glory – Wahiba Hall (IRE)
Came back into training in early August, he looks great and will follow a similar programme to last year. He has been a very good horse for us winning those valuable staying chases at Haydock. Unfortunately, having won the Grand National Trial there in February, it looks like he may lose it. I thought he ran a grand race in the Ultima Handicap Chase at the Cheltenham Festival. A real winter horse who stays well, it would be great if he could sneak in at the bottom of the weights in the Grand National but he will need to climb the weights beforehand. We will look at all those good staying handicaps at Haydock again and hopefully he will have another successful year.

FLORIDA DREAMS (IRE) 7 b g Doyen (IRE) – First Line (GER)
Successful on his reappearance at Hexham, we thought he would win a big handicap hurdle last season. He ran some good races in defeat including when fifth in the Greatwood Hurdle at Cheltenham, plus he wasn't beaten far in the Morebattle Hurdle at Kelso. Runner-up at Ayr's Scottish National meeting in the spring, he will go novice chasing this season. We have schooled him over fences and that has gone well. Two and a half miles is his trip, although I think he may stay three miles eventually. His owner has an arrangement with Brian Hughes who will ride him this season. He doesn't want the ground too soft.

GINTIME (IRE) 5 b m Mount Nelson – Irish Lass (IRE)
Runner-up on her debut in a mares' bumper at Carlisle before Christmas, she was too keen next time at Ayr. Fourth at Sedgefield on her final start, she has strengthened up during the summer and will be aimed at mares' novice hurdles over two miles. I would put a line through her last two runs and give her the benefit of the doubt.

HIGH DANCER 5 b g Norse Dancer (IRE) – Up High
An Irish point winner, he joined us during the summer having won over hurdles at Haydock during the spring for James Ewart. Runner-up at Kelso last time, he is rated 114 and we have the option of staying over hurdles or going novice handicap chasing. Still lightly raced, he will hopefully continue to improve.

JAPETUS 4 b g Sea The Moon (GER) – Zaminast
A Juddmonte cast off who we bought last year, he is a lovely horse who did nothing wrong in bumpers. We operated on his wind before he ran and he kept on improving. Runner-up on his debut at Kelso, he won next time at Newcastle before cantering to victory under his penalty at Hexham in April. He is improving rapidly and is a very nice horse for the future. Ready to go novice hurdling, he jumps brilliantly and loves it. Two miles is his trip because he isn't short of speed.

JEHOL DE THAIX (FR) 6 b g Masked Marvel – Luperca (FR)
Having shaped well on his debut in a bumper at Uttoxeter and over hurdles at Kelso, he was a bit disappointing thereafter. Things didn't happen for him in two runs at Ayr during the second half of the season. We have given him a long break and hopefully he can bounce back this year. Owned by a lovely man, Frank Bird, he is on a good mark if we can get him back to his earlier promise.

JO COKO (FR) 6 b g Cokoriko (FR) – Trevoloise (FR)
Previously trained by James Ewart, he was placed over hurdles at Haydock and Ayr last season and is rated 114. Brian (Hughes) rode him on each start and feels he is capable of winning races. He appears to stay well and handles testing ground.

LADY WALK ON BYE (IRE) 4 b f Walk In The Park (IRE) – On The Way Home (IRE)
Related to Harbour Pilot and Get Me Out of Here, she is a lovely big filly we acquired at the Tattersalls Derby Sale in Ireland last year. Owned by Mrs and Miss Sellars, she will be running in mares' bumpers this winter and I like her a lot.

LATOSCA DU HOUX (FR) 4 gr f Gris De Gris (IRE) – La Lorelei (FR)
Another big unraced filly who is owned by the Cheltenham For Breakfast syndicate, she is a nice type who will be campaigned in mares' bumpers.

LA ZOUBIDA (FR) 5 b m Authorized (IRE) – Titi Jolie (FR)
She is a nice mare who made her debut in a decent bumper at Sedgefield on Boxing Day. Runner-up behind a subsequent Listed winner, she confirmed that promise when going one better at Market Rasen next time. Her syndicate had a hospitality box at Aintree's Grand National meeting and were keen for her to run in the Grade 2 mares' bumper. She found the ground quick enough but wasn't disgraced and the experience she gained will stand her in good stead. She has schooled well and will run in mares' novice hurdles over two and two and a half miles. We are hoping she will gain some black type at some stage.

LUCKIE DEVIL (IRE) 5 br g Pillar Coral – Uimhir A Seacht (IRE)
Half-brother to Luckie Seven, he was runner-up on his debut in a bumper at Newcastle in March. We then sent him to Kelso for a similar event two months later thinking he would nearly win. However, he unseated Danny (McMenamin) twice on the way to the start and we should have pulled him out. We let him take his chance and he didn't run to form and was disappointing. Given a good break since, he jumps well and will contest novice hurdles over two and two and a half miles.

LUCKIE SEVEN (IRE) 7 b g Soldier of Fortune (IRE) – Uimhir A Seacht (IRE)
Remains lightly raced having had an issue with his feet last season. A dual winner over hurdles, he ran well for a long way at Uttoxeter during the summer. It wasn't a bad race either and we will give him a few more runs over hurdles for experience purposes. It won't be long before he goes chasing though. He likes decent ground and is capable of winning more races.

MILCREE (IRE) 7 b g Milan – Glencree Spirit (IRE)
Unable to run last season due to minor niggling problems, he is back in work following his summer holiday and we are looking forward to sending him over fences. He won a point-to-point for Brian Harding and was progressive over hurdles the previous season. A horse with plenty

of ability, he hasn't had a lot of racing and ought to make a lovely chaser. His mark of 117 is fair and we will start him off in a novices' handicap chase over two and a half miles.

NAB WOOD (IRE) 8 b g Court Cave (IRE) – Glenark (IRE)
A grand horse who ran some good races in defeat last season. Runner-up at Ayr in January, the race wasn't run to suit him at Kelso last time. We are going to keep him over hurdles and I think he is capable of winning a nice race this year. Two and a half miles on soft ground and a decent pace to aim at is ideal because he is a strong traveller who jumps well. He isn't short of ability.

NELLS SON 10 b g Trans Island – Miss Nellie (IRE)
A homebred owned by David and Nicky Robinson, he won two nice prizes last season, a Graduation chase at Carlisle and the inaugural running of the Richard Landale Memorial Handicap Chase at Kelso. Officially rated 146, he is a useful horse who will continue to contest the good two mile handicap chases. He handles testing ground and likes a strongly run race.

PARISENCORE (FR) 9 b g Walk In The Park (IRE) – Folk Dancing (FR)
Tough and genuine, he is consistent and has picked up plenty of prize-money over the years. A winner at Perth last season, he was runner-up in the Castleford Chase at Wetherby over Christmas. He jumps well and prefers better ground and will continue in two mile handicap chases.

PRESIDENT SCOTTIE (IRE) 7 b g Milan – Kinard True (IRE)
Still a novice over fences, it may prove a blessing in disguise because he gained plenty of experience last season. He ran well on his chasing debut at Haydock finishing second and wasn't disgraced in his subsequent runs. Even though he jumps well, he was inclined to spend quite a lot of time in the air at his fences on occasions. Rated 121, he wants a trip and soft ground and I could envisage him running in some of those long distance chases one day. Races like the Borders National at Kelso and Eider Chase at Newcastle could suit him.

RUBY ISLAND 8 ch m Trans Island – Midnight Mayhem (IRE)
Joined us last season, she was consistent over hurdles being placed three times before winning at Ayr in March. We then stepped her up to three miles for the first time at the Scottish Grand National meeting, but I don't think she stayed. The plan is for her to go over fences and we will run her in mares' novice chases over two and a half miles. It would be nice to think she could gain some black type at some stage.

SMOKERINGINTHEDARK (IRE) 5 b g Shantou (USA) – Res Ipsa Loquitur (IRE)
He is a nice horse who beat a subsequent Grade 2 winner (Jet To Vegas) on his hurdles debut at Musselburgh in December. Placed twice since, his future lies over fences having finished runner-up in a point-to-point for Colin Bowe in Ireland. However, we will give him a few more runs over hurdles beforehand with two and a half miles being his trip. His mark of 120 is fair.

SOFT RISK (FR) 9 b g My Risk (FR) – Douce Ambiance (FR)
An impressive winner on his chasing debut at Ayr nearly two years ago, he has been sidelined since. He is back in now though and hopefully we can keep him right because he possesses a huge amount of ability. His owner James Westoll has been a great supporter of the yard over the years and a real enthusiast. He jumps brilliantly and it is a case of fingers crossed we get a clear run with him.

SUNNYVILLA (IRE) 10 b g Mustameet (USA) - Shenamar (IRE)
Purchased at the Doncaster Spring Sales last year, he has only raced twice for us winning impressively at Haydock at Christmas. We were going to take him back to Haydock next time, but his blood wasn't right. He wants heavy ground and we struggled to find suitable conditions during the second half of the season. We ran him at Ayr in February and, considering he struck into himself early on, he did well to finish second. He is usually a very good jumper but didn't jump well that day and we know why. Back cantering, he needs a wet winter and will continue in two mile handicap chases.

THE KALOOKI KID 7 gr g Gentlewave (IRE) - Wild Blueberry (IRE)
Took well to fences and enjoyed a good season winning twice, including the Scottish Champion Chase at Musselburgh in February. We ran him in Grade 1 company at Aintree in the spring on the advice of Davy Russell and, while he struggled at that level, the experience he gained won't have been lost on him. He has done very well during the summer and we will aim him at some of the good handicap chases over two and a half miles. There is every chance we will take him back to Musselburgh in February with such good prize-money on offer. Good to soft ground is ideal because he doesn't want extremes.

THEY'RE CHANCERS (IRE) 5 b g Milan - Valentines Lady (IRE)
A half-brother to Grade 1 winning chaser Edwulf, he is one of two lovely young horses owned by Paul & Clare Rooney. His work at home has always been good and we were fairly confident when taking him to Ayr in January. He did everything right during the race gliding to the front and winning in good style. We schooled him over hurdles in the spring and he has spent the summer with Jason Maguire doing plenty of roadwork. Physically, he looks a three miles chaser in the making, but he isn't slow and will start off in a National Hunt novices' hurdle over two miles before stepping up in trip later on. He is a smashing horse.

UPON TWEED (IRE) 5 b g Berkshire (IRE) - Catchers Day (IRE)
A very nice horse who we thought was a fair sort before he made his debut in a bumper at Newcastle in February. Brian Harding rode him in a piece of work at home and came back in grinning like a cheshire cat. I didn't need to ask him what he thought of him afterwards. An impressive winner, the sectionals were very good and the form received a boost when the runner-up ran well at the Punchestown Festival next time. It was a good performance and there were a queue of people inquiring about him afterwards. He has been subsequently sold to Eddie Melville, who has been a great owner for us over the years, including with my father. He has had some decent horses, most notably Grade 2 winner Eduard. A good jumper, he is ready to go novice hurdling and will start off over two miles. I think he could run over any trip.

WANDERINGINTHEDARK (IRE) 5 b g Soldier of Fortune (IRE) - Miss Fleming
Similar to They're Chancers, he is a lovely young horse belonging to the Rooney's. He does everything well at home and we thought he was the better of the pair before they both ran. Forward going at home, he made his debut at Ayr in March and looked all set to win when hitting the front in the homestraight. He was very green though and showed his inexperience in the closing stages. Still raw, the experience will have done him good and he will go hurdling. A big strapping horse, we will find a suitable National Hunt novice hurdle over two miles to begin with.

YOUNG GETAWAY (IRE) 6 b g Getaway (GER) – The Youngone (IRE)
From the family of triple Grade 1 winning hurdler Iktitaf, he is a fine big horse who will be going over fences this season. Rated 112, I think he is well handicapped and he should improve as a chaser. He won nicely over hurdles at Newcastle and was unlucky not to follow up at Hexham having got boxed in on the run-in. Not short of speed, he will be running in two mile novice handicap chases.

Unnamed (IRE) 5 b g Getaway (GER) – Ayleoola (IRE)
Half-brother to the useful hurdler Break My Soul, he was bought as a three year old and has needed time. He looks a nice horse and will run in a bumper before Christmas.

Unnamed (IRE) 4 b g Poet's Word (IRE) – Doyen's Glory (IRE)
From the family of China Rock, he is a grand big horse who we bought at the Goffs Arkle Sale as a three year old. For sale, he will make his debut in a bumper in the Autumn.

We have a nice team of bumper horses who were in pre-training in Ireland last year, then the weather turned against us, so we let them off. They are all back in work now and have done well during the summer.

TRAINER'S HORSE TO FOLLOW: YOUNG GETAWAY

Lucinda RUSSELL

Stables: Arlary House Stables, Milnathort, Kinross, Tayside.
2024/2025: 74 Winners / 545 Runners 14% Prize-Money £1,044,330
www.lucindarussell.com

AHOY SENOR (IRE) 10 b g Dylan Thomas (IRE) – Dara Supreme (IRE)
He has enjoyed a good summer and we are very pleased with him. In all likelihood, he will reappear in the Grade 2 Old Roan Chase at Aintree (26th October) once again. Third in the race last year, he will follow a similar programme culminating in the Cheltenham Gold Cup and the Bowl at Aintree in the spring. Last season's Gold Cup was frustrating because he appeared to be still going well when falling.

ALLFOR (IRE) 4 b g Mahler – Tiffiny Gale (IRE)
An old fashioned type with a great attitude, he is a lovely horse we bought for a new owner to the yard at the Cheltenham April Sale. Runner-up in his point-to-point in Ireland during the spring, I think he will suit our style of training. He is likely to go straight over hurdles and should be suited by soft ground.

ANACONDA (FR) 3 b g Chachnak (FR) – Ana's Best (FR)
Only three, he gained plenty of experience on the Flat and over hurdles in France. Runner-up three times on the Flat, Tom Malone claimed him after winning over hurdles at Compiegne in May. We were keen to acquire a juvenile hurdler to run at Musselburgh and he fits the bill. A beautiful looking horse, we are looking forward to seeing what he can do.

APPLE AWAY (IRE) 8 b m Arctic Cosmos (USA) – Dr A Day (IRE)
Looks well following her summer break, she was consistent throughout last season finishing second in Listed mares' chases at Market Rasen and Newbury. She has been subsequently awarded the Grand National Trial at Haydock on a technicality having finished runner-up. A strong stayer, we will mix between mares' chases and the good staying handicap chases.

BELLEFILLE (FR) 3 b f Beaumec De Houelle (FR) – Manouka (FR)
By a sire we like, she was bought as a two year old at the Arqana Summer Sale last year. She has a good attitude and is one of a team of very nice three year olds who will be running in junior bumpers / hurdles. We like the three year old series and keen to support it.

BIG JOHN WAYNE (IRE) 7 b g Shantou (USA) – Balwaney (FR)
Unfortunately, he got struck into when finishing second over hurdles at Worcester last Autumn. That meant he missed the remainder of the season but is back in work now. A fine big horse with loads of ability, he won an Irish point and is built for fences. He will go novice handicap chasing over three miles. He stays well.

BIGLESISBACK 5 b m Walk In The Park (IRE) – Asturienne
She is a nice mare who is eligible for the GBB bonuses and will go mares' novice hurdling this season. We were keen to run her in a bumper in the spring over here, but the ground dried out. We therefore ran her at the Punchestown Festival and she acquitted herself well having got hampered on the hometurn. She will be suited by stepping up to two and a half miles over hurdles.

BOLD LIGHT (IRE) 8 ch g Leading Light (IRE) – Turmoss (FR)
A three times winner over hurdles last season, he has been a super horse. His lad Reece adores him and has done a great job with him. He will probably jump fences later on but, in the meantime, he will continue over hurdles. Suited by two and a half miles plus, he likes Musselburgh and we will campaign him in decent handicaps off his mark of 127.

CABALLO DE GUERRA (IRE) 4 br g Soldier of Fortune (IRE) – Lindy Lou
Homebred, he is from a good family and is a lovely type. Placed in his first two starts in bumpers at Wetherby and Ayr, he was immature but has settled down and will be running in two and a half miles novice hurdles.

CADELL (IRE) 7 b g Mahler – Prettyasapicture
Owned by the Kelso Lowflyers, his main target is the Borders National at Kelso (7th December) with the likelihood of one run at the same track beforehand. Twice a winner over fences at Wetherby and Kelso last season, he stays well and should continue to give his owners a lot of fun.

CHANONRY POINT (IRE) 5 b m Affinisea (IRE) – Dance Cover (IRE)
A sweet mare who won her Irish point in January and we bought her a fortnight later at the Cheltenham Sales. We gave her a couple of runs in bumpers in the spring winning in good style at Musselburgh. Third against the geldings at Kelso next time, she is tough and will go mares' novice hurdling. We like her.

CHOOSE A COPPER (IRE) 7 b g Well Chosen – Printing Copper (IRE)
A winner on his chasing debut at Hexham last Autumn, he promised a lot last season but didn't progress in the manner we expected. We are hoping he will improve this year and haven't ruled out the possibility of putting some headgear on at some stage. Two and a half miles suits him, although he may stay further. We will do plenty of schooling with him.

COCONUT MAN 4 b g Telescope (IRE) – Belle Amis
Trained in Ireland by Jonathan Fogarty, he finished runner-up in his point-to-point during the spring. Subsequently bought at the Cheltenham April Sale, he can only improve and his future ultimately lies over fences. Only four, we might give him a run in a bumper before going hurdling. One for the future, we like him.

CONMAN JOHN (IRE) 5 br g Malinas (GER) – Shanclough (IRE)
A lovely straightforward horse, we like him a lot. An impressive winner of a point-to-point in Ireland in November, we purchased him less than a fortnight later. Runner-up in a bumper at Newcastle in February, he then ran very well in a hotly contested bumper at the Punchestown Festival. Ready to go hurdling over two and a half miles, he will hopefully win his maiden / novice before stepping up in grade. He is a very nice young horse.

COSMIC BLIZZARD (IRE) 6 b g Arctic Cosmos (USA) – Tara Belle (IRE)
Purchased at the Goffs UK Spring Sale, he is a half-brother to the useful Waterford Whispers and came highly recommended by his previous trainer Sam Curling. A maiden under Rules, he did well in point-to-points winning on four occasions and could be favourably treated over hurdles and fences. Scu (Peter Scudamore) has been riding him at home and we love him. Three miles appears to be his trip.

DE LEGISLATOR (IRE) 8 b g Shirocco (GER) – Reynard's Glen (IRE)
Sidelined for almost two years, it was great to see him win over fences at Wetherby last season. He has had a few niggles but is a talented horse who remains fairly treated. We fitted him with cheekpieces at Wetherby and they definitely helped. He likes soft ground and stays well and will hopefully progress over fences.

DERRYHASSEN PADDY (IRE) 6 b g Arctic Cosmos (USA) – Kerrie Girl (IRE)
A very exciting prospect for novice chasing, he is immense and I can't wait to see him jumping fences. A high-class novice hurdler last season, he won twice at Uttoxeter and Windsor before finishing third in the Grade 1 Albert Bartlett Novices' Hurdle at the Cheltenham Festival. It was an excellent run. A winning pointer, he jumps well and his ultimate target is the Grade 1 Brown Advisory Novices' Chase at Cheltenham in March. If the ground is suitable, he could start off over two and a half miles at Wetherby (31st October). Three miles is his trip and he is very much at home on a big galloping track.

DOUBLY BLESSED (IRE) 4 br g Vadamos (FR) – Mrs Jay Dee (IRE)
A lovely big horse with a lot of class, we like him a lot. From the same source as Conman John, namely Rob James in Ireland, he was acquired at the Goffs UK Spring Sale following his impressive win in a point-to-point. He moves well at home and may not want it too soft. We will probably start him off in a bumper.

EAGLES REPRIEVE (IRE) 4 b g Wings of Eagles (FR) – Oscar's Reprieve (IRE)
Half-brother to Welsh National winner Secret Reprieve, he is bred to stay well and gained valuable experience in a junior bumper / hurdles last season. A winner at Wetherby on his debut, he was then runner-up twice over hurdles at Haydock and Carlisle. A resolute galloper, he will continue novice hurdling over two and a half miles plus.

ESPRIT DU POTIER (FR) 6 gr g Montmartre (FR) – Absent Minded
Back in work having missed the whole of last season, he is a useful horse who loves testing ground. A dual bumper and hurdles winner, he is rated 128 and will stay over hurdles for the time being. Suited by two and a half miles plus, we will be aiming him at some decent handicaps.

FOX'S FANCY (IRE) 7 b m Kayf Tara – Nonnetia (FR)
A half-sister to one of our Grand National winners One For Arthur, she is named after Derek (Fox), who loves her. While she isn't as robust as her brother, she has loads of scope and should improve switching to fences. Placed twice over hurdles at Ayr in the spring, she stays well.

FROM THE CLOUDS (FR) 8 b g No Risk At All (FR) – Saffarona
Another returning from a spell on the sidelines, he was progressive in novice hurdles the previous season. He remains lightly raced and will go novice handicap chasing over two miles. Placed in Irish points, he jumps well and handles soft/heavy ground. He should make a nice chaser.

HEADS OF HARPS 8 b g Flemensfirth (USA) – Dametori (FR)
Has only raced three times for us improving with each outing last season. Runner-up at Wetherby on his penultimate start, we dropped him back to two miles at Ayr next time and he won impressively. He remains at the right end of the handicap and will be campaigned in two and two and a half miles handicap chases. He is a lovely horse and still unexposed.

HOURMAN (FR) 4 ch g Masked Marvel – Next Dream (FR)
Bought as a two year old at the Arqana Summer Sale in France, the intention was to run him in junior events last season but it never materialised. However, he is in good shape and will probably start off in a bumper before going hurdling. He jumps well.

HUMBLE JUMBLE (IRE) 5 b g Jet Away – Taylors Storm (IRE)
Surprised us when winning a bumper at Kelso on his debut in November displaying a good attitude in the process. A strong galloper, he will go novice hurdling and, while we will start him off over two miles, he will stay further.

HUNTERS SPRING 4 b f Nayef (USA) – Last Supper
She is a nice filly who did well in bumpers winning on her debut at Newcastle. Runner-up at the same track last time, she has schooled very well over hurdles and will be running in mares' only events over two miles. She loves jumping.

IDEM (FR) 7 b g Rail Link – Reflexion (FR)
Twice a winner at Kelso last term, he ran well in a Pertemps qualifier at Musselburgh in February and wasn't disgraced in the final at the Cheltenham Festival. Suited by two mile six plus, we haven't decided whether to stay over hurdles or go chasing. We will probably school him over fences and then make a decision. He is a decent horse who stays well.

IMPERFECTLYPERFECT (IRE) 5 b g Walk In The Park (IRE) - Ballyknock Hill (IRE)
My dark horse, I really like him and feel he has got a lot to offer. Runner-up in the second of his two Irish point-to-points, we bought him at the Goffs UK Coral Gold Cup Sale in late November. He ran twice for us in bumpers finishing third at Kelso before winning nicely at Hexham in the spring. A chaser in the making, he should make his mark in two and a half to three mile novice hurdles this season.

INIS OIRR (IRE) 8 b g Ocovango - Peace Time Beauty (IRE)
Needs to go right-handed, his main target is the Edinburgh National at Musselburgh in February, which he won a couple of seasons ago. We will look at some suitable races en route but he doesn't want the ground too soft. The handicapper has dropped him a few pounds since the start of last season.

INOX ALLEN (FR) 7 br g Masked Marvel - Bienvenue Allen (FR)
A horse we have always liked and a dual winner over hurdles, we weren't convinced he was going to make a chaser. However, he won in good style at Perth in the spring when fitted with a visor for the first time. That will have hopefully built his confidence and he can develop into a progressive sort over two and a half miles. He likes soft ground.

JESSMARVEL (FR) 3 b g Masked Marvel - Jessamine (FR)
Another very nice three year old who we bought in France last year. I think he is lovely and have retained a share in him. Measuring 16.2hh, he is one for the junior series this season and he leads all the young horses at home. We have always loved him.

JET OF STARS (IRE) 4 b g Jet Away - Gilt Ridden (IRE)
From a very good family, he is a half-brother to the Paddy Power Gold Cup winner Johns Spirit and is an exciting prospect. Owned by Jimmy Fyffe and yours truly, he was bought at the Cheltenham Festival Sale in March and is a lovely horse for the future. An impressive winner of his point-to-point for Denis Murphy in Ireland, he is only four and there is a lot of improvement to come. His work at home has been very good and we will probably start him off in a bumper.

JET TO VEGAS (IRE) 6 b g Jet Away - Jet Setting Fiona (IRE)
A Grade 2 winning novice hurdler, we are excited about the prospect of him going novice chasing. Progressive over hurdles, he won twice at Ayr and Kelso, including the Premier Novices' Hurdle at the latter track in March. Fourth in the Grade 1 Top Novices' Hurdle at Aintree last time, we should have run him in the two and a half miles novice the following day. His homework is very good and he will go over fences. Two and a half miles is his trip.

JOHNNY RINGO 4 b g Twilight Son - Florett (IRE)
A winner over seven furlongs on the Flat, he did well in juvenile hurdles scoring at Musselburgh on New Year's Day. Placed twice at the track, too, he may stay further than two miles and isn't badly treated off 117. He will go handicap hurdling.

JUPITER DES MOTTES (FR) 6 b g Castle Du Berlais (FR) - Pour Toi Georges (FR)
He is a lovely staying prospect who joined us last season. A winner on his hurdles debut at Newcastle over two and a half miles, he was then runner-up at Ayr under his penalty. Stepped up to three miles for the first time in a Listed novice hurdle at Perth in the spring, he ran well and will improve over fences. He jumps and stays well and enjoys soft ground, he will go novice handicap chasing.

KING OF ANSWERS (IRE) 6 br g Malinas (GER) – Queen of Questions (IRE)
Owned by The Kings Counsel syndicate, he is another we feel will improve once tackling fences. He won over hurdles at Newcastle and was runner-up at Perth last time. Rated 128, he stays three miles plus and it wouldn't surprise me if he developed into an Ultima Handicap Chase type horse at the Cheltenham Festival. We will start him off in a suitable novices' handicap chase in the Autumn.

KINGSTON JAMES (IRE) 6 b g Kingston Hill – Jemima Jay (IRE)
A UK point winner, he won over hurdles at Hexham and Musselburgh before finishing second in a competitive handicap hurdle at Ayr's Scottish National meeting. A superb jumper, he is ready to go novice chasing and we are excited about him running over two miles over fences.

KOOL RAOUL (FR) 5 b g Great Pretender (IRE) – Douma Desbois (FR)
He is a nice young horse who ran well in bumpers finishing second at Musselburgh and wasn't beaten far at Kelso next time. Workmanlike, he keeps galloping and will benefit from tackling two and a half miles over hurdles this winter. He has a good attitude.

LETS MINGLE (IRE) 5 b m Walk In The Park (IRE) – Thessalienne (FR)
Not over big, she is a lovely mare who should continue to improve. A former pointer, she ran well in the spring finishing third at Ayr's Scottish National meeting before winning at Perth in May. Long-term, she is a chaser in the making but will continue over hurdles for the time being. Still eligible for mares' novice hurdles, she is on a fair mark.

LINALENE (FR) 4 gr g Rail Link – Quristine (FR)
Placed in junior bumpers at Aintree and Bangor, he has matured a lot during the summer and we have been pleased with him. He likes soft ground and will start off in a two mile novice hurdle. He is a chaser in the making.

LITLEANGEL DUSEUIL (FR) 4 b f American Devil (FR) – Shany De Loriol (FR)
An interesting prospect we bought at the Arqana Summer Sale in July. She won on the Flat at Fontainebleau in March before switching to hurdles. A thirteen lengths winner at the same track four weeks later, she was then runner-up at Auteuil. We have operated on her soft palate since arriving and have the option of running her in mares' hurdles or going over fences. She is a big filly measuring 16.2hh and would receive a healthy age and sex allowance in novice chases.

MAGIC GLOVES (IRE) 4 br f Jet Away – Shamrock Queen (IRE)
Progressive in Irish points winning on her third start, we bought her at the Cheltenham April Sale. She is a sweet filly who works well at home and we are hoping she can develop into another Apple Away. She will contest mares' bumpers.

MALAYALAM (FR) 5 b g Masked Marvel – Frivolite (FR)
Similar to Magic Gloves, he was acquired at the Cheltenham April Sale having run in three Irish points for Jonathan Fogarty. A big strong horse, Scu has been riding him at home and his work has been good. He is a stayer and will go novice hurdling. He reminds me of One For Arthur.

MARCH ON OXO (IRE) 4 b g Walk In The Park (IRE) – Betty Roe (IRE)
Half-brother to the useful Sandor Clegane, Tom (Scudamore) trained him to finish second in an English point-to-point so we have known him for a while. A work in progress, we need to keep a lid on him, but he is a very nice horse who could be a proper one. We will run him in a bumper to begin with.

MARVEL MAGIC (FR) 3 b g Masked Marvel – Dame Magic (FR)
Sharper than our other three year olds, I loved him at the sales and was keen to buy him. He goes nicely at home and is one to look forward to in junior bumpers in the Autumn onwards.

MOON PHASES (IRE) 6 ch g Ol'Man River (IRE) – El Mighty Twelve (IRE)
From the family of Snake Roll, he is a nice horse who ran in an Irish point before we bought him a couple of years ago. Runner-up on his hurdles debut at Ayr last spring, he wants soft ground and will appreciate stepping up to two and a half miles.

MYRETOWN (IRE) 8 b g Dylan Thomas (IRE) – Miss Platinum (IRE)
Produced a brilliant performance to win the Ultima Handicap Chase at the Cheltenham Festival. I thought Patrick (Wadge) was very brave on him because he had suffered a horrible fall at Windsor in January and we weren't sure he was ready for such a race. His jumping was superb. He has always been an awesome jumper but has struggled when having to fiddle at a fence. He has improved since stepping up to three miles and, having only raced a handful of times over fences, I think he will continue to progress. His first main target is the Coral Gold Cup at Newbury (29th November) and he will run in the Edinburgh Gin Chase at Kelso (25th October) beforehand.

NETYWELL (FR) 8 b g Willywell (FR) – Netova (FR)
Enjoyed a really good campaign the previous season winning three times. Runner-up at Kelso in March, he loves soft ground and is capable of winning more races. He has matured with age with two miles on barely raceable ground being his optimum conditions.

OLD GREGORIAN 6 b g Jack Hobbs – Thankyou Very Much
Progressive over hurdles last year, he won twice at Kelso and Wetherby and was placed in the Morebattle Hurdle at the former track in March. Rated 123, we have schooled him over fences and he has been very good. He is one to look forward to in two mile novice handicap chases.

OUT OF THE WOODS (FR) 5 b g Ectot – Fabiola (GER)
Laid back and straightforward at home, he comes alive when he goes to the races. We were delighted with his win on his debut in a bumper at Ayr early in the New Year before running respectably in the Go North series final bumper at Kelso in the spring. Ready to go novice hurdling, he will be suited by two and a half miles. We like him.

PRIMOZ (IRE) 7 b g Westerner – Be Mine Tonight (IRE)
A useful horse who won twice over fences at Wetherby and Kelso. He benefited from being treated for gastric ulcers and we thought he would run well in the Grand Annual Chase at the Cheltenham Festival but he missed the start and is a horse who likes to lead or race prominently. He has been hobdayed during the summer and we will aim him at decent two mile handicap chases, although he doesn't want the ground too soft.

RATTLING ROAD (IRE) 8 b g Arctic Cosmos (USA) – Rossa Parks (IRE)
He improved a lot over fences winning at Hexham and Newcastle. The step up to two and a half miles suited him, too, plus he loves jumping. Rated 119, we will try him over three miles at some stage and he will be campaigned in handicap chases over two and a half miles plus.

ROCHEVAL (FR) 5 b g Kapgarde (FR) – County Fun (FR)
Lightly raced last season, he is a lovely horse who struggled with a kissing spine. Runner-up at Kelso in February, he was leading when falling at the second last at the same venue the following month. We were very pleased with his run at the Punchestown Festival finishing sixth in a big field handicap hurdle series final. I would think he will remain over hurdles for the time being, although we have the option of schooling him over fences with a view to going novice chasing later on. Two and a half miles is ideal.

SARACEN BEAU (IRE) 6 gr g Mount Nelson – Caroline Fontenail (IRE)
A nice straightforward horse who joined us before Christmas, we like him a lot. He has only run once for us finishing third at Kelso in the spring. A fine big horse and very much a chaser in the making, he will go over fences and should stay further. He appears to prefer better ground.

SLEEDAGH (IRE) 5 b g Milan – Tullyglush (IRE)
Another future chaser, we have been big fans of his sire over the years. Placed in an Irish point, we bought him at the Cheltenham December Sale. He ran well in a bumper at Perth in the spring and will improve in novice hurdles this winter. We will start him off over two miles and he is a horse we really like.

SMOKE TRAIL (IRE) 4 b g Jet Away – Jennycomewest (IRE)
Not over big, he is a bonny horse who won the second of his two Irish point-to-points in late April. We bought him at the Goffs UK Spring Sale and he belongs to The Caledonian Racing Society, who are always keen to have runners at Kelso. He is working nicely at home and we are pleased with him. In all likelihood, he will go straight over hurdles.

SPADESTEP (IRE) 6 b g Jukebox Jury (IRE) – Glibin (IRE)
A half-brother to dual Grade 2 winner Tommy's Oscar, we purchased him at the Cheltenham November Sale having won his only point-to-point for Colin Bowe last Autumn. Narrowly beaten in both runs over hurdles at Carlisle and Perth in the spring, he was unlucky not to get his head in front. He jumps well and will go novice chasing over two and two and a half miles.

STRIDE ON (IRE) 5 b g Walk In The Park (IRE) – Mohboss
A really nice horse whose future lies over fences. He is a fine big horse who ran twice in bumpers finishing third at Ayr last Autumn before winning at Newcastle in January. Given his size, he can only improve and will spend this season in novice hurdles before going chasing the following year.

THE HATCHET (IRE) 5 b g Vadamos (FR) – Kelloura (IRE)
Runner-up in a point-to-point in Ireland in December, we bought him at the Cheltenham Sales less than a week later. He is better than he showed in two bumpers at Ayr and Perth in the spring. We have given him a break since and he is another for novice hurdles at tracks such as Ayr and Kelso this winter.

TIMEFORTOM (IRE) 5 ch g Soldier of Fortune (IRE) – Bell Walks Day (IRE)
Another buy from the Goffs UK Spring Sale, he reminds me of our Scottish National winner Mighty Thunder. He raced in three point-to-points in Ireland winning his latest start and gives the impression he is going to stay well. Good to soft ground appears to suit him and he will go straight over hurdles. I like him.

TRAPRAIN LAW (FR) 7 gr g Martaline – Pina

Despite running some good races in defeat, including in the Scottish Champion Chase at Musselburgh and the Grand Annual Chase at Cheltenham, the weather scuppered him. He wants soft / heavy ground and is a very good horse when encountering his favoured conditions. Two miles on testing ground is ideal.

TRIPLE CROWN TED (IRE) 5 b g Walk In The Park (IRE) – This Is Bollyduff (IRE)

A very nice young horse who we thought would run well in both his starts in bumpers at Ayr. Runner-up on each occasion, he belongs to One For Arthur's owners and is a lovely horse for the future. A staying chaser in the making, he will run in two and a half miles plus novice hurdles this season before going over fences next year. We have always loved him.

VISUAL IMPACT (IRE) 6 b m Westerner – Miss Mayberry (IRE)

Consistent over hurdles, she finished runner-up on three occasions and is capable of winning races. Set to go over fences, she stays well and handles soft ground. Two and a half to three mile novice handicap chases will be on her agenda.

WAL BUCK'S (FR) 6 b g Buck's Boum (FR) – Walsamelle (FR)

Took well to fences winning in good style at Haydock over Christmas having been narrowly beaten at Wetherby on his previous start. An out and out stayer, he looks an ideal candidate for the regional Nationals and hopefully he will continue to progress.

WALK ON QUEST (IRE) 6 b g Walk In The Park (IRE) – Aure Antique (FR)

A real improver, he took very well to fences winning four times, including twice at Kelso. He has strengthened and I think he will continue to progress. Even though his wins were over shorter trips, he ought to stay three miles and we will campaign him in some decent handicap chases.

WALKING ON A DREAM (IRE) 6 b g Walk In The Park (IRE) – Connaught Hall (IRE)

Runner-up in three point-to-points, he is a big horse who we have minded until he goes chasing. A winner over hurdles at Ayr in early January, we ran him in the Grade 2 Rossington Main Novices' Hurdle at Haydock next time. We have always liked him and given him plenty of time. Rated 113, he will start off in a two miles novices' handicap chase and we will see how far he can progress.

WHISTLE STOP TOUR (IRE) 7 b g Saddex – For A While (IRE)

A lovely type who won over fences at Kelso and Ayr last season. We ran him in the Ultima Handicap Chase at the Cheltenham Festival, it came too early in his chasing career and things didn't go to plan. Very much a stayer, the Grand National is his long-term target, but he needs to climb the ratings in the meantime.

TRAINER'S HORSE TO FOLLOW: IMPERFECTLYPERFECT

Dan SKELTON

Stables: Lodge Hill, Shelfield Green, Shelfield, Alcester, Warwickshire.
2024/2025: 179 Winners / 996 Runners 18% Prize-Money £3,374,474
www.danskeltonracing.com

ACE OF SPADES (FR) 6 b g Dink (FR) – Alingo's Lass (IRE)
He had a good season over hurdles winning twice, including at Cheltenham in November. Runner-up in a three miles handicap hurdle at Ayr's Scottish National meeting on his final start, he will continue down the hurdle route and we will campaign him in the decent staying handicaps. The *Betfair* Stayers' Handicap Hurdle at Haydock (22nd November) is a possible target.

BE AWARE (FR) 6 gr g Martaline – Kendova (FR)
Had a good year without getting his head in front being placed in two valuable handicap hurdles. Runner-up in the Greatwood Hurdle at Cheltenham in November, he was then third in the Ladbrokes Handicap Hurdle at Ascot before Christmas. We then purposely kept him fresh for the Coral Cup at the Cheltenham Festival and thought he would run well. He ran respectably and we have always thought he would make a better horse over fences. He will go two mile novice chasing and we have big aspirations for him.

BIG CADILLAC (IRE) 5 ch g Soldier of Fortune (IRE) – Askrosy (IRE)
A big horse who won his point-to-point in Ireland for Pat Doyle, he has taken time hence we didn't run him until January. He won his bumper at Chepstow in good style and is very much a staying type. We won't run him until the rain arrives and, while he will start off over two and a half miles, he will eventually be a three miler.

BOOMBAWN (IRE) 8 b g Dylan Thomas (IRE) – Well Clad (IRE)
Enjoyed a good season over fences winning the Grade 2 Rising Stars Novices' Chase at Wincanton and finishing runner-up in the Grade 2 Pendil Novices' Chase at Kempton. Fourth in Grade 1 company at Aintree, his form got stronger as the season progressed. The Grade 2 Old Roan Chase at Aintree (26th October) looks a good starting point followed by the Grade 2 Copybet 1965 Chase at Ascot (22nd November). I think he will continue to be competitive in good races with two and a half miles on decent ground being ideal.

BOSSMAN JACK 5 b g Jack Hobbs – Lindeman (IRE)
Half-brother to dual Grade 2 winner Gidleigh Park, he is a very nice horse who will go novice hurdling. He won in good style on his debut in a bumper at Wincanton in January, picking up well in the homestraight. We liked him beforehand and it was nice to see him do it on the track. He will start off over two miles.

BRACE FOR LANDING (IRE) 4 b g Wings of Eagles (FR) – Annie Grit (IRE)
A big horse who looks really nice, he raced twice over hurdles at Compiegne in France during the spring. Runner-up last time, he will spend this season in novice hurdles over two and two and a half miles before going chasing in twelve months time. He could develop into an EBF Final type horse in the spring.

BRECHARNON (FR) 4 b g Goliath Du Berlais (FR) - Athene (GER)
We bought him at the Aintree Sale in April having won a bumper at Chepstow for Tom Weston the previous month. He has a nice way of going and has a very good attitude. I like him a lot and he will either contest another bumper or go straight over hurdles in the Autumn.

CARLENRIG (IRE) 5 ch g Soldier of Fortune (IRE) - Tenmoku
Owned by Highclere Thoroughbred Racing, he won a point-to-point at Hexham in December by fifteen lengths before being bought privately. A fine big horse, he is not really one for bumpers and will therefore go novice hurdling. He looks a nice horse.

CATCH HIM DERRY (IRE) 7 b g Milan - Pretty Present (IRE)
An improver over hurdles last season winning twice at Newton Abbot and Exeter, he was then third in the Pertemps Final at the Cheltenham Festival. He will go novice chasing and I think he will continue to progress. Suited by two and a half miles plus, I hope he will develop into a Graded performer over fences and could be a Welsh National horse one day.

COOLTOBECARELESS (IRE) 4 b g Maxios - Honours Stride (IRE)
Successful in his only point-to-point for Colin Bowe in Ireland, he is a lovely straightforward horse. Only four, we will run him in a bumper and, if he wins, then we will try him in a higher grade.

COUNTRY MILE (IRE) 6 b g Ocovango - Uncatchable (IRE)
Twice a winner over hurdles at Ayr and Cheltenham, he had a mixed year. Runner-up in a Grade 2 at Haydock, he was very good on occasions but hasn't been the easiest to train. The ground was bad when we ran him in the Grade 1 Formby Novices' Hurdle at Aintree and we decided to give him time. Placed in a UK point, he will go novice chasing over two miles and could start off at Uttoxeter (5th October).

DALSTON LAD (IRE) 5 b g Ocavango - Miss Platinum (IRE)
A promising young horse, we are very pleased with him and looking forward to going novice hurdling. Former winning pointer, he won his first two bumpers at Ayr and Aintree. Over the top by the time the Cheltenham Festival bumper came around, the experience he gained there will help him. He will run over two and a half to three miles and something like the Grade 2 Bristol Novices' Hurdle at Cheltenham (13th December) over three miles could suit him.

DOUBLE MEASURE (FR) 4 ch g Goliath Du Berlais (FR) - Regba (FR)
Still babyish, he didn't surprise us when winning a bumper first time out at Uttoxeter during the spring. He can only improve and has pleased us during the summer. He will go novice hurdling starting off over two miles and is promising. I think he is a fair horse.

DOYEN QUEST (IRE) 7 ch g Doyen (IRE) - Queen Of Questions (IRE)
Had a good season over hurdles finishing second in the Silver Trophy at Chepstow before winning twice at Cheltenham and Warwick. Successful on his chasing debut at the latter track in May, we were keen to get some experience into him before putting him away for the summer. His first target is the Listed Robert Mottram Memorial Trophy Novices' Chase at Chepstow (12th October) over two miles three. Then, all being well, he will run in the Grade 2 Rising Stars Novices' Chase at Wincanton (8th November). Even though he has won over three miles, I think he is at his best over two and a half miles.

DUTCH CORNER (IRE) 4 ch g Getaway (GER) – Lightning Breeze (IRE)
A half-brother to four times Grade 1 and Cheltenham Festival winner Yorkhill, he is a very nice horse who we like a lot. Of all the four year olds we ran in bumpers last spring, he is the one we would like another go with. We can't believe he didn't win. He didn't get the clearest of runs and wasn't beaten far in third. We will take it steady with him, but he is a good horse and one to look forward to in novice hurdles.

EDELAK (IRE) 3 b c Almanzor (FR) – Edelmira (IRE)
We have a few three year old's by Almanzor who will go juvenile hurdling. Progressive on the Flat for Johnny Murtagh in Ireland, he won easily at the Galway Festival and is rated 87. He handles soft ground, stays well and looks ideal to go jumping with.

ETALON (IRE) 8 br g Sholokhov (IRE) – So You Said (IRE)
Having won his first three races over fences as a novice, he hasn't quite progressed as much as we hoped finding it tough last season. However, he got it together in the spring winning at Perth. Rated 139 over fences, there is lots more to be done with him and we will try and maximise that in two mile handicap chases.

FORTHFACTOR (IRE) 4 b g Wings of Eagles (FR) – Kitty Russell (IRE)
We have done well with horses we have purchased out of Tom Weston's yard and he could be another. He won a bumper at Hereford in February and appears to have a good attitude. Straightforward, he should improve and will go novice hurdling.

FORTUNE DE MER (IRE) 5 ch g Doyen (IRE) – Creation (FR)
A useful horse who we really fancied to run well in the Cheltenham Festival bumper but he had had enough by the spring. We learned how to ride him earlier in the season winning in a cheeky manner in a Listed bumper at Cheltenham's November meeting. He has done well during the summer and will go novice hurdling over two miles in the Autumn. We may start him off in a maiden hurdle at Uttoxeter (5th October) before aiming him at the Grade 2 *Sky Bet* Sharp Novices' Hurdle at Cheltenham (24th October). He possesses plenty of speed.

GETAWHISKEY 5 gr m Getaway (GER) – Whisky Rose (IRE)
A smart mare who won first time out at Carlisle before finishing fourth in a Listed bumper at Market Rasen. She will go mares' novice hurdling and I think she will improve for going jumping and contest some of the better novice events. We will start her off over two miles.

GIANTSGRAVE (IRE) 5 b g Walk In The Park (IRE) – Poppy Baloo (IRE)
Another smart horse who I like a lot, we are hoping he will take high rank amongst this season's novice hurdlers. Runner-up in an Irish point, he won a bumper at Ffos Las in January and we decided to give him time after that. Even though he will begin over two miles over hurdles, it won't be long before he is running over two and a half miles. Long-term, he will stay three miles.

GREAT FLEET (IRE) 5 b g Doyen (IRE) – Rosa Fleet (IRE)
Ex-pointer, he won a bumper at Market Rasen on his first run for us with his stamina coming into play. It was horrific ground when running below par next time in a Listed event at Newbury in February. He will go novice hurdling.

GREY DAWNING (IRE) 8 gr g Flemensfirth (USA) – Lady Wagtail (IRE)
He is in good form at home and we are aiming him at the Grade 1 *Betfair* Chase at Haydock (22nd November) first time out when he is fresh. Last year's race was frustrating because he ran so well until getting caught on the run-in. Without the rain, it may have been a different result. We will keep him to left-handed tracks this season and make a plan after Haydock.

GWENNIE MAY BOY (IRE) 7 b g Mahler – Samsha (IRE)
Won the Grade 2 Rendlesham Hurdle at Haydock in February and is ready to go novice chasing. He stays well and we will start him off in a beginners / novice chase in October.

HARRY LOWES (IRE) 4 b g Walk In The Park (IRE) – Dazza
Owned by J.P.McManus, he arrived during the summer and is a lovely horse who raced in two point-to-points for Derek O'Connor in Ireland, winning last time. It is early days, but he is a nice type and we like him a lot. He will go novice hurdling.

HIDDEN HISTORY 7 bb g Schiaparelli (GER) – Bollin Judith
Joined us earlier in the year, he won on his first run for us at Uttoxeter before finishing a close second at Perth during the spring. Two and a half miles is his trip and he will go novice chasing. We feel he will improve for the switch to fences.

HITINTHEHEADLINES (IRE) 4 bb g Harzand (IRE) – Larnalee (IRE)
Won his only point in Ireland for Denis Murphy, we bought him privately and he has a great attitude. He does everything nicely at home and we will start him off in a bumper at either Chepstow (12th October) or Cheltenham (25th October).

HOE JOLY SMOKE 7 b g Black Sam Bellamy (IRE) – My Miss Lucy
A dual winner over three miles at Sandown last season, we targeted the Bet365 Gold Cup at the same track on the final day of the season but he didn't stay. That told us he isn't an out and out stayer and we will therefore aim him at the decent three miles handicap chases. The Native River Handicap Chase at Chepstow (11th October) is his first target.

HONKY TONK HIGHWAY (IRE) 6 b m Milan – St Gregory (IRE)
Dual Listed winner in a bumper and over hurdles at Sandown, she hung when narrowly beaten over three miles at Windsor last time. She has undergone surgery on her knees since and is a tough mare who stays well. We will keep her over hurdles and aim her at good staying events.

JOYEAUX MACHIN (FR) 8 b g Saddler Maker (IRE) – Ya D'La Joie (FR)
Arrived from Ireland last Autumn and ran some very good races in defeat. Runner-up in valuable handicaps at Ascot and Uttoxeter, it was frustrating to get beaten on the latter occasion. He will continue in the good staying handicap hurdles and looks ideal for the *Betfair* Stayers' Handicap Hurdle at Haydock (22nd November).

JUST GOLDEN (IRE) 5 b g Flemensfirth (USA) – Golden Songbird (IRE)
Unassuming, he could be a really nice horse. We ran him twice in bumpers last season finishing runner-up on his debut at Hereford before going one better at Chepstow. He will stay three miles eventually but will start off over two miles over hurdles. He loves his job.

KABRAL DU MATHAN (FR) 5 b g Pastorius (GER) – Nasthazya (FR)
A very good horse who joined us during the summer, he has some high-class form. Runner-up in the Ladbrokes Handicap Hurdle at Ascot and Scottish Champion Hurdle, he reminds me of L'Eau Du Sud, who had a similar level of form over hurdles. The plan is for him to go novice chasing over two and two and a half miles. I am not sure where he will start but we are hoping he will develop into a Graded novice chaser.

KADASTRAL (FR) 5 b g Cokoriko (FR) – Parallele (FR)
Looked very good in bumpers last season improving from his debut at Kempton to winning the Goffs Hundred Grand Bumper at Newbury in the spring. Straightforward, he has grown a lot during the summer and will continue to get stronger. We will start him off over two miles over hurdles and won't be in a hurry to go up in trip. If he wins his maiden / novice hurdle during the Autumn, it is not difficult to envisage him running in the Grade 1 Formby Novices' Hurdle at Aintree (26th December).

KALDOUN DES ROCS (FR) 3 b g Earnshaw (USA) – Tamkevi (FR)
A really nice recruit from France, he finished second on his hurdles debut at Compiegne in March and it proved a strong race. Still a baby, he was quite narrow when arriving and we are going to be patient with him. He will continue in juvenile hurdles this season, but I think he could be very smart one day.

KATEIRA 8 b m Kayf Tara – Raitera (FR)
Despite winning a Listed mares' hurdle at Kempton and being narrowly beaten in the Grade 2 Yorkshire Rose Mares' Hurdle at Doncaster, she endured a slightly frustrating season. We were planning to run her in the spring but she suffered with a back issue. She will follow a similar campaign starting off in the Grade 2 West Yorkshire Hurdle at Wetherby (1st November) once again.

KEOPS DES BORDES (FR) 5 b g Tunis (POL) – Carmen Des Bordes (FR)
A point-to-point winner in Ireland, we thought he'd win on his debut for us in a bumper at Warwick on New Year's Eve. However, I think he was beaten by a very good horse (No Drama This End) and haven't lost faith in him. A chaser in the making, jumping fences will bring out the best in him but he will have no trouble winning races over hurdles this season. We will aim him at some good races over two and a half miles plus. Long-term, I can't wait for him to jump fences.

KILBAKANTO (IRE) 6 ch g Malinas (GER) – Maca Rince (IRE)
A nice straightforward horse, he has a good attitude and we received a positive report about him before he ran in his point-to-point in December. It was encouraging to see him win and we gave him plenty of time to acclimatise after arriving. We nearly ran him in a bumper in the spring, but the ground dried out. He has had a good summer and I think he will make a useful novice hurdler. We will start him off over two miles.

L'EAU DU SUD (FR) 7 gr g Lord Du Sud (FR) – Eaux Fortes (FR)
Looks well following his summer holiday, he had a very good season over fences winning four times, including the Grade 1 Henry VIII Novices' Chase at Sandown and Grade 2s at Cheltenham and Warwick. Not beaten far in the Arkle Trophy at Cheltenham in March, he ran well but was over the top by Aintree. Officially rated 155, there are plenty of options for him this season. We

could start him off in a valuable two miles handicap chase at Ascot (1st November) or continue down the Graded route and look at the Haldon Gold Cup at Exeter (7th November) or Shloer Chase at Cheltenham (14th November). We know he stays two and a half miles, which brings the Grade 2 Peterborough Chase at Huntingdon (7th December) into consideration.

LAFFER CURVE 4 bl f Jack Hobbs - Martiloo (FR)
Fourth in a bumper at Ascot in February when trained by Tom Weston, we bought her privately and she is a beautiful filly. She has done unbelievably well during the summer and is capable of winning a mares' bumper in the Autumn before going hurdling. A future chaser, she is exciting.

LARGY BELTER (IRE) 5 b g Youmzain (IRE) - Iffett (IRE)
A big strong horse who was bought at the Cheltenham January Sale having finished fourth in a point and runner-up in a bumper at Fairyhouse on New Year's Day for Stuart Crawford. We liked him in the spring and he has done well since arriving. He will spend this season in novice hurdles before going chasing in twelve months time.

LE BEAU MADRIK (FR) 4 gr g Beaumec De Houelle (FR) - Boma Has (FR)
A very nice horse who ran well on his debut in a bumper at Plumpton on Easter Sunday. Unfortunately, Willie (Mullins) brought one over and beat us, but it was still a really good run. He will improve a great deal and will contest another bumper and then we will decide whether to aim him at a Listed / Graded event or go novice hurdling.

LEAUMEC DE MEE (FR) 4 b g Beaumec De Houelle (FR) - Finesse De Mee (FR)
We don't usually run many four year olds in bumpers during the spring but we did this time around. Despite being a big raw baby, he is French bred and a more forward type than most of them. Narrowly beaten at Kempton in March, he will improve a lot for that and should make a really nice two mile novice hurdler.

LET IT RAIN 6 b m Kayf Tara - Tazzarine (FR)
Unbeaten in bumpers, including a Listed event against geldings at Ascot, she won over hurdles at Wetherby in November. Unfortunately, she cut through her tendon during the race and therefore missed the remainder of the season. We have given her plenty of time off and, all being well, she will be back in action after Christmas. Officially rated 120, she is well treated and will run in two miles handicap hurdles. We still don't know how good she is.

LIRONE DU SEUIL (FR) 4 b g Masked Marvel - Brume Du Seuil (FR)
Raced twice in France, including when runner-up over hurdles at Fontainebleau in February. Physically, he has improved a lot during the summer and we like him. Still a maiden, he will go novice hurdling in the Autumn and looks a nice prospect.

LISTENTOYOURHEART (IRE) 6 br m Getaway (GER) - Illwalktheline (IRE)
She had a good year in mares' novice hurdles winning her first three starts, including a Listed event at Newbury's Winter Festival. Fourth in a similar contest at Taunton over Christmas, it was tough under her penalty. She will continue over hurdles and I think she will do well again during the Autumn before we give her a break in the winter. She prefers better ground with two miles being her trip. The Listed mares' hurdle at Wetherby (1st November) is a possible starting point.

LIVE CONTI (FR) 4 b g Cokoriko (FR) – Valdivia (IRE)

A really nice horse who is getting stronger and I think he will continue to improve. Successful on his only start over hurdles at Auteuil last Autumn before we bought him, he won at Wetherby in February before we ran him in the Grade 1 four year old hurdle at Aintree. He took us by surprise with how well he travelled during the race before finishing second. Only four, he will stay over hurdles and could reappear in the Masterson Holdings Hurdle at Cheltenham (25th October), if it rains a lot. We hope he will be competing in more Graded events by the spring. We will keep him to two miles.

LORIKO (FR) 4 b g Cokoriko (FR) – Theme Song (FR)

Placed in both starts in AQPS Flat races in France, he was runner-up on his hurdles debut at Auteuil in March. We have been pleased with him since arriving and he will continue in novice hurdles. He looks more of a hurdler than chaser.

MADARA (FR) 6 b g Doctor Dino (FR) – Becquascenthe (FR)

Joined us in November last year and ran two very good races. Fourth in the Paddy Power Gold Cup at Cheltenham, I can't believe he got beaten in the December Gold Cup over the same C&D a month later. Off since, he won't be back until the second half of the season.

MILLE ET UNE VIES (FR) 3 gr f The Grey Gatsby (IRE) – Avacapa (FR)

Translated means 1001 lives, she is a very nice filly who was sent to us during the summer. Still a maiden, she was placed in all three starts over hurdles at Auteuil in France, including in Listed and Grade 3 events. Her form is strong and we are going to aim high with her.

MINELLA MARATHON 4 b g Blue Bresil (FR) – Saint Goustan (FR)

Owned by Ronnie Bartlett, he won a point-to-point for John Nallen in Ireland in March before being bought at the Aintree Sale. He has a very good attitude and the further he went in his point, the better he looked. Two and two and a half mile novice hurdles will be his job this season.

MOMENTS IN TIME (IRE) 4 gr g Kingston Hill – Wyndham Rose (IRE)

It is early days, but he bolted up in his only Irish point in the spring and the reports were positive beforehand. He handles soft ground and will spend this season in bumpers. He will go novice hurdling next season.

MONEYGARROW (IRE) 5 b g Shantou (USA) – Laren (GER)

A nice horse who showed a good level of form in bumpers last season. He won at Chepstow in the Autumn before finishing runner-up behind a very good horse (Windbeneathmywings) in a Listed contest at Ascot. We thought he would win next time at Kempton, but he was over the top by then. He will go novice hurdling over two and a half miles with the Grade 2 Persian War Novices' Hurdle at Chepstow (10th October) his first target.

MR HOPE STREET (IRE) 7 br g Jet Away – The Scorpion Queen (IRE)

We are dying for him to go novice chasing having done well over hurdles. A three times winner last year, he is 16.3h and is built for fences. He stays well and I think he will continue to improve. Rated 128, he will be progressive in novice handicap chases.

MYDADDYPADDY (IRE) 4 b g Walk In The Park (IRE) – Debdebdeb

An exciting prospect who we think is very smart, he looked really good when winning his bumper at Huntingdon in early March. He had a racecourse gallop beforehand and it was good to see him confirm it on the track. We did our best not to run him again because he is only four and, if he stays injury free, he has a bright future. He will go novice hurdling over two miles.

PHINEAS BUNCE (IRE) 4 b g Walk In The Park (IRE) – Keep Face (FR)

Ran twice in bumpers and surprised us because he doesn't show a lot at home. Fourth on his debut at Wincanton, he produced an even better run next time and was unlucky not to win at Doncaster in March. A chaser in the making, he should continue to improve and is a nice horse for novice hurdles. We will start him off over two miles and we like him.

PONY SOPRANO (IRE) 6 b g Blue Bresil (FR) – Milanese Queen

Looked good when winning on his hurdling debut at Exeter last Autumn. We then ran him in a Grade 2 novice at Sandown, but I don't think he was ready for it. Still a young horse lacking experience, I am not sure he mentally applied himself and his season slipped away thereafter. Given a good break during the summer, we need to get him back to the level he showed at Exeter. He will go novice chasing.

PRECIOUS MAN (FR) 3 ch g Almanzor (FR) – Preciously (FR)

A smart recruit from France, he raced twice at Auteuil finishing second on his first start before winning next time. It is early days, but he has grown two or three inches since arriving and is one to look forward to. We could start him off at a low level under a penalty in juvenile hurdles or we might look at the early season Graded events, which tend to attract the same horses.

PRIVATE DANCER (FR) 3 b g Almanzor (FR) – Maia Dancer (FR)

Another three year old from France by Almanzor, he is a really nice horse who was placed in both his starts on the Flat. I loved the manner in which he picked up on his second run and the fact he handles soft ground makes him a good candidate for jumping. He has the form in the book and is a lovely prospect for juvenile hurdling.

PROTEKTORAT (FR) 10 b g Saint Des Saints (FR) – Protektion (FR)

He is a credit to himself and once again he ran some very good races last season. A winner of the Fleur De Lys Chase at Windsor in January, he was runner-up in the Grade 1 Melling Chase at Aintree and the Grade 2 Peterborough Chase either side of that. He has earned £912,869 in prize-money and we are going to try and get him to the £1 million. His two big targets are the Charlie Hall Chase at Wetherby (1st November) and the Fleur De Lys Chase at Windsor in January once again.

QUAVISTE (FR) 5 b g Authorized (IRE) – Fliegend

Took us by surprise when winning a bumper at Huntingdon on his debut in February. We thought he was nice but were worried he wouldn't settle. However, Harry (Skelton) did a great job and I think it is possible to upgrade the performance. Over the top when running in the Grade 2 championship bumper at Aintree, he will go novice hurdling over two miles. One could envisage him running in the good two mile handicap hurdles in the spring.

REAL QUARTZ (IRE) 5 bb g Soldier of Fortune (IRE) – Miss Elderberry (IRE)
An Irish point winner for Sam Curling, we bought him at the Goffs UK Coral Gold Cup Sale in late November. He is a very nice horse who was ready to run in the spring but there was no rain. He looks good at home and the expectations for him are high. A big powerful horse, he looked tough in his point-to-point and we will start him off over two miles over hurdles. If he wins his maiden / novice hurdle first time out, we will look towards a Graded race.

ROYAL INFANTRY (IRE) 6 br g Soldier of Fortune (IRE) – Sovereign Lass (IRE)
Dual winner over hurdles at Chepstow and Haydock, he will probably stay hurdling with the Silver Trophy at Chepstow (11th October) a possible early season target. Effective over two and a half and two miles six, he could be a three miler by the end of the season. He got the trip well when finishing second in a Listed novice hurdle at Perth last spring. Earlier in the year, he had disappointed in the Grade 2 Rossington Main Novices' Hurdle at Haydock. He looked in trouble after two flights that day and got lost halfway through the race. We tinkered with his wind afterwards.

SERVICE MINIMUM (FR) 5 ch m Doctor Dino (FR) – Zanzibelle (FR)
Consistent, she is a nice solid mare who was placed in three bumpers before winning twice over hurdles. Successful at Ludlow and Worcester during the spring and summer, she has benefited from stepping up in trip and prefers better ground. We are hoping she will gain some black type at some stage.

SHEEZER DANCER (FR) 4 ch f Jeu St Eloi (FR) – Danse Cantilienne (FR)
We really like her and hope she will develop into a candidate for the Grade 2 Dawn Run Mares' Novices' Hurdle at Cheltenham in March. Physically, she is one of the most improved horses in the yard during the summer. Third in a mares' bumper at Cheltenham in April, Harry (Skelton) dropped her in and took her wide. She travelled well and finished off her race and wasn't beaten far by the winner (Poetisa) who was sold for a lot of money. I was impressed with her and she will be running in mares' novice hurdles over two miles.

SHINAGO THEYSS (FR) 3 b f Goliath Du Berlais (FR) – Shinaway (FR)
A winner of her only start over hurdles at Dieppe in France in May, I loved her attitude. While she isn't over big, she is tough and made of muscle. She enjoys her job and we will aim her at the Listed Wensleydale Juvenile Hurdle at Wetherby (31st October).

SINNATRA (IRE) 5 b g Walk In The Park (IRE) – Youngborogal (IRE)
Arrived during the summer having shown a good level of form in bumpers last season. A big horse and a chaser in the making, we won't be over racing him this year. He will go novice hurdling and should stay two and a half miles. We will start him off in November and I would like to think he will be Graded class.

SOLDIER REEVES (IRE) 4 b g Soldier of Fortune (IRE) – Benny's Fagartha (IRE)
Runner-up in a three runner point-to-point in Ireland in March, we bought him at the Cheltenham Festival Sale. The winner (Midnight Jukebox) was sold for a lot of money and I loved the way he came back at the finish. Only four, he looks tough and will begin in bumpers.

SUNRAY SHADOW 6 b g Blue Bresil (FR) – Silver Spinner

A bumper and novice hurdle winner, he had a little problem following his run at Market Rasen in December and therefore missed the remainder of the season. Back in work, he remains promising but has got to go and do it on the track. We will give him a run in a handicap hurdle, but it won't be long before he goes novice chasing. Related to a three mile winner, we will step him up in trip at some stage.

SUPREME MALINAS (IRE) 5 b m Malinas (GER) – Native Supreme (IRE)

A lovely mare with the heart of a lion, she showed a good level of form in bumpers. We were surprised when she was beaten at Newton Abbot on her first start for us last Autumn but it transpired to be a strong race. She then won a Listed mares' event at Huntingdon in December. It became tough under a penalty thereafter but she still acquitted herself well at Windsor and Sandown. She loves soft ground and will go mares' novice hurdling over two and two and a half miles.

SYTADEL (FR) 3 b g City Light (FR) – Giralda (FR)

Twice raced on the Flat in France, he was an impressive five lengths winner over a mile and a half at Le Lion D'Angers in May. Bought to go juvenile hurdling, we have gelded him since arriving and given him a break. He stays well and handles soft ground.

THE MAD POET (IRE) 4 b g Poet's Word (IRE) – Zariyana (IRE)

Along with Dutch Corner and Keop Des Bordes, we thought he would win a bumper last season. He still ran well at Wetherby finishing second and remains highly regarded. We will try and win a bumper on his reappearance and then possibly have a crack at a Listed or Graded event. He is a fair horse who will make an even better five year old.

THE NEW LION 6 b g Kayf Tara – Raitera (FR)

He looks fabulous following his summer break at Martinstown Stud. J.P.(McManus) and his team always do a great job. He had an exceptional season winning all four starts including the Grade 1 Challow Novices' Hurdle at Newbury and Turners Novices' Hurdle at the Cheltenham Festival. It was fantastic to be part of it and it was good to end the hoodoo of the Challow Hurdle, although it never bothered me beforehand. He matured with each run and certainly isn't slow. We are therefore going to head down the Champion Hurdle route and that will be his main target. It is our job to get him in the best form we can at Cheltenham in March. The plan is for him to reappear in the Grade 1 Fighting Fifth Hurdle at Newcastle (29th November). I don't know whether we will aim him at the Christmas Hurdle on Boxing Day because it is a different type of track and we have never felt he was a two miles Kempton horse. We won't be doing anything we are not comfortable with.

THISTLE ASK (IRE) 8 b g Ask – Thistle Lane (IRE)

Bought at the Goffs UK Spring Sale, we had our eye on a few and he looked good when winning at Musselburgh in February. Rated 115, he has only raced twice over fences and there are plenty of two and two and a half miles handicap chases. If we can get him high enough, he could be competitive in some of those class 2 and 3 handicaps.

TORMUND GIANTSBANE (IRE) 5 b g Mount Nelson – Roc N Roe (IRE)

From the family of Roksana, he exceeded our expectations last season because we didn't view him as a bumper horse and thought he may be too green. However, he won at Worcester during the Autumn seeing it out well before finishing second at Warwick under his penalty. The experience he gained will stand him in good stead and I think he is a decent horse. He should keep improving and will go novice hurdling over two and a half miles.

TRANQUIL SEA (IRE) 5 ch g Teofilo (IRE) – Finata
Arrived during the summer and is a horse who had quite a reputation before he even raced. He possibly didn't hit the headlines they expected but he looks an interesting horse. His form indicates he has run well over two and three miles but hasn't been tried in between. We haven't worked him yet but will be looking to start him off in two and a half mile handicap hurdles during the Autumn. He could develop into a Lanzarote Hurdle type horse at Kempton in January.

TWISTTHENIGHTAWAY (IRE) 5 b m Walk In The Park (IRE) – Ballinahow Lady (IRE)
Quite smart, she is a nice mare but not really a bumper type. She has a big round shoulder and finished third on her debut at Warwick in November. We will start her in two miles mares' novice hurdles before benefiting from stepping up to two and a half miles plus. Long-term, chasing will be her job.

VANGO CAN GO (IRE) 4 b g Ocovango – Our Katie (IRE)
A hardy staying type, he was runner-up in his Irish point and I liked the way he finished off. He has a good attitude and will run in a bumper in the Autumn.

TRAINER'S HORSE TO FOLLOW: MYDADDYPADDY

Jamie SNOWDEN

Stables: Folly House, Upper Lambourn, Berkshire.
2024/2025: 62 Winners / 294 Runners 21% Prize-Money £801,776
www.jamiesnowdenracing.co.uk

A PATH TO RONDA (IRE) 5 gr m Getaway (GER) – Dusty Too
Half-sister to dual Cheltenham Festival winner Simonsig, she is well related and a lovely mare. It was a bit of a surprise when she won on her debut in a mares' bumper at Uttoxeter on New Year's Eve. We then ran her in a Listed mares' bumper at Sandown in the spring and she finished a good fourth. That run can be upgraded, too, because she slipped leaving the backstraight and nearly came down. We will start her off in a two miles mares' hurdle in the Autumn and see how far she can progress.

ADMIRAL STEWART (IRE) 6 b g Soldier of Fortune (IRE) – Ivy Queen (IRE)
A former pointer in Ireland, he won in good style on his hurdles debut at Ffos Las in November and was runner-up at Ayr on his final outing. We were keen to run him again, but he needs soft ground and it dried up in the spring. The BHA are going to put on some 'winners of one' hurdle races this season and we may give him another run over hurdles before going chasing. Two and a half miles on soft ground is ideal and I think he is fairly treated off 122. He should make a lovely chaser.

AUDACIOUS ANNIE 6 b m Jack Hobbs – Annie's Answer (IRE)
Half-sister to our Cheltenham Festival winning mare You Wear It Well, who is in foal to Walk In The Park, she is a cracking mare. She did well in the spring winning twice over hurdles at Wetherby and Warwick. Officially rated 111, she remains on a nice mark and will contest two and a half miles handicap hurdles.

CE MI RUN (IRE) 5 ch m Flemensfirth (USA) – Buche De Noel (FR)
Out of a French mare we trained, she ran in a couple of bumpers last season. Narrowly beaten on her debut at Newcastle, she confirmed the promise winning nicely next time at Sedgefield in the spring. She is ready to go hurdling and will be suited by two and a half miles.

CENTAURI STAR (IRE) 4 ch g Diamond Boy (FR) – Beautiful Tune (FR)
Well bred, we bought him at the Cheltenham Festival Sale in March having run in two point-to-points. He hails from a small yard in Ireland (trainer is also a school teacher) and hopefully there is plenty of improvement to come. Runner-up last time, he is only four and will start off in a bumper. I like him.

CINQUENTA (FR) 5 b g Cokoriko (FR) – Opaline Song (FR)
Third in each of his runs in bumpers, I am amazed he didn't manage to win one. He is a nice sort who I like and, while we will start him off over two miles over hurdles, he will benefit from stepping up in distance later on.

COLONEL HARRY (IRE) 8 ch g Shirocco (GER) – Stateable Case (IRE)
A Grade 2 winning chaser, he didn't have much luck last season. Runner-up in the Listed Colin Parker Memorial Chase at Carlisle on his reappearance, he then ran well for a long way in the Coral Gold Cup at Newbury but ultimately didn't stay. We then dropped him back in trip for another valuable handicap chase at Cheltenham on New Year's Day and he was still in contention when falling at the fourth last. Unfortunately, he got an infection in a back leg and spent time in hospital. Thankfully, he is back cantering and we will be aiming him at the good handicap chases over two and a half miles on soft ground. Underfoot conditions are important to him and he could be ideal for the December Gold Cup at Cheltenham (13th December).

DATSALRIGHTCHARLIE (IRE) 5 b g Kingston Hill – First Act
A slower burner, he is a big horse who has been given time to mature. We gave him a run in a bumper at Doncaster in late January before winning over hurdles at Huntingdon in the spring. Eligible for novice hurdles until the end of November, we will try and win another under a penalty. His future lies over fences and there is every chance he will go novice chasing later in the season. Two and a half miles suits him.

EPIC WEST (IRE) 6 b g Mount Nelson – Silver Stream (IRE)
Half-brother to the ill-fated Grade 3 winner Complete Unknown, he won an Irish point prior to joining us and did well over hurdles last season. Twice a winner at Carlisle and Plumpton, he was then runner-up at Fontwell and incurred an injury in the process. We were aiming him at the EBF Final at Sandown in March in a bid to emulate his older sibling, but he required time off and has had a long break. Officially rated 120, he will go over fences and I think he will make a lovely novice chaser. Novice handicap chases over two and two and a half miles will be his target.

FINE SHOT 5 b g Jack Hobbs – Midsummer Magic

Bred by the late HM Queen Elizabeth II, we are delighted to be training for HM The King & HM The Queen and he is a very nice horse. From the family of Close Touch and Open Hearted, he is well bred and shaped promisingly on his debut. Placed in a bumper at Huntingdon in February, he stayed on well and the form has worked out (second, seventh, ninth won since). He will go novice hurdling starting off over two miles.

FRESH PERSPECTIVE 5 b g New Approach (IRE) – Tea Blossom

A UK point winner for Will Biddick, he is a nice horse who won a bumper at Uttoxeter in good style on his first run for us. We then ran him in a Listed event at Ascot before Christmas, but it was too much for him. He got wound up in the paddock beforehand and the whole occasion got to him. I would put a line through that – we left him off for the remainder of the season and he has matured since. A horse I like, he will go novice hurdling.

GA LAW (FR) 9 b g Sinndar (IRE) – Law (FR)

He has been a legend for us over the years and, even though he didn't win last season, he ran some very good races in defeat. Runner-up in the Paddy Power Gold Cup at Cheltenham, a race he won in 2022, he was also placed in the Grade 2 Oaksey Chase at Sandown for a second consecutive year. Raised three pounds since to a mark of 155, he is a victim of his own consistency. He prefers decent ground and we think he will stay three miles nowadays. With that in mind, it is possible we will aim him at the Charlie Hall Chase at Wetherby (1st November).

GIT MAKER (FR) 9 b g Saddler Maker (IRE) – Bamos (FR)

Runner-up behind the subsequent Gold Cup winner (Inothewayurthinkin) in the Kim Muir at the Cheltenham Festival and placed in the Scottish National the previous season, nothing fell right for him last year. He wants soft ground and conditions weren't in his favour at either Haydock or Cheltenham last term. Back in following his summer holiday, the Welsh National at Chepstow (27th December) is his target with one run beforehand.

HANDLETHEKETTLE (IRE) 6 b g Youmzain (IRE) – Tooreen (IRE)

He has been a star winning four times over hurdles. Progressive during the spring / summer, he likes decent ground and is now rated 126. Two and a half miles handicap hurdles are on his agenda with the Silver Trophy at Chepstow (11th October) his target.

HOLLYGROVE CHA CHA (IRE) 5 b m Affinisea (IRE) – Hollygrove Rumba (IRE)

A super mare, she has been a star for us winning both her starts in bumpers before developing into a high-class novice hurdler last season. Following wins at Ludlow and Fontwell, she won the Grade 2 Jane Seymour Mares' Novices' Hurdle at Sandown in February. It has been a lucky race for us winning it three times in the last five years. Pulled up in Grade 2 Dawn Run Mares' Novices' Hurdle at Cheltenham last time, she found it too sharp. Effective with cut in the ground, she stays well and we are looking forward to sending her over fences. Two and a half miles mares' novice chases with ease in the ground are her aim.

JACKSTELL (FR) 6 ch g No Risk At All (FR) – Prestelle (FR)

Owned by Value Racing Club, he is a bumper winner in Ireland and has been consistent since joining us. Runner-up at Huntingdon and Ascot, he was also placed at Lingfield and Hereford last season. Back in work, he is rated 110 and will contest novice handicap hurdles over two and two and a half miles.

JOHNNY'S JURY (IRE) 5 gr g Jukebox Jury (IRE) – Sainte Baronne (FR)
Yet to run for us, he is a lovely horse we bought out of Nicky Henderson's yard at the Goffs UK January Sale. A half-brother to Cheltenham Festival winner Appreciate It, he finished third on his debut over hurdles at Ffos Las ten days prior to the sale and the form has worked out well. We were keen to give him plenty of time and he is an interesting prospect for novice hurdles. Suited by soft ground, he stays well and it wouldn't surprise me if he emerged as a contender for the EBF Final at Sandown in March, a race we won last year with Laurens Bay.

JULIUS DES PICTONS (FR) 6 b g Cokoriko (FR) – Visga Des Pictons (FR)
A high-class novice hurdler last season, he provided us with our first Grade 1 win in the Sefton Novices' Hurdle at Aintree in the spring. Officially rated 138, he was suited by stepping up to three miles for the first time. Unfortunately, he came back a bit jarred up and has had an easy time since. The plan was to send him novice chasing but things are on hold at the moment and we haven't decided whether to be patient and leave him off until next season.

KERNIE D'AIRY (FR) 5 b m It's Gino (GER) – Purda D'Airy (FR)
She is a nice mare who won her only start in an AQPS Flat race in France in impressive style. We bought her at the Goffs UK Coral Gold Cup Sale in late November. She was disappointing in a Listed bumper at Newbury in February but it may have come too soon. The French horses often need time to acclimatise and we have given her a long break since. A big strong mare, she looked good in her bumper in France and I hope she will make a nice mares' novice hurdler.

KOSAC D'OUDAIRIES (FR) 5 ch g Castle Du Berlais (FR) – Une D'Oudairies (FR)
A point winner, he loves soft ground and is one for two and a half miles plus novice hurdles this season. He raced three times in bumpers last term, including when running creditably in a strongly contested event at Newton Abbot on his first start for us last Autumn. Third next time at Catterick, he enjoyed the conditions at Ffos Las on his latest outing making all and winning comfortably. He stays well and will come into his own at tracks like Chepstow and Ffos Las.

LA CONQUIERE (FR) 6 b m Le Havre (IRE) – Montebella (FR)
A smart mare who was narrowly beaten on her debut in a bumper at Thurles before Christmas when trained by Denis Leahy. Bought privately soon afterwards, we gave her some time before throwing her in at the deep end in a Grade 2 mares' bumper at Aintree's Grand National meeting. Her work at home beforehand had been good and she ran an excellent race finishing a close second. The form is very solid and she is one to look forward to in mares' novice hurdles this season. She has plenty of zip and will start off over two miles.

LA MARQUISE (FR) 5 b m Beaumec De Houelle (FR) – Manhattan Princess
Another smart mare who did well in bumpers the previous season winning twice and being placed in the Grade 2 mares' bumper at Aintree. Successful on her hurdles debut at Ludlow last Autumn, she was never right thereafter. Disappointing at Newbury over Christmas, we purposely left her off after that. Still quite weak last year, she has grown and strengthened during the summer and come back in looking much bigger. Indeed, she looks amazing. It is not ideal the fact she is no longer a novice with limited experience, but we will have a look at some of the newly designed 'winners of one' hurdle races for her.

LADY TADITA 4 ch f Masterstroke (USA) – Fabrika

From a very good family, she made a promising start to her career when showing a nice turn of foot before winning decisively in a bumper at Huntingdon in November. Still weak last year, we have given her time to mature and she is another nice prospect for mares' novice hurdles.

LAURENS BAY (FR) 6 b g Youmzain (IRE) – Hey Laura (FR)

Dual winner over hurdles, he came good in the spring winning the EBF Final at Sandown, which is a lovely race to win. Prior to that, he had finished runner-up twice, which was frustrating, before winning at Huntingdon. The combination of two and a half miles and slow ground really suited him at Sandown and he produced a very good performance. A former Irish pointer, the plan is for him to go novice chasing and, while two and a half miles is his trip for the time being, I think he will eventually be a three miler.

LEGENDARY LUKE (IRE) 5 b g Soldier of Fortune (IRE) – Mo Bury (IRE)

Related to Cheltenham Gold Cup winner Native River, he won his Irish point-to-point for Sean Doyle in March. We purchased him at the Aintree Sale the following month and he is a lovely horse who I like a lot. There is every chance we will give him a run in a bumper before going novice hurdling.

LIVINGIT DU LARGE (FR) 4 b g Nirvana Du Berlais (FR) – Kayagua (FR)

One of the first winners in the UK for his sire, he raced twice in junior 'National Hunt' hurdles last winter. Green on his debut at Warwick, he finished third before winning next time at Chepstow. Eligible for novice hurdles without a penalty this season, he will stay further than two miles and is a lovely young horse.

MARCHE D'ALIGRE (FR) 4 b g Seahenge (USA) – Simplon

A ten furlongs winner on the Flat in France, we bought him at the Arqana Summer Sale last year. He looked very good on his first two runs over hurdles winning easily at Wetherby before finishing runner-up in the Grade 2 Finale Juvenile Hurdle at Chepstow over Christmas – both of those were on soft ground. He didn't run as well in his three subsequent starts, which were all on quicker ground. A big horse who we considered sending novice chasing receiving his four year old allowance, we have decided to stay over hurdles. Two miles handicap hurdles on soft ground are the plan. Rated 118, he is on a workable mark.

MAXIMUM OFFERS (IRE) 6 b g Getaway (GER) – Gaye Lady (IRE)

Half-brother to Scorpion Sid who we trained to win four races, he was placed in a bumper at Carlisle before running three times over hurdles last season. A winner at Huntingdon in March, he was then second under a penalty at Newcastle last time. We will try and win another novice under a penalty but it won't be long before he goes novice chasing. He wants two and a half miles plus and ought to make a nice staying chaser.

MILPAT (FR) 3 b g Cokoriko (FR) – Gulip (FR)

By the same sire as Julius Des Pictons, he is a classy type who we bought privately during the summer. Runner-up in an AQPS Flat race at Moulins in April, we have given him plenty of time since arriving. A very interesting horse, there are a few options for him, including running in junior bumpers or going juvenile hurdling. We are going to be patient with him because he is a lovely horse for the future.

ONLY THE BOLD (IRE) 10 b g Jeremy (USA) - Cloghoge Lady (IRE)
Joined us last season and provided his owners Value Racing Club with a wonderful day at Uttoxeter in June when winning the Summer Cup under a masterful ride by Gavin (Sheehan). It was only his third run for us having been unlucky at Ludlow on his reappearance when making a mistake at the fourth last. A running on third at Aintree in the spring, the Summer Cup was always the plan and it was great to see it come to fruition. Given a break since, he stays very well and handles soft ground. Officially rated 130, the Welsh National at Chepstow (27th December) is his target.

PASSING WELL (FR) 8 b g Coastal Path - Passing Lore (FR)
He is another who has been earmarked for the Welsh National, although he is only rated 125 and therefore could do with rising in the weights. Consistent last season without getting his head in front, he was unlucky not to win the Surrey National at Lingfield. Placed in the Eider Chase and Midlands National at Newcastle and Uttoxeter respectively, he ran well in both considering the ground wasn't soft enough for him. Capable of winning a good staying handicap chase, he wants testing ground.

QUEEN OF THE VALE (IRE) 5 b m Malinas (GER) - Elsie (IRE)
Unbeaten in two bumpers at Worcester last summer, she had an injury afterwards and has been on the sidelines since. However, she is back now and will contest mares' novice hurdles.

REBEL TRIBESMAN (IRE) 4 b g Crystal Ocean - You Should Know Me (IRE)
A half-brother to Filey Bay, who was placed in the *Betfair* and County Hurdles, he is a lovely horse we acquired at the Goffs UK Spring Sale at Doncaster. Third in a UK point at Garthorpe in April, he then won a PTP bumper at Aintree the following month. He showed a good turn of foot and will go novice hurdling over two miles.

RIDE LIKE A GIRL (IRE) 4 b f Beaumec De Houelle (FR) - Arizona Air (GER)
A well bred filly, she was progressive in bumpers last season. Placed at Stratford and Newbury, she then won in good style at Huntingdon in the spring. Not short of speed, she will run in mares' novice hurdles.

ROYALE NAVY (FR) 4 b f Born To Sea (IRE) - Aero Navale (FR)
She is a very nice filly who we bought at the Goffs UK Spring Sale. Twice raced in Irish points for Rob James, she was runner-up on her debut before going one better next time. Only four, she will contest a mares' bumper in the Autumn and is a filly I like a lot.

SENATOR (FR) 3 ch g Doctor Dino (FR) - Presidente Line (FR)
An exciting prospect who was placed in two runs on the Flat in France during the spring/summer. From the family of Grade 1 winning hurdler Porticello, he is a lovely horse who was purchased at the Arqana Summer Sale in July. Jumping bred, he looks smart and will go juvenile hurdling.

SHE IS FOR ME BOYS 6 b m Clovis Du Berlais (FR) - Bet Davis (IRE)
Won a point-to-point in Ireland prior to joining us in the Autumn. Sent hurdling in the spring, she did well winning twice at Fontwell. The plan is for her to go mares' novice chasing in the Autumn. She is quick enough for two miles but ideally wants further.

SILVER HILL (IRE) 5 b g Shirocco (GER) – Coole Aris (IRE)
A workmanlike winner on his debut in a bumper at Market Rasen in December, he then finished fourth under a penalty at Sandown. He handles soft ground, stays well and will go novice hurdling over two and a half miles.

SMOKEHOUSE (IRE) 4 br g Maxios – Crystal Pearl
He is a big strong horse who won a point-to-point for Andy Slattery in Ireland in the spring. Well related, we bought him at the Aintree Grand National Sale in April and gives the impression he will be suited by some cut in the ground. We haven't decided whether he will have a run in a bumper or go straight over hurdles.

STYLE DE FOLIE (FR) 4 b g Vol De Nuit – Anowe De Jelois (FR)
An expensive store, he nearly ran in a bumper last spring but had a sinus issue. We therefore left him off and he has had a good break during the summer. He is a lovely looking horse who will start off in a bumper in the Autumn.

TIPTOPTIM (IRE) 5 b g Mount Nelson – Lady Perella
Related to Grade 1 winning hurdler Grumeti, he won his only point for Donnchadh Doyle in Ireland. Third on his debut for us in a bumper at Plumpton in December, the form worked out well. He then won easily at Newcastle making all. I think he will make a smart novice hurdler this season.

TOMMY PICKLES (IRE) 5 b g Shirocco (GER) – Carrig Millie (IRE)
A ten lengths winner of his point-to-point in Ireland, we bought him at the Cheltenham January Sale. He is a lovely big horse who we have taken our time with because of his size. Ready to go novice hurdling, he handles soft ground.

TORNEO (FR) 5 b g Toronado (IRE) – Abbronzatissima (IRE)
Ex-French, he was a useful juvenile hurdler the previous season. We decided to send him novice chasing and take advantage of his four year old allowance last term. He progressed with each start winning at Taunton and Chepstow and still held every chance when falling at the third last at Ayr's Scottish National meeting last time. Rated 122, he will be campaigned in two mile handicap chases and I hope he will continue to improve.

WENDIGO (FR) 6 br g Great Pretender (IRE) – Biche D'Oo (FR)
One of our stand out horses, he was a high-class novice hurdler last season winning twice at Ludlow and Wetherby. Runner-up in the Grade 1 Challow Novices' Hurdle at Newbury in between, he also ran very well in the Grade 1 Albert Bartlett Novices' Hurdle at the Cheltenham Festival. He was fifth and unlucky not to finish closer after being hampered at the second last. I think he would have been third otherwise. Rated 143 over hurdles, his future lies over fences and I hope he will develop in a very smart novice chaser. We will start him off over two and a half miles.

TRAINER'S HORSE TO FOLLOW: WENDIGO

CHANGING CODES

The feature highlights a selection of Flat horses set to go jumping for the first time this winter. Last season's article produced **15 winners** from 48 runners (31%) and showed a **PROFIT of £412.40** (£10 stake). The selections included Graded winners **BLUE LEMONS (2 wins), EAST INDIA DOCK (3), MR PERCY (16/1), NATURALLY NIMBLE (33/1)** and Fred Winter Juvenile Handicap Hurdle winner **PUTURHANDSTOGETHER (17/2)**.

Joseph O'Brien has served this section well during recent years - the last two winners of the Fred Winter Juvenile Hurdle have featured - and the County Kilkenny based trainer is reportedly looking forward to running **KIBRIS** in juvenile hurdles this winter. Owned by Simon Munir & Isaac Souede, the Lope De Vega gelding is rated 89 on the Flat. A €155,000 yearling, he was a half length winner at the Curragh (1m : Yielding/Soft) as a two year old. Without a victory in four runs this year, he reappeared in the Group 3 Ballysax Stakes at Leopardstown (1m 2f : Good/Yielding) during the spring. Less than ten lengths behind subsequent Group 1 winners Delacroix (Coral Eclipse & Irish Champion Stakes) and Lambourn (Epsom & Irish Derby), he was castrated towards the end of May before returning from a break of 107 days. Fifth in a conditions event at Roscommon (1m 2f : Soft) in early September, he was less than seven lengths behind stablemate Viking Invasion.

Stablemate **GLENROYAL** is also due to going hurdling having earned an official rating of 77 on the level. Bred for jumping, the Australia gelding is a half-brother to Lagostovegas who was rated 145 over hurdles and a Royal Ascot winner for Willie Mullins, in addition to the Irish Cesarewitch winner Magellan Strait. Placed at Ballinrobe (1m 1f) and Tipperary (1m 1f), he appreciated the step up to middle distances when beating older horses in a twelve furlongs handicap at the Galway Festival (Soft) at the end of July. Powering clear in the homestraight, he won by two lengths off 66 (wore cheekpieces). The fact he handles slow ground and stays well is encouraging for his hurdling career.

Co.Kildare handler **Ross O'Sullivan** had a personal best season over jumps last winter with 22 winners, including a couple of Listed winners at Listowel and Fairyhouse. The Co.Kildare trainer is looking forward to running the ex-French three year old **BIBE MUS** over obstacles this Autumn and beyond. A ten furlongs winner at Lyon (Very Soft) in October last year for Yoann Bonnefoy, he was subsequently bought for €125,000 at the Arqana Autumn Sale by Anthony Bromley on behalf of Simon Munir and Isaac Souede. The Camelot gelding has run twice for his new connections during the summer, including when four and a quarter lengths fifth in a competitive three year old handicap at the Galway Festival (1m 4f : Yielding) in July. He may have found the ground too lively in a premier handicap at Killarney (1m 6f : Good) next time. Lightly raced, he is bred to stay and copes with soft surfaces.

It is hoped the lightly raced **MO CHROI** goes juvenile hurdling having run well on both starts on the Flat for **Gavin Cromwell**. A €62,000 breeze-up buy, he belied his odds of 33/1 when an eyecatching third on his debut on the AW at Dundalk (1m) in November. Less than four lengths behind the 110 rated and Group 3 placed Purview, he stayed on well under Gary Carroll. Off the track for 196 days, the son of Galiway appreciated the step up to ten furlongs when winning a maiden at Fairyhouse (Good) in June. Leading close home, he edged out Iron Fist (won since) with the 92 rated Local Lad three and a half lengths further back in third. The fourth Happy

Pharoah won his next two starts before finishing runner-up at Listed level (rated 99). Owner Patrick Sheanon has tasted Graded juvenile hurdle success with Bottler'secret and Hello Neighbour during the last couple of seasons. The same patron could have another exciting prospect on his hands.

* *

Newmarket trainer **James Owen** has done particularly well with his juvenile hurdlers during the last couple of seasons. Burdett Road, East India Dock, Liam Swagger and Opec all won Pattern races during their first season over jumps.

His team for the 2025/2026 campaign includes: **AMMES** is rated 90 on the Flat and was gelded in August. A twelve furlongs winner at Chepstow (Good) in May, the son of No Nay Never was sixth in the King George V Handicap at Royal Ascot before finishing runner-up behind the 103 rated Push The Limit in a valuable three year old handicap at 'Glorious' Goodwood (1m 4f : Good/Soft). He has only raced eight times and looks ideal for hurdling having schooled 'very well.'

HALLELUJAH U belongs to The Gredley Family and is a dual winner on the level (rated 100). Successful at Thirsk (1m 4f) in handicap company in May, the son of Pinatubo was then two and a quarter lengths sixth in the Group 2 Queens Vase Stakes at Royal Ascot (1m 6f : Good/ Firm). Gelded soon after his run at 'Glorious' Goodwood in early August, his trainer expects him to running over jumps towards the end of October.

Another Gredley Family owned three year old who has been transferred to Green Ridge Stables is the 87 rated **KATE O'RILEY**. Previously in training with Michael Bell, the Sea The Moon filly is a half-sister to Ascot Gold Cup winner Big Orange. Successful in two of her six starts, both victories were gained at Wolverhampton, including over a mile and a half in March. Fifth in the Listed Cheshire Oaks behind the subsequent triple Group 1 winner Minnie Hauk, she was only beaten six and a half lengths. Fillies' juvenile hurdles will be on her agenda with black type the aim. Reported to have been 'schooling well,' she will be in action during October.

TRAD JAZZ is another three year old filly by Sea The Moon who showed a good level of form on the Flat. The grey won her first two starts at Kempton (1m & 1m 3f) before contesting the Listed Pretty Polly Stakes at Newmarket's Guineas meeting (1m 2f). Well beaten, she performed much better next time when two and a half lengths fourth in the Listed Height of Fashion Stakes at Goodwood (1m 2f : Good) in May. The third Never Let Go won at Royal Ascot next time. While her entry in the Epsom Oaks was never fulfilled, she is a well regarded filly who could be smart over timber.

The 2024 Epsom Derby runner-up **AMBIENTE FRIENDLY** is also set to embark on a hurdling career towards the end of October / early November having been schooled. Rated 105 on the Flat, he was a top-class three year old winning the Listed Lingfield Derby Trial before finishing second behind City of Troy at Epsom. Placed in the Irish Derby at the Curragh, too, he has found it tough this summer. Gelded in June, the son of Gleneagles could have his enthusiasm rekindled by eight flights of hurdles.

* *

Flat jockey Billy Garritty recommended the **Mick & David Easterby** trained **CAPLA LAZARUS** was included having won two of his eight races on the Flat. Officially rated 79, the Phoenix of Spain gelding was due to go hurdling last season. A dual winner over ten furlongs at Redcar (Good) and Ayr (Soft), he stayed on in fourth in a Racing League Handicap at Chepstow (1m 2f : Good/Soft) in early August. Reported to have schooled well, he is versatile in terms of underfoot conditions and ought to win races over two miles on the northern circuit.

Dan Skelton has a strong looking team of juvenile hurdlers comprising of recruits from France and Ireland. **EDELAK** was owned and bred by the late HH Aga Khan and was progressive for Johnny Murtagh during the summer. A son of Almanzor who has been gelded since joining Paul Nicholls' former assistant, he was narrowly beaten by the 92 rated Delta at Fairyhouse (1m 4f : Good/Yielding) in June. Fitted with blinkers for the first time at the Galway Festival (1m 4f : Yielding/Soft), he was ridden by apprentice Miss Georgie Benson and, having led over two out, powered away in the homestraight to win by four and a half lengths (third won since). Only five and a half lengths behind subsequent Group 1 St Leger and Goodwood Cup winner Scandinavia at Navan (1m 2f : Good) earlier in the year, he hails from the family of Ascot Gold Cup winners Enzeli and Estimate. Owned by Carsberg, Rafftery and Stennett, he could be a high-class hurdler.

Harry Derham has taken charge of the ex-Tom Clover trained **GALLIVANTED** having purchased the three year old for 70,000gns at the Newmarket July Sales. By the same sire as Grade 1 winning hurdlers Gala Marceau and Vauban, the son of Galiway only raced three times on the Flat. Placed at Kempton (1m) as a juvenile, he returned from an absence of 232 days to win at the same track in May appreciating the step up to a mile and a half. Sent off 4/6 favourite, he led inside the final furlong and scored by a neck. The fourth (Belgravian), who was beaten nearly seven lengths, has won four times since and is rated 96. Gelded since joining Paul Nicholls' nephew, he is rated 79 on the Flat and is owned by Bathurst-Norman, Ramsay & Tufnell. He could be useful.

Scottish handler **Iain Jardine** is reportedly planning to run his 101 rated Flat racer **TIERNAN** in juvenile hurdles this campaign. A well bred gelded son of Dubawi, he was a Godolphin cast off who was bought unraced for 18,000gns in January. Despite remaining a maiden after four starts, the three year old has run some excellent races in defeat, including when beaten less than a length in the Listed Glasgow Stakes at Hamilton (1m 3f : Good) in July. The runner-up Arabian Force finished a length third in the Group 2 Great Voltigeur Stakes at York next time. From the family of Ebor winner Litigant, he stays well and handles slow ground. One could envisage him making his hurdles debut at Musselburgh on New Year's day before making an impact in the Scottish Triumph Hurdle at the same venue in February with former champion jockey Brian Hughes on board.

FRENCH REVOLUTION

In addition to those included in the *Top 40 Prospects*, this feature highlights the most exciting prospects to have been purchased from across the English Channel who will be plying their trade in Britain and Ireland this season. Last year's selections produced 24 winners, including Grade 1 winner **MURCIA**, plus **KARNIQUET, KAROLINE BANBOU, KAWABOOMGA, KISS WILL** and **KITZBUHEL**. Other winners included **EPINEPHRINE (11/1), KIKIJO (9/2), LAST KINGDOM (10/1)** and **QUANTOCK HILLS (11/2)**.

The list of subsequent Grade 1 winners from previous editions contains **A PLUS TARD, BLUE LORD, BURNING VICTORY, CAPODANNO, DEFI DU SEUIL, EL FABIOLO, ESPOIR D'ALLEN, GAILLARD DU MESNIL, GALA MARCEAU, IMPAIRE ET PASSE, IRISH POINT, KLASSICAL DREAM, MONMIRAL** and **QUILIXIOS**.

There is an extensive list of over 50 new recruits and, similar to previous years, a number of the write-ups have been accompanied by comments from triple French champion jockey **James Reveley**. The 36 year old has ridden 16 Grade 1 winners, including the Grande Course de Haies d'Auteuil – the French Champion Hurdle - at Auteuil twice. As discussed, James steered the aforementioned El Clavel to victory in May, ten years on from Un Temps Pour Tout's success.

AGUELLID (FR) 4 ch g Goliath Du Berlais (FR) – Green Hope (FR)
Big, scopey chestnut by Goliath Du Berlais, he raced twice for Daniela Mele finishing around ten lengths sixth on his Flat debut at Craon (RH : 1m 6f) in late August last year. A fortnight later, he made his jumping bow in the colts and geldings version of the Prix Finot at Auteuil (LH : 2m 2f : Very Soft). Racing prominently, Lucas Zuliani's mount led with over a circuit to run and was still in front between the final two flights. Headed before the last, he kept on and was less than four lengths behind the winner Musique Maestro (runner-up in a Grade 1 hurdle in May). The second Neverchangedoctor has won a Listed hurdle since. Bought soon afterwards by **J.P.McManus**, he has been given plenty of time to mature at Martinstown Stud in Co.Limerick before going into training with **Philip Hobbs** and **Johnson White** at the beginning of August. One could envisage him starting off in a maiden hurdle at either Chepstow or Exeter in the Autumn.
Reveley's Remarks: **"Daniela Mele always targets the Prix Finot and invariably runs nice horses in it. I finished second aboard Neverchangedoctor and he is a useful horse. The form is good."**

BERTUTEA (FR) 3 bb g Beaumec De Houelle (FR) – La Vertu (FR)
One of a handful of potentially smart recruits acquired by **Gigginstown House Stud,** the three year old gelded son of Beaumec De Houelle raced four times for Mickael Seror, including twice over hurdles. A length and a half scorer at Lyon (RH : 1m 2f : AW) in January on his second run on the Flat, his attentions were turned to jumping in the spring. Bryony Frost partnered him in both starts at Auteuil being placed on each occasion. Seven lengths behind The Mighty Celt (Listed placed twice) and Precious Man (won since) in the Prix Rush (1m 7f : Heavy) in mid March, he stayed on well after the last having been patiently ridden. Less than three weeks later, he was two lengths second behind Midnight Cowboy (Grade 3 placed next time) in another conditions hurdle at the Parisian track (1m 7f : Very Soft). Taken wide, he challenged along the stands rail and held every chance on the run-in. Four lengths clear of the third, the fourth won

a Listed hurdle next time. A good jumper, he is a useful prospect for juvenile hurdles for **Willie Mullins**.

Reveley's Remarks: **"I rode in both races, including aboard The Mighty Celt in the Prix Rush, and the form is decent. Bertutea finished well each time and should do well for his new connections."**

BLUE SEABHAC (FR) 3 b g Seabhac (USA) – Ivanka (FR)

The German bred pair El Dancer and United provided **Lucy Wadham** with Graded hurdle success between 2005 and 2009. The Newmarket based handler has taken charge of this once raced gelding who was acquired for €150,000 at the Arqana Online Sale in late March by owner **James Summers**. A former stablemate of the aforementioned Bertutea, the Seabhac gelding was three lengths runner-up on his hurdles bow at Fontainebleau (LH : 1m 7f : Very Soft) in March. Ridden by Baptiste Le Clerc, he wore a noseband and raced in behind the leaders until making headway in the homestraight. Having allowed the winner (Champlatreux) to get first run, he stayed on after the last. The first three pulled eleven lengths clear and the form has been boosted with the third (twice), fourth, sixth and sixth winning subsequently. Blue Seabhac looks scopey with plenty of size and the type to progress with age. It will be disappointing if he can't make his mark in juvenile hurdles in the UK.

BRACE FOR LANDING (IRE) 4 b g Wings of Eagles (FR) – Annie Grit (IRE)

Owned by **Robert Kirkland and Neil & Alfie Smith**, the four year old was bought by Anthony Bromley having showm promise in two runs for Noel George and Amanda Zetterholm. Fourth on his debut at Compiegne (LH : 2m 2f : Heavy), he was beaten around nine lengths behind Leader Sport (won again since). Running over the same C&D a month later, he stayed on well in second having got tapped for speed approaching the penultimate flight. A length and three quarters behind Laccio Conti, he has plenty of size and is a chaser in the making. However, he is expected to make his mark over two and a half miles plus over hurdles for **Dan Skelton** this winter.

CORNELIENNE (IRE) 4 bb f Golden Horn – Australienne (IRE)

A dark one for the Grade 2 Dawn Run Mares' Novices' Hurdle at the Cheltenham Festival in March. French trainer Christophe Ferland was responsible for the 2020 winner Concertista and the Chantilly based handler was in charge of this Golden Horn filly. Successful in 2 of her 8 races, she won at Longchamp (1m 2f : Heavy) and La Teste De Buch (RH : 1m 4f : Good) last year before finishing a neck second in Listed company at Fontainebleau (1m 7f : Very Soft) in November. Unexposed over middle distances / staying trips, she was bought for €250,000 at the Arqana December Sale and is owned by **J.P.McManus**. The four year old was sent into training with **Joseph O'Brien** and is very much one to look out for in mares' novice hurdles.

DSCHINGIS DESIRE (FR) 3 b f Dschingis Secret (GER) – Neckara (GER)

Mathieu Brasme trained this once raced filly to win on her Flat debut at Argentan (RH : 1m 4f : Soft) in April. Contesting a fourteen runner event, she was partnered by Hugo Journiac and was held up during the early stages. Making ground on the outside towards the end of the backstraight, she came with her challenge inside the final quarter of a mile. Leading close home, she led close home to prevail by a neck from Viento De Levante (runner-up in three handicaps since). The third and fifth have scored subsequently. Bought privately by **Gigginstown House Stud**, she has joined **Willie Mullins** and will go juvenile hurdling. She can only improve with experience.

FORT DINO (FR) 4 b g Doctor Dino (FR) – Scarletts Fortune (FR)

Twice raced over hurdles for Hugo Merienne, he was nine lengths fourth on his debut at Dieppe (RH : 2m : Soft) at the beginning of May – made a mistake at the second and never a threat to easy winner Kind of Mix. Thirty days later, he produced an improved performance when beating ten rivals by upwards of seven lengths at Auteuil (2m 1f : Very Soft). In behind the leaders turning for home, he produced a bold leap at the second last to join the principals before taking charge along the stands rail. Stretching clear on the run-in, the further the four year old went, the better he looked. The runner-up Litleangel Duseuil was subsequently sold for €70,000 and has joined Lucinda Russell. Bought privately on behalf of **Mark E.Phelan**, the gelded son of Doctor Dino is now in training with **Henry De Bromhead** and is an interesting prospect for novice hurdles.

FOU DE TOI (FR) 4 b g Motivator – Finella (FR)

From the same source as Grade 1 winning stablemate Kargese, namely Donatien Sourdeau de Beauregard, the Motivator gelding wore a hood, noseband and tongue tie on his hurdles bow at Auteuil (1m 7f : Very Soft) in May last year. Anchored in rear, he jumped crisply and moved smoothly into contention on the approach to the hometurn. Clement Lefebvre's mount produced a good jump at the penultimate flight and held every chance. Faring best of the debutants, he was four lengths third behind Apollon Du Luy and Sauvignon (both won Listed hurdles since, although the former has been disappointing since joining Paul Nicholls) in receipt of six and eight pounds respectively. Six and a half lengths clear of the fourth, he was subsequently bought privately on behalf of **Joe and Marie Donnelly** but has yet to race for **Willie Mullins** having been given plenty of time since arriving at Closutton. Nicolas Bertran De Balandra, who has been involved with Grade 1 winners A Plus Tard, Editeur Du Gite, Goshen, Quilixios, Salvator Mundi, Sire Du Berlais and Teahupoo, commented in December: **"A juvenile I was involved with that sold to Willie (Mullins), that I really liked a lot, was Fou De Toi. I hope he's very good, I liked him a lot."** The four year old could be *Sky Bet* Supreme Novices' Hurdle material.

FREE SPIRIT (FR) 4 ch g Muhtathir – Musikaline (FR)

By the same sire as the multiple Grade 1 winner Envoi Allen, he was owned in France by the legendary Walter Connors and trained by Daniela Mele. Twice raced over hurdles, he was seven and a half lengths runner-up behind Hassadam in the Prix Emilius at Auteuil (2m 2f : Heavy) in late October – Teahupoo won the same race in 2024. Returning to action at Dieppe (RH : 2m 1f : Soft) in June, the chestnut (wore a noseband) sat in behind the longtime leader until jumping to the front at the third last. Stretching away soon afterwards, his advantage was diminished on the run-in and the four year old was all out to hold the late thrust of previous winner Darling De Chamdou with the pair ten lengths clear of the remainder. The Muhtathir gelding will sport the **Mrs Audrey Turley** silks, of Galopin Des Champs fame, and is residing with **Willie Mullins**. He is eligible for novice hurdles.

GOLD CAST (FR) 3 b f Telecaster – Shannon Marigold (FR)

Paul Nicholls turned to trusted ally Anthony Bromley at the Arqana Summer Sale in July and returned with two high profile signings. They included this progressive filly who was acquired for €300,000 and is now owned by **Brooks, Stewart & Vogt**. She raced three times over hurdles at Auteuil for Mickael Seror improving with each start. A well beaten ninth in the fillies' version of the Prix Wild Monarch (1m 7f : Very Soft) in April, she performed much better over C&D nearly three weeks later. Less than eight lengths fourth in another conditions event behind

Panthere Verte (second won next time), the Telecaster filly shed her maiden tag at the third time of asking in late May (2m 1f : Very Soft). Stepping up in trip, she sat close to the pace racing enthusiastically under Bryony Frost. Leading on the run-in, she stayed on stoutly to beat Malaisie by a short neck with a length and three quarters back to the third. She looks tailormade for races such as the Listed Coral Fillies' Juvenile Hurdle at Newbury (28th November) and Listed Byerley Stud Mares' Novices' Hurdle at Taunton (30th December).

JUST ENNEMI (FR) 5 ch g Kamsin (GER) – Aubane (FR)

Owner / former jockey **David Maxwell** transferred this dual hurdles winner to **Harry Derham** last Autumn and he is an interesting proposition for handicap hurdles this winter before going chasing later on. Out of a Listed winning mare and a half-brother to Perfect Impulse (runner-up twice in the Grade 1 Grand Steeple-Chase de Paris), he was handled in his native country by Dominique Bressou winning two of his three races over the smaller obstacles. A nineteen lengths scorer on his first run over hurdles at Argentan (RH : 2m 1f : Very Soft) in October 2023, he was purchased by Maxwell soon afterwards. A well held sixth in a conditions hurdle at Auteuil (2m 1f : Heavy) in March, he was nearly thirty lengths behind the winner (King Conti – third in a Grade 2 hurdle next time) with some smart horses filling the frame. Absent for 189 days, he contested a similar event over the same C&D (Very Soft) in September. Sporting a noseband and racing handily under Gabin Meunier, he led at the penultimate flight before staying on strongly to beat Majestika by four and a half lengths. The form has been boosted with the third, fourth, fifth, eighth and ninth winning since. Allocated a mark of 128, such a rating may underestimate the Kamsin gelding. The Gerry Feilden Handicap Hurdle at Newbury (29th November) looks an ideal target – his young trainer sent out Brentford Hope (off 133 in 2023) and Queens Gamble (130 in 2024) to be placed in recent years.

KAI LUNG (FR) 3 b g Galway – Panda Queen (FR)

Purchased by the **Slaneyville Syndicate**, of Lecky Watson and Schindlers Hunt fame, he may not be one of **Willie Mullins**' leading juvenile hurdlers this winter, but is interesting nevertheless. Trained by Francois Rohaut, he only won one of his six races on the Flat but never raced beyond ten furlongs. The son of Galway could be open to significant improvement over two miles. A two and a half lengths winner at Tarbes (RH : 7.5f : Soft) in April, he then finished runner-up over a mile and a quarter at the same venue (Soft) in early June. Staying on under sympathetic handling, he was beaten a length and quarter by Jean-Claude Rouget's Maneki (won again since). Consistent, he was bought for €80,000 at the Arqana Summer Sale and could be the sort to develop into a Fred Winter Juvenile Hurdle contender next spring.

KALDOUN DES ROCS (FR) 3 b g Earnshaw (USA) – Tamkevi (FR)

Hector Lageneste and Guillaume Macaire trained the once raced gelding to finish second at Compiegne (LH : 2m : Heavy) in early March – Triumph Hurdle winner Quilixios won the same race in 2020. A big, rangy gelding he travelled well in behind the leader before sharing the advantage turning for home. Holding every chance after the second last, Lucas Zuliani's mount couldn't withstand the challenge of Wild Bill Hickok (won at Listed level since) and was beaten a length and a half with a further two and a half lengths back to the third (won next time). Snapped up by **Dan Skelton**, he is owned by **Eventist Group Limited** and is a smashing long-term prospect.

Reveley's Remarks: **"It is one of the first three year old hurdles of the season and I rode the winner (Wild Bill Hickok). We like our horse and I know the runner-up was fancied on the day. I think the form is solid and he looks a nice type."**

KOLIATH DE COUELY (FR) 4 b g Goliath Du Berlais (FR) – Kolivana (FR)
Beaten in a driving on his hurdles bow at Le Lion D'Angers (LH : 2m 2f : Soft) in June, the four year old led soon after the fourth last and was still in front jumping the final flight. Headed on the run-in, Laurent & Matheo Viel's runner kept on well only to be denied by Marvel Delablairie with three lengths back to the third. The form is modest but the Goliath Du Berlais gelding has size and scope and remains a maiden. Purchased by **Willie Mullins** for €150,000 at the Arqana Summer Sale, he will carry the colours of the trainer's wife Jackie.

LARINKA (FR) 4 b f Martinborough – Madrika (FR)
By the same sire as triple Grade 1 winner Majborough, the unbeaten filly hails from the same source, too, namely Daniela Mele. Making her racecourse bow in a fourteen runner AQPS Flat race at Saumur (LH : 1m 7f : Good/Soft) in March, she dominated from an early stage. In front with over two circuits to run, the four year old galloped on relentlessly in the homestraight to win hard held by six and a half lengths (third won since). She looked above average and, not surprisingly, **J.P.McManus** acquired the filly and **Willie Mullins** is now training her. She looks Dawn Run Mares' Novices' Hurdle material.
NB: Even though the ground was described as good to soft, it resembled a ploughed field.

LAS CANALS (FR) 4 b g Cokoriko (FR) – Daviere (FR)
Olly Greenall and **Josh Guerriero** have been well served by ex-French horses sired by Cokoriko in recent seasons. Homme Public is a Grade 2 winner, while Iroko won the Martin Pipe Conditional Jockeys' Hurdle at the Cheltenham Festival in 2023. Hopes are high that the former Louise Carberry trained four year old Las Canals will develop into a smart performer, too. Half length winner of an AQPS Flat race at Argentan (RH : 1m 4f : Very Soft) in October last year, he came down the middle of the track before leading inside the final furlong (third and fifth won subsequently). A month later, he finished around ten lengths third on his hurdles debut at Compiegne (LH : 2m 1f : Heavy). Given an educational ride, he was in rear for the majority of the race until making eyecatching headway after the second last. The winner Coeur D'Amour followed up in Grade 3 company next time, while the runner-up The Workaholic has won twice over fences since. Transferred to Cheshire soon afterwards, he is owned by **The Nevers Racing Partnership III** syndicate and is a cracking prospect for novice hurdles.

LAURETS D'ESTRUVAL (FR) 4 b g Saint Des Saints (FR) – Brise D'Estruval (FR)
The four year old raced once for Hector Lageneste and Guillaume Macaire finishing runner-up in a newcomers event over hurdles at Pau (RH : 2m : Heavy) in December. Partnered by Kevin Nabet, the Saint Des Saints gelding was anchored in rear along the rail until making headway towards the end of the backstraight. He then moved into contention after the second last but couldn't reel in Lovely Guy (won twice more since, including at Listed level) on the run-in. Beaten a length and a quarter, he was five lengths clear of the third. Purchased in January by **Willie Mullins**, he is owned by **Rich & Susannah Ricci** and looks a surefire winner of a maiden hurdle before hopefully going on to better things. Burrows Saint, Let's Dance and Vautour have all provided the Ricci family with big race success courtesy of the same source.

LA VALSERINE (FR) 4 b f No Risk At All (FR) – Brookdale (FR)
Half-brother to dual Grade 3 winner Kandy Park, the No Risk At All filly came with a strong challenge on the outside before pulling away to win on her debut in an AQPS Flat race at Fontainebleau (LH : 1m 7f : Very Soft) in February. Trained by Daniela Mele, she was patiently ridden amongst the eleven runner field before moving to the outside early in the homestraight.

Picking up well, she hit the front inside the final 150 yards before crossing the line a length and a quarter clear of Lieira (won since). The third (Lady Magic) has won twice since and is now in training with Tom Symonds, while the sixth (Leader D'Allier) won his next five starts, including a Grade 3 and has joined Willie Mullins. A fine prospect for mares' novice hurdles, she is owned by **Kenny Alexander** and is trained by **Willie Mullins**.

LE DESTRIER (IRE) 6 b h Le Havre (IRE) – Quanzhou (FR)
Polish owner **Stawomir Pegza** sent a select bunch of horses to **Willie Mullins** last year, including Hipop De Loire who has run well twice in the *Sky Bet* Ebor and won over hurdles at the Galway Festival. The six year old Le Destrier was another and it is hoped a hurdling career on his agenda having won 5 of his 11 races on the Flat. All five wins were gained in Poland, including twice at Sluzewicz (1m 5f : Good/Soft) in 2023. Fifth in a Group 1 at Hoppegarten (1m 4f : Good), the son of Le Havre was a neck second in a Listed event at Lyon (LH : 1m 4f : Very Soft) in June last year. Bidding to make all, he was only headed close home by Andre Fabre's Sacred Spirit (placed in a Group 2 since) with two and a half lengths back to the third. Off since, he has the size for hurdling and has been given time since arriving at Closutton in January.

LE DIVIN ENFANT (FR) 4 b g Saint Des Saints (FR) – Quinine De Mazille (FR)
Full-brother to Philip Hobbs & Johnson White's 144 rated chaser Imperial Saint, the four year old raced twice in France for Davide Satalia. Less than five lengths fourth in an AQPS Flat race at Vichy (RH : 1m 4f : Good) in July last year, he then filled the same position on his hurdles bow in the Prix Isopani at Auteuil (2m 2f : Heavy) in October. Racing enthusiastically in behind the leaders, he jumped and travelled well and held every chance approaching the second last. Pulled to the stands rail, he couldn't match the finishing kick of Grade 1 winner Lulamba but stayed on to finish around ten lengths behind the subsequent Nicky Henderson trained winner (third won since and Grade 3 placed). Purchased by **Willie Mullins** on behalf of **Miss M.A.Masterson**, of Appreciate It and Champ Kiely fame, the Saint Des Saints gelding will make his Irish debut in a maiden hurdle before hopefully making an impact in Graded events.

LEO WOOD (FR) 4 b g Cokoriko (FR) – Ruth (FR)
Once raced, the four year old is a half-brother to Grade 1 winning chaser Franco De Port and is owned by **Lady J.H.Parker** and trained by **Kim Bailey & Mat Nicholls**. Handled in his native country by Noel George & Amanda Zetterholm, he was a €46,000 store and made his debut in a fifteen runner hurdle at Compiegne (LH : 2m 2f : Very Soft) in April. Sharing the lead during the early stages, he turned for home amongst the leading pack and kept on in encouraging fashion. Two and a half lengths behind Laccio Conti and stablemate Brace For Landing (joined Dan Skelton), he was a further five lengths clear of the fourth. The Cokoriko gelding was acquired the following month and will be suited by two and a half miles plus novice hurdles.

LET'S LOVE (FR) 4 b g Voiladenuo (FR) – Sably (FR)
Jerome Delaunay was in charge of this once raced four year old when filling third position in a fifteen runner hurdle at Compiegne (LH : 2m 1f : Heavy) in November last year. Ridden by Clement Lefebvre, he ran a race full of promise and the form has worked out particularly well. Jumping well in midfield, he is a fine big scopey horse who moved up smoothly in behind the leaders on the final circuit. He stayed on stoutly after the second last to finish two lengths behind the unbeaten and potentially top-class Lascar Du Mathan (won again since) and Miss Maelys (2 from 2 since). Less than three weeks later, he was purchased for €75,000 at the Arqana Autumn Sale by **Venetia Williams** on behalf of **David Maxwell**. Significantly, Maxwell

owned the winner at the time. A chaser in the making, he will spend this season in novice hurdles and could prove a shrewd acquisition.

LIMIER D'ARTHEL (FR) 3 b g Cokoriko (FR) – Bellone d'Arthel (FR)
Seven times Grade 1 winner Defi Du Seuil began his career in French bumpers for Emmanuel Clayeux. The Voix Du Nord gelding won 14 of his 25 starts for **J.P.McManus** and **Philip Hobbs** earning £627,611 in total prize-money. The same combination took charge of another ex-Clayeux inmate, Limier D'Arthel, last year. The son of Cokoriko caught the eye on his AQPS Flat race debut at Lignieres (LH : 1m 4f : Heavy) in March 2024. Short of room on the far rail, he stayed on strongly once in the clear to finish fourth behind Lincoln Du Seuil. Beaten five and a half lengths, he confirmed the promise with a bloodless win at Moulins (RH : 1m 4f : Soft) a fortnight later. Keen during the early stages, he was held up before moving closer to the pace halfway down the backstraight. Sent to the front turning for home (400 metres out), he stretched away to win by nine lengths. The second, third and fourth have won since. Bought soon afterwards, he was due to go juvenile hurdling last season but a skin condition has delayed his jumping debut. Expect him to make up for lost time this winter and evoke memories of the top-class Defi Du Seuil.

LIRONE DU SEUIL (FR) 4 b g Masked Marvel – Brume Du Seuil (FR)
Owned by **Colm Donlon**, the four year old has reportedly thrived physically since joining **Dan Skelton** in the spring. Trained by Mickael Seror, he was around a dozen lengths sixth behind the aforementioned Limier D'Arthel in an AQPS Flat race at Moulins (1m 4f : Soft) in April last year. Ten months later, the Masked Marvel gelding reappeared over hurdles at Fontainebleau (LH : 2m 1f : Very Soft) and caught the eye finishing strongly in second. In rear in the fourteen runner event, he was patiently ridden before pulled to the outside turning for home. Still seventh jumping the last, he stormed home to get within three and a half lengths of the winner Rock Me Charly (won again). The third has also won since. Still a maiden with size and scope, he should have no trouble winning novice hurdles.

LIVIO (FR) 4 b g Cokoriko (FR) – Etoile Du Berger (FR)
Belied his lack of experience to win a Grade 3 AQPS Flat race at Lyon (LH : 1m 4f : Very Soft) in September last year on his racecourse debut for Lucie Pontoir. Racing keenly on the outside early on, the Cokoriko gelding was well positioned leaving the backstraight. Pushed along when the tempo lifted turning for home, he picked up well to wear down Landmaderlo (1 from 5 since) close home in a bunch finish. A half length scorer, he still looked raw and is open to considerable improvement. The twelve furlongs event has been won by subsequent Grade 1 winners Valseur Lido (2012) and Delta Work (2016). **Willie Mullins** purchased the four year old for €260,000 at the Arqana Arc Sale the following month and he is owned by **Mrs Rebecca Jane, Twigden, H.O.S.Syndicate** and **Anthony O'Leary**. He ought to make a smart two mile novice hurdler.

LORIKO (FR) 4 b g Cokoriko (FR) – Theme Song (FR)
Owned by **Cherry Knoll Farm, M.Ward and Dan Skelton**, he is another potentially useful addition for the last named. Thrice raced for Anne-Sophie Pacault, of Espoir D'Allen fame, the Cokoriko gelding was placed in AQPS Flat races at Le Mans (LH : 1m 7f : Very Soft) and Lignieres (LH : 1m 4f : Very Soft) in the space of four weeks in November last year. Switched to hurdles in the spring, the four year old was three and a half lengths runner-up in a conditions event at Auteuil (2m 1f : Heavy) in March. Held up in last, he was still sixth jumping the penultimate flight

before staying on to grab the runners-up berth. Three and a half lengths behind Lombo Sacre, he was two and a half lengths clear of the third. More of a hurdling type, he gives the impression a step up to middle distances over timber will suit.

MACAO (FR) 3 ch g Telecaster – Cour d'Eau Ludique (FR)
Owner **Peter Davies** has enjoyed plenty of big race successes with **Venetia Williams** in recent seasons with Djelo (triple Grade 2 winner), Fontaine Collonges (Rowland Meyrick Chase) and Frero Banbou (Rehearsal Chase). The same partnership are responsible for this hugely exciting unbeaten three year old who was bought for €320,000 at the Arqana Summer Sale. Under the tutelage of Henri-Francois Devin (trained six times Grade 1 winner Sharjah), the son of Telecaster was a six lengths winner of a four runner AQPS Flat race at Lyon (LH : 1m 4f : Good/Soft) in June. Making all the running under Dorian Provost, he upped the tempo early in the straight before stretching away. Eased down close home, the runner-up Mysoko Star has won a Grade 3 since, while the third and fourth haven't raced since. Juvenile hurdling will presumably be on the agenda and the three year old is very much one to look forward to.

MACKTOAD (FR) 3 gr g Beaumec De Houelle (FR) – Toady (FR)
Purchased for €125,000 at the Arqana Summer Sale in July by **Gary & Josh Moore**, he is another unbeaten once raced three year old. Half-brother to six times French bumper winner Ginola, the grey was trained by Alain Couetil. Making his debut in an eight runner AQPS Flat race at Vichy (RH : 1m 4f : Good/Soft) in late May, he still looked raw and can only improve. Racing in mid division, the Beaumec De Houelle gelding mounted his challenge on the outside in the homestraight knuckling down well to get the better of the luckless Misty Morning (hemmed in at a crucial stage) by a neck. The runner-up has won since and the fourth (Macshadow Des Crai) is now owned by Million In Mind and has joined Nicky Henderson. Described as 'a big horse and a racy type' by Gary Moore, he will go juvenile hurdling and has the ingredients to be above average.

MADNESS D'ELLE (FR) 3 b g Moises Has (FR) – Voulay (FR)
Another former Daniela Mele inmate who arrived at Closutton during the summer. Owned by **Rich & Susannah Ricci**, the Moises Has gelding was six and a quarter lengths third in the Prix Gemix, a conditions hurdle at Auteuil (1m 7f : Very Soft) in May. Typical of his previous trainer, he possesses an abundance of scope and will jump fences eventually. Sat in behind the leading duo Shannon Maestro (runner-up in Listed hurdle since) and Mongary, he appeared to be delivered perfectly after the second last but was unable to reel in the front two. He was three and a half lengths clear of the fourth. A three year old with plenty of potential, he is another cracking prospect for **Willie Mullins** and the Ricci family.

MAJOLIQUE (FR) 3 b f Tigron (USA) – Voix Romaine (FR)
Owner **Kenny Alexander** and trainer **Willie Mullins** tasted Grade 1 juvenile hurdle success with the filly Murcia at Aintree last spring. The pairing will be hoping lightning strikes twice with this unbeaten Flat racer. Previously handed by Florian Bellemere, the daughter of Tigron was a narrow winner of a seven runner unraced fillies' maiden at Longchamp (RH : 1m 2f : Good/Soft) in mid May. Drawn widest, she soon slotted in behind the leaders before moving strongly into contention inside the final quarter of a mile. Augustin Madamet's mount was forced to sit and suffer for a few strides. However, once seeing daylight, she picked up well hitting the front inside to win going away by a short neck. The runner-up Velikaya and fifth have won since. Open to considerable improvement, she has plenty of size and no shortage of talent either.

MANGE TOUT (FR) 3 b f Born To Sea (IRE) – Brune Ecossaise (FR)

Mightily impressive on her hurdles debut at Compiegne (LH : 2m : Very Soft) in May, the Born To Sea filly was trained by Elisabeth Allaire and is a half-sister to five times Grade 1 winner Impaire Et Passe. Fitted with a hood and tongue tie and racing prominently, she took over with a circuit to run and dominated thereafter. Switched to the stands rail, she sauntered clear to win by fifteen lengths. The form is questionable, but she was in a different league to her eight opponents. Significantly, **Gordon Elliott** was in attendance and the filly was purchased soon afterwards on behalf of **Robcour**. A slick and accurate jumper, the well bred three year old could take some pegging back in Graded events this winter.

MANITA (FR) 3 gr f Moises Has (FR) – Mastermambo (IRE)

French trainer Yannick Fouin has been a terrific source for owners **Rich and Susannah Ricci** over the years with Lossiemouth and Min winning 14 Grade 1 races between them. The same handler is responsible for this once raced filly, who chased home the highly regarded Manlaga on her debut at Auteuil (1m 7f : Heavy) in mid March. Contesting a twelve runner conditions hurdle at the Parisian track, the grey filly raced prominently and was well positioned approaching the second last. Upsides the leader over the last couple of flights, she couldn't match the winner's acceleration. However, she kept on well to fill the runners-up berth and was three lengths clear of the third. The fourth (Olga De Kiev) has won a Grade 3 hurdle since. She joined **Willie Mullins** the following month and is an exciting juvenile hurdle prospect.

MANOIR DE MIRANDE (FR) 3 b g It's Gino (GER) – Gingerly (FR)

A former stablemate of the aforementioned Loriko, the It's Gino gelding was a two and a half lengths winner of a twelve runner AQPS Flat race at Moulins (RH : 1m 4f : Very Soft) in early April. Anne-Sophie Pacault's runner looked a smart prospect quickening up to lead approaching the final two furlongs before pulling away. Eased down close home, he was value for more than the winning margin. A fine big three year old, the fifth has won since, while the runner-up (Milpat) and third (Macshadow Des Crai) have joined Jamie Snowden and Nicky Henderson respectively. **Gigginstown House Stud** were quick to acquire the winner and he looks another useful juvenile prospect for **Gordon Elliott**.

MARCO DU SEUIL (FR) 3 b g Galiway – Cibelle Du Seuil (FR)

Half-brother to the 151 rated four times Grade 3 winning chaser Hercule Du Seuil, he is another terrific prospect to have joined **Gordon Elliott** during the summer. Owned by **Robcour**, the Galiway gelding beat four previous winners on his debut in a Grade 3 AQPS Flat race at Le Lion D'Angers (LH : 1m 4f : Good/Soft) in late July. Trained by Mickael Seror, he was the only debutant in the seven strong field and was positioned in third along the rail during the early stages. Mounting his challenge turning for home, he was pulled to the outside and pushed into the lead under hands and heels. A two lengths victor, Augustin Madamet's mount was firmly on top. Bought soon afterwards, he has plenty of substance physically and ought to jump fences one day.

MILLE ET UNE VIES (FR) 3 gr f The Grey Gatsby (IRE) – Avacapa (FR)

A well bred filly, she raced three times over hurdles for Francois Nicolle being placed on each occasion, including in Listed and Grade 3 company. Ten and a half lengths third behind Delmegan at Auteuil (1m 7f : Heavy) in late March on her debut, she was beaten a neck by the same rival over the same C&D less than a month later. Having chased Elisabeth Allaire's winner throughout, she had closed the gap approaching the last and the pair were involved in a protracted duel on the run-in. Three lengths clear of the third, the grey managed to reverse the form next time they met in a Grade 3 hurdle at the Parisian track (2m 1f : Very Soft) in May. However, she was still beaten eight lengths by Olga De Kiev who had finished behind her on their previous start. Leading down the back straight on the final circuit, she was headed approaching the final flight before keeping on at the one pace. Subsequently bought by **Johnny De La Hey** and sent to **Dan Skelton**, she jumps and stays well and one could envisage her being positively ridden in juvenile hurdles this winter. The Grade 2 Finale Juvenile Hurdle at Chepstow (27th December) could be to her taste - very much in the mould of the stable's 2019 winner Allmankind.

MILPAT (FR) 3 b g Cokoriko (FR) - Gulip (FR)
Bought for €29,000 as a two year old, he shaped encouragingly on his debut in an AQPS Flat race at Moulins (RH : 1m 4f : Very Soft) in April. Trained by Mathieu Pitart, he was no match for the aforementioned Manoir De Mirande but stayed on well in second and was two lengths clear of the third. A tall son of Cokoriko, he raced in mid division before moving up on the outside early in the homestraight. Bought privately by **Jamie Snowden** on behalf of the **McNeill Family & Stone Family**, he is by the same stallion as the stable's first Grade 1 winner Julius Des Pictons. He is likely to go juvenile hurdling but won't be over raced this campaign.

MINO DES MOTTES (FR) 3 b g It's Gino (GER) - Ulyssa Des Mottes (FR)
Etienne D'Andigne trained subsequent triple Grade 1 winner and Champion Hurdle runner-up Irish Point to win one of his three AQPS Flat races in 2021. The same handler was also responsible for this twice raced three year old who is now in the ownership of **Gigginstown House Stud**. The It's Gino gelding made a rather undistinguished start to his career when unseating his rider on his debut at Granville (RH : 1m 4f) in late June. Sharing second position and travelling strongly, he parted company with his jockey Lenny Kulik towards the end of the backstraight. None the worse and back in action ten days later, he showed what he is capable of by defeating seven rivals by upwards of a length and a quarter at Senonnes (RH : 1m 4f : Good/Soft). The trainer's son Olivier took over in the saddle and the partnership made virtually all the running. Leading with over a circuit to run, he dictated throughout upping the tempo early in the homestraight. Pushed out to win comfortably, he never looked like being headed. The runner-up (Magic Bede) finished around two lengths fourth behind the aforementioned Marco Du Seuil in a Grade 3 event next time. Likely to join either Gordon Elliott or Willie Mullins, he is another cracking juvenile hurdle prospect for Eddie and Michael O'Leary's operation.

MODE AVION (FR) 3 b g Taj Mahal (IRE) - Galatica De Thaix (FR)
Half-brother to Willie Mullins' 129 rated hurdler Last Kingdom, he hails from the same source, namely Laurent & Matheo Viel. A length and three quarters winner of an AQPS Flat race at Le Lion D'Angers (LH : 1m 4f : Very Soft) in April, he won going away in the manner of a decent sort. Wearing a noseband, the Taj Mahal gelding lobbed away in rear before starting his challenge early in the homestraight. Switched to the outside, his rider never had to get too serious pushing him to the front and extending away. The runner-up won next time. Purchased by **Gigginstown House Stud**, he will form part of **Gordon Elliott**'s formidable team of juvenile hurdlers this term.

MOJITO DES MOTTES (FR) 3 b g Clovis Du Berlais (FR) - Magie Des Landes (FR)
Described as 'strong and possessing a good attitude,' by his trainer **Ben Pauling**, the Clovis Du Berlais gelding spent a few weeks at Naunton Downs Estate in sleepy Gloucestershire during the

spring before being transported to Martinstown Stud for the summer. Owned by **J.P.McManus**, he was a three parts of a length winner on his hurdles debut at Moulins (RH : 2m 1f : Very Soft) in March when trained by Francois Nicolle - Grade 1 winning juvenile hurdlers Monmiral and Quilixos began their careers with the same handler. Racing in mid division, Angelo Zuliani's mount made headway on the inside rounding the hometurn. Switched to the outside, he joined the leader Metronomique at the second last before staying on dourly to edge out Noel George & Amanda Zetterholm's runner by three parts of a length with ten lengths back to the third. The second has won over fences since. He could be the type to develop into a Fred Winter Juvenile Hurdle prospect at Cheltenham in March.
Reveley's Remarks: **"I rode the second (Metronomique) and Noel George couldn't believe he got beaten. I suspect the winner is a decent horse."**

MONT STAR (FR) 3 b g Clovis Du Berlais (FR) – English Star (FR)
Jerry Planque trained the twice raced son of Clovis Du Berlais in his native country. Six and a half lengths fourth on his debut in an AQPS Flat race at Machecoul (LH : 1m 4f : Very Soft) in mid March, he was no match for the emphatic winner Match Amical but stayed on to good effect having been ridden patiently in rear. Less than four weeks later, he was positively ridden from the front only to find the unbeaten Mabriska (2 from 2) too good at Senonnes (RH : 1m 4f : Soft). Beaten two and a half lengths, the Alain Couetil trained winner looks above average and there was no disgrace in the performance. Headed at the 400 metres pole, he stuck to his task two and a half lengths in arrears. The fourth has won since. Purchased by owner **Mark E.Phelan**, he has joined **Henry De Bromhead** and will go juvenile hurdling.

NIGHTMARE HAS (FR) 3 b g Doctor Dino (FR) – Nice To Meet You (FR)
A half-brother to the Grade 2 winning juvenile hurdler Nietzsche Has, he was bought for €150,000 as a two year old at the Arqana Summer Sale last year. Owned by **Robcour** and trained by **Gordon Elliott**, he will be targeted at the new series of NH Academy Hurdle races in Ireland - they begin in October 2025 and are open to three year olds horses who haven't run on the Flat or under National Hunt rules. The well bred Doctor Dino gelding could clean up in such events.

PARCHMENT (FR) 3 b g Triple Threat (FR) – Flower Burg (FR)
Owned by **John White & Anne Underhill**, the Triple Threat gelding joined **David Pipe** during the summer. Trained in France by Noel George & Amanda Zetterholm, he was given a confident ride by James Reveley when scoring on his debut at Clairefontaine (RH : 2m : Very Soft) in mid June. Positioned in rear in the twelve runner event, he made smooth headway along the inside rail towards the end of the backstraight. Jumping to the front at the last, he was pushed out to readily beat Pourquoi Pas Papa (sold for €200,000 and has joined Paul Nicholls) by a length and a half. The third and fourth have boosted the form by winning subsequently. Set to go juvenile hurdling for the Pond House team, he looks a useful acquisition and his new owners have had plenty of success with the Pipe team with Pattern race winners Dynaste, Israel Champ and Ramses De Teillee.
Reveley's Remarks: **"We thought he would run well at Clairefontaine and he did it nicely. He is a horse with a lot of speed and will be suited by better ground in the UK."**

POURQUOI PAS PAPA (FR) 3 b g Manatee – Pourquoi Pas Elle (FR)
Runner-up behind the aforementioned Parchment, it was an encouraging start to his career at Clairefontaine (2m : Very Soft) in June. Trained by David Cottin, the Manatee gelding raced

prominently throughout and, having been tapped for speed soon after the second last, Gabin Meunier's mount rallied gamely on the run-in to regain the runners-up berth. Beaten a length and a half, the third and fourth have won since. **Paul Nicholls** and leading agent Anthony Bromley combined at the Arqana Summer Sale in early July and acquired the three year old for €200,000. Owned by **Bell, Lyons, James and Hill**, the fact he is a maiden is a bonus and he ought to be a force in juvenile hurdles this winter.

PRECIOUS MAN (FR) 3 ch g Almanzor (FR) – Preciously (FR)
Another exciting three year old owned by **Johnny De La Hey** and trained by **Dan Skelton**. The Almanzor gelding raced twice over hurdles at Auteuil during the spring and looks Graded material. Ridden by Lucas Zuliani on his debut in the Prix Rush (1m 7f : Heavy) in March, he stayed on in second behind the Coolmore owned The Mighty Celt (Listed placed twice since). Beaten four lengths, he had the aforementioned Bertutea three lengths behind in third. Off 73 days, he returned to the Parisian track in late May and appreciated the step up in distance (2m 1f : Very Soft) collaring Novak in the shadows of the post. Patiently ridden throughout, he moved up between the third and second last flights before throwing down his challenge on the run-in. Winning by a head, the pair pulled eight lengths clear of the third (won since). Bought soon afterwards, he has reportedly thrived since joining Team Skelton growing a couple of inches. The Grade 2 Prestbury Juvenile Hurdle at Cheltenham's November meeting (15th) could be ideal for his UK debut – his yard won it with Allmankind in 2019.
Reveley's Remarks: **"Novak, who finished second behind him at Auteuil last time, is a nice horse who Noel George likes a lot. The form is strong and he is a nice prospect for the UK."**

ROC DINO (FR) 4 ch g Doctor Dino (FR) – Presidente Line (FR)
Willie Mullins has purchased subsequent Graded performers Blood Destiny, Franco De Port and Haut En Couleurs from Gabriel Leenders in recent years and Ireland's champion trainer has returned to the same source for this thrice raced maiden. An €85,000 yearling out of a Listed hurdle winning mare, he raced three times over hurdles in France improving with each outing. Only seventh on his debut at Pau (RH : 2m 1f : Heavy) in December, he stepped up on that effort over the same C&D a couple of months later when a length and a quarter runner-up behind Lovely Dino (won over fences since). Leading at the last, he was reeled in close home. He rounded off his French career when a good third behind Lord Brett (Listed placed twice since) and Leho (won since) at Auteuil (2m 2f : Heavy) in February. Partnered by former champion jockey Felix De Giles, the four year old made headway along the rail down the backstraight before joining the leaders at the second last. In front at the final flight, he was run out of it by the Francois Nicolle and Daniela Mele trained runners. Beaten two and a half lengths, he is owned by **Barnane Stud & Hollywood Stud** and shouldn't have any trouble winning a maiden hurdle in Ireland. With three hurdle runs under his belt, he could be a player in some valuable handicaps in the spring.

SAINT BACO (FR) 4 b g Cokoriko (FR) – Saint Vigne (FR)
There were two divisions of the Prix Finot at Auteuil (2m 2f : Very Soft) in September last year with the second one being run in a much quicker time – 4m 13.09s compared to 4m 16.48s in division one. This Daniela Mele trained Cokoriko gelding was beaten narrowly in third behind subsequent Grade 1 runner-up Musique Maestro and Listed winner Neverchangedoctor. A half-brother to Cheltenham Festival winner Saint Roi, Clement Lefebvre's mount travelled strongly holding every chance in the homestraight. A good looking individual with plenty of size and scope, **Willie Mullins** acquired him the following month on behalf of **Michael Hilary Burke**.

Given time to settle into his new surroundings, he has got a bright future and can make an impact in Graded novice hurdles over two and two and a half miles this year.

SALVE CAMELIA (IRE) 4 ch f Le Havre (IRE) – Salve Haya (IRE)
Half-sister to 130 rated hurdler and 96 rated Flat racer Sea of Sands, the Le Havre filly has joined her older sibling at Closutton and is set to go mares' novice hurdling for **Willie Mullins**. Owned by **Ballylinch Stud**, she raced five times on the Flat for Francis-Henri Graffard last year. Runner-up twice at Saint-Cloud (1m 7f : Very Soft) and Senonnes (RH : 1m 6f : Good/Soft) – wore cheekpieces for the first time - she got off the mark at the fifth attempt in maiden company at Lyon (LH : 1m 4f : Soft) in September 2024. Racing prominently behind the leaders, she outstayed Guardian in the closing stages to score by three parts of a length with the pair six and a half lengths clear of the third. The second, third and fourth have won since.

SENATOR (FR) 3 ch g Doctor Dino (FR) – Presidente Line (FR)
A full-brother to the aforementioned Roc Dino, he ran twice on the Flat for Alain Couetil being placed on both occasions. Having raced in midfield, the son of Doctor Dino stayed on strongly to finish third in a fourteen runner event at Vichy (RH : 1m 4f : Good/Soft) in late May. Beaten around two lengths, he returned to action a month later in a similar event at Chateaubriant (RH : 1m 5f : Soft). Set plenty to do in the sixteen runner contest, he made headway leaving the backstraight before challenging on the outside. While he failed to trouble the decisive winner Talgat, he finished well in third. Four lengths in arrears, the runner-up has got one better since. Purchased at the Arqana Summer Sale for €140,000, he has joined **Jamie Snowden** and is owned by **Mr Thomas Mold**. From the family of the ill-fated Grade 1 winning hurdler Porticello, he ought to make his mark in juvenile hurdles.

SHINAGO THEYSS (FR) 3 b f Goliath Du Berlais (FR) – Shinaway (FR)
Owned by **Babbitt Racing**, she is another string to **Dan Skelton**'s juvenile hurdle bow for 2025/2026. Previously handled by Mme Marine Pineda, she was a four lengths winner on her hurdles bow at Dieppe (RH : 1m 7f : Soft) at the beginning of May. Fifteen unraced horses lined up and she was partnered by Simon Planque. Racing in midfield towards the outside, the daughter of Goliath Du Berlais made stealthy headway on the final circuit to sit in behind the leader at the end of the backstraight. Leading after the last, she quickened away in good style. The form has been franked with the second and fourth (twice) scoring subsequently. Bought privately, she looks capable of making an impact in three year old fillies' black type races for her new connections.
Reveley's Remarks: **"She is a well bred filly who won in good style on her debut. She did the job well and is an interesting prospect for juvenile hurdles in the UK."**

TAHAA (FR) 4 gr f Beaumec De Houelle (FR) – La Pinede
A half-sister to Jonjo O'Neill's four times winning chaser Le Domaniale, she was trained in her native country by Donatien Sourdeau De Beauregard, who was also responsible for Grade 1 winning filly Kargese. A grey filly by Beaumec De Houelle, she beat fifteen rivals by upwards of two lengths in a conditions hurdle at Compiegne (LH : 2m 2f : Very Soft) in April on her only start. Racing handily on the outside, she moved up stylishly rounding the hometurn. Switched off the rail after the second last, she led at the final flight. Despite getting in tight, she picked up well on the run-in stretching clear to beat the Noel George & Amanda Zetterholm trained Nirisque (joined Henry De Bromhead). Eligible for novice hurdles until the end of November, she was bought privately by **Robcour** and is trained by **Joseph O'Brien**. She looks a smashing prospect.

THEWOODCORNER (FR) 3 b g The Grey Gatsby (IRE) – Goldy Hauty (FR)
Nicky Henderson trained Grade 2 winning hurdler Aigle D'Or. The Halling gelding began his career on the Flat in France when trained by Henri-Alex Pantall. The Seven Barrows team have acquired another ex-Flat racer from the same source in the twice raced Thewoodcorner. Owned by **Axom**, the son of The Grey Gatsby was only ninth on his debut at Durtal (RH : 1m 2f : Heavy) in December last year. Three and a half months later, he was a different proposition when defeating thirteen opponents at Saumur (LH : 1m 7f : Soft) and relishing the step up in distance in the process. Sat in behind the principals, he was pushed into the lead rounding the final turn before staying on strongly to prevail narrowly. The first two pulled eleven lengths clear of the third. The runner-up Optimus has won over hurdles since. Stamina appears his strong suit, which will stand him in good stead for juvenile hurdles.

ZEKRET (FR) 3 ch c Zarak (FR) – Anjella (GER)
Purchased by agent Alex Elliott for €520,000 at the Arqana Summer Sale, he is an exciting juvenile hurdle prospect for **Robcour** and **Joseph O'Brien**. The son of Zarak, who was previously owned by Al Shaqab, raced four times on the Flat for Andre Fabre. A length winner on his sole start as a two year old, he beat seven opponents at Deauville (1m : Heavy) in October last year. Half a length runner-up in a conditions event at Longchamp (1m 3f : Very Soft) in April, the winner (Parachutiste) has subsequently won at Listed level and finished third in the Group 2 Niel at Longchamp. A month later, he finished a staying on fifth in the Group 3 Prix Hocquart over the same C&D (Soft). Lightly raced and unexposed, he stays well and handles testing ground.

IRISH POINTERS

Expert **DECLAN PHELAN** highlights the point-to-pointers to follow from across the Irish Sea who will race under Rules this winter. Last year's feature unearthed **39 winners** from 130 runners (30%). The selections included Grade 1 winners **FINAL DEMAND** & **POTTERS CHARM**, plus **DERRYHASSEN PADDY, GORAIBHMAITHAGAT (16/1)** and unbeaten Listed bumper winner **SOBER GLORY**. In the 2023/2024 edition, Declan nominated the first **THREE** home in the **2024 Cheltenham Festival bumper** – **JASMIN DE VAUX (9/2), ROMEO COOLIO (18/1) & JALON D'OUDAIRIES (3/1)**. The best in the business, Declan has once again penned his invaluable article regarding those horses who caught his eye 'between the flags' in the Emerald Isle last winter/spring.

ASH HOBBS (IRE) 4 br f Jack Hobbs – Fly Town (IRE)
Trainer: Henry De BROMHEAD   Form Figures: 1
A cheap €4,500 store, her modest dam won a two miles chase. A tall rangy bay mare with one rear white sock. She competed for Wexford handler Harley Dunne in her only point engagement. If one considers the 2024/25 campaign was somewhat of a disaster for Harley, from a string of over 40 young horses, he managed just two winners from 86 runners, as one of the winners, Ash Hobbs was swimming against the prevailing tide and can certainly be upgraded. Her date with the pointing game happened at Ballycahane (Left-Handed : Yielding) in March: in a seven runner mares' maiden for four-year-olds, given a slowly run opening two miles, she sat in the first three throughout. Rounding the home bend with two to jump, Ash Hobbs suddenly turned up the heat, quickened away to establish a half dozen lengths advantage, and never gave her rivals a chance to reel her in.Her stock certainly rose in the sales ring at the Cheltenham Festival

Tattersalls auction, fetching a price of £170,000. There may be questionable substance to the form of the Ballycahane victory, however, she looks like a talented and straight forward lady and can make an impact on the track and could elevate to mares Graded class as a hurdler or chaser.

BENTRAGHHILL (IRE) 4 b g Getaway (GER) – Itsalark (IRE)
Trainer: Willie MULLINS Form Figures: 3
Fine specimen: a €35,000 foal, he is a sibling to multiple winners, including Party Central, a product of the renowned Motherway nursery in Youghal, Yellowford Farm. Sporting the Dennison colours, he figured in one point, at Fairyhouse (Right-Handed : Yielding) in April. He did little wrong in the contest, but he had the misfortune to be trapped in a pocket when the pace increased away from the second last. By the time he found racing room, his goose was cooked, nonetheless he kept on nicely for little pressure to grab the bronze, defeated three lengths. One sensed had he a second serve at the tie, a different outcome may have arisen. Team Closutton certainly gave him the benefit of the doubt, bidding €150,000 to add him to their team. At face value, this gelding has fewer buttons pushed than other contemporaries within the four-year old crop, and he may have more in the way of untapped potential.

BEST TRUMP (IRE) 4 b g Walk In The Park (IRE) – Samsha (IRE)
Trainer: Jonjo & A.J.O'NEILL Form Figures: 1
Well-proportioned bay gelding, sibling to winners, amongst them Gwennie May Boy, acquired by team McManus at a tariff of €72,000 at the store sales. Posted to Derek O'Connor for a pointing education, the handler took the reins in the 2m 4f four-year-old maiden at Knockanard (RH : Heavy): the partnership supplanted in the betting ring due to a punt on main rival Mister St Eloi. With four to jump, the market rival exited after an incident with another horse, and in truth Best Trump, who had been held up in the rear of a five-runner race, simply slipped through to lead at the final fence and won without any real test. Impossible to estimate his standing judged on winning a messy race, if forced to call it, an educated guess would rank him a 120-130 style handicapper as opposed to star material.

BUD FOX (IRE) 4 b g Walk In The Park (IRE) – Flaviana (IRE)
Trainer: Gavin CROMWELL Form Figures: 11
Medium sized bay gelding, dam a four-time winner when handled by Jessica Harrington (2m - 2m 4f on good ground being her cup of tea). The Bleahan family based in East Galway are one of the leading nurseries in the West of Ireland producing jump store stock for the premier sales like the Tattersalls Ireland Derby and Land Rover auctions. Their past alma mater include Sizing Europe and loads of top Skelton stock. It appears they failed to get Bud Fox ready in time to sell during the summer of 2024 and instead decided to take a punt and send him 30 miles down the road to fellow Galwegian, Derek O Connor, to try and sell via a point performance. The gelding was obviously quick to come to hand as Derek partnered him in one of the first four-year-old maidens of the campaign at Bellharbour (LH : Good/Yielding) in February. He sat off the leaders and had to roust his mount into serious action after three out. Turning into the home straight four deep, the horse found for encouragement and quickened up nicely to take the measure of market rival, the ill-fated Pierrot, by two lengths. The victory guaranteed a pay day for all, as the Bleahan family cashed in, selling to Gavin Cromwell. The youngster's stock rose further as he made an instant impact on the track proper: again steered by Derek O'Connor, once he found racing room off the final bend, he soon put a Punchestown Festival bumper to bed, scoring by four and a quarter lengths in a 25 runner affair. Classy, but not necessarily a

cruise/bridle type, it is a positive characteristic that he will produce under pressure and he has bright aspirations of Graded success as a novice hurdler and he can comfortably command a jumps rating north of 130.

CRISTAL D'ESTRUVAL (IRE) 4 b g Crystal Ocean - Aurore D'Estruval (FR)
Trainer: Harry DERHAM Form Figures: 1

Robust, well defined bay gelding: €70,000 foal, dam 3-times winner and runner-up in the Grade 1 Fighting Fifth Hurdle for John Quinn. Produced by Colin Bowe for one of the divisions of the four-year-old geldings maiden at Lisronagh (LH : Heavy) in February. With Barry O'Neill aboard, the tactic deployed was to sit close to the pace throughout. In a race which was run at a modest pace, from the third last, two runners counted. It seemed as though Cristal D'Estruval was going to play second fiddle to No Walkover coming to the final fence: he compounded his prospects with a sloppy jump at the fence: luck was in his corner, as No Walkover (tack problems) appeared to pull himself up fifty yards from the winning line and with Cristal D'Estruval to his credit rallying, he snatched the gift by a neck. By an up and coming (yet unproven) sire, he proved to be a desirable object when auctioned at the Cheltenham Festival Sale and made the vendors a bounty of £400,000. Judged on Lisronagh, he has an impressive physique and a touch of class and potential: to my eyes there was no 'wow' factor, and team Derham will have work on their hands if they aspire to develop the gelding into a top tier performer. He is game, which will translate to track success, his dam is a progeny of Nickname, whose stock tend to be in their pomp on soft/heavy, so he might be one in his element during deep winter conditions.

CRYSTAL ISLAND (IRE) 4 b g Crystal Ocean - Je T'Aime (IRE)
Trainer: Nicky HENDERSON Form Figures: 1

Stout, powerfully built, bay gelding: €60,000 store from modest French jumps clan. Handled by Eamonn Doyle, one of the younger siblings in the Monbeg operation, he debuted at Rathcannon (LH : Good) in April. To the fore from early doors, he travelled along in his comfort zone: upping the tempo from three out, he burned off his rivals one by one: although a little deliberate at the final fence, which cost him momentum, he managed to get rolling again and drew away to win by more than three lengths. Loads of potential, yet still rather raw and wet between the ears, a fair verdict. Sold to Nicky Henderson for £205,000, he will be a more than decent novice hurdler, capable of obliging in the 2m to 2m 6f range and further down the line he can mould into a Graded class middle distance chaser. There may be a valuable pot to be won with him in due course and I would be positive on his future prospects.

FAIRY PARK (IRE) 4 b f Walk In The Park (IRE) - Fairy Hill (IRE)
Trainer: Joe TIZZARD Form Figures: 1

Imposing, ball of muscle, bay lady: her dam is a half-sister to Bellshill: she was an expensive €58,000 foal. Housed with Colin Bowe, she ventured to Dromahane (LH : Good/Yielding) in April to debut in a four-year-old mares' maiden. Most comfortable in the jumping department, she tracked the long-time leader, Time To Give, until putting on the indicator after three out and then stamping her authority on proceedings, as she drove clear to score by eight lengths. Notable, she clocked the fastest time of the day at the fixture, a very rare accomplishment by a mare, given the card contained other high class maiden races. With Time To Give subsequently recording her own maiden win weeks later at Ballindenisk, the form looks reliable. Fairy Park transferred via a private deal on behalf of Brocade Racing to the Tizzard stable and she will certainly make an impression in mares' hurdles and chases in the UK. Her optimum trip may be in the 2m 4f - 3 miles ballpark and it remains to be seen if she will prove as effective on a softer surface. Climbing to a rating of 130+ is a probability and she may therefore be either a Graded quality track jumper or on the fringes of that level. One of the top five mares from the 2025 spring contingent of mares aged four.

GEE FORCE FLYER (IRE) 5 b g Jet Away – Forge Field (IRE)
Trainer: Olly MURPHY Form Figures: 1
Well-formed bay with white spots on crown and nose: a member of an ordinary jumps clan, his brother is the 110 hurdler, Forged Well. A €42,000 store. One of a select group of young horses Olly Murphy entrusted to Cork based handler Michael Kennedy to nurture before they would head over to his UK base. Looked like a most straight forward and accomplished individual on his sole run, at Boulta (LH: Yielding) in December. Figuring in a warm maiden, with the top point yards represented, his jockey Johnny Barry parked towards the rear, and the combination popped away, minding their own business: in driving rain, Gee Force Flyer closed on the leaders on the way to three out. Ever advancing, he took the lead between the last two fences and asserted without pressure to triumph by two lengths...the picture postcard perfect introduction. In time, the form was complimented as during the spring, the third, fifth and sixth home at Boulta attained their own maiden point wins. He returned to Olly Murphy during the spring and he is nicely teed up to make a fair impact as a track racer. He has gears and a competitive attitude and one to respect. He had no issues with the yielding, good/soft style Irish ground, and given his style of movement, he may prefer a range of ground from soft to good. Over time, he may not have the ammunition to be a threat at the top table of the jumps game, a realistic ambition could be to land a valuable handicap either over hurdles or fences, with 2m 4f quite possibly his optimum.

GOULMICHETTE (FR) 5 b m No Risk At All (FR) – La Bezizais (FR)
Trainer: TBC Form Figures: 1
Muscular bay mare, €40,000 store from a plain equine clan. Debuted for the Monbegs at the Quakerstown (LH : Yielding) Easter Sunday fixture and managed to spreadeagle an eleven runner five and six year old mares' maiden field. Driving through to lead after halfway, leading into the final circuit, she gradually upped the pace and her rivals suffered, eventually powering away to record a 20 lengths success. Given three subsequent point winners were amongst her victims, the form has some strength to it. It was notable how fluent she skipped over her obstacles and she looks a natural in the jumping department. She can make waves as a Graded novice hurdler and she will enjoy middle distances (2m 4f). Sold for €170,000 at the Punchestown Festival Sale, she was knocked down to Noel Fehily and may have been purchased for a private client rather than for the Fehily syndicates.

GREEN HINT (IRE) 4 gr g Crystal Ocean – Hint of Grey (IRE)
Trainer: Willie MULLINS Form Figures: 12
Chunky grey, dam six times winner (3 Flat, 3 jumps), a €50,000 store for the double green, Munir/Souede partnership. Housed with the Crawfords to start his career in points. He made the journey south to race at what was a new track at Daramona House in Longford (LH : Yielding/Soft): hidden towards the rear of a tightly packed seven runner maiden, he advanced through to position in second place away from the fourth last fence. Jumping crisply, he landed in front after two out, and then kept up a solid tempo to edge clear and win by over two lengths without his jockey getting serious. An ideal winning debut, hinting of plenty more to come. As a graduate of the 2024 Goffs Defender Sale, he was qualified to run in the linked valuable bumper at the Punchestown Festival (2m : Yielding). In a maximum bumper field of 18 runners,

the grey was to the fore, forcing a nice pace: rounding the final bend, he was swamped by challengers and when headed looked set to drop out of the picture: to his credit, he illustrated steely resolution, to the extent, he rallied and up against the rail, was a staying on second at the winning post, suffering a defeat of under two lengths. Punchestown proved two items: he is a 2m 4f and upwards specialist and is as game as a pebble. Progeny of a new sire on the jumps scene, one well touted, the double green enjoyed many memorable days with Bristol De Mai and, in Green Hint, they could have their next grey star, one bound to yield plenty of exciting pay days.

HALFTHEWORLDAWAY (IRE) 4 b m Jet Away – Ballela To Moscow (IRE)
Trainer: Oliver GREENALL & Josh GUERRIERO Form Figures: 2
Angular bay mare with white stamp on crown: dam a sibling of 2022 Thyestes winner Longhouse Poet: a smart stores sale purchase at €9,000 for the Murphys and professional jockey Richie Deegan. Partnered by the trainer, Luke Murphy, she figured in one of the more upper class four-year-old mares' maidens run during the spring of 2025. The handler must have trusted in her ability because on the stiff galloping circuit at Curraghmore (RH : Soft), the mare set a solid tempo from the beginning, testing stamina. She jumped economically and had all bar Lime On Gin cooked by the final bend: she was reeled in by Lime On Gin approaching the last fence, going down by three lengths but a wide margin clear of the rest. On a day of quality racing at Curraghmore, the race clocked the fastest time, and Halftheworldaway played a major role on the clock. Her debut performance in defeat impressed Oliver Greenall & Josh Guerriero, as the team forked out €130,000 to acquire this young mare. An honest lady with a high cruise speed, she will be effective as a conditions hurdler/chaser in due course and can be placed to win a mares' bumper up north and hold her own to a fair standard as a novice hurdler.

HARDLY SURPRISING (IRE) 4 b g Affinisea (IRE) – Inquisitive Look
Trainer: Harry FRY Form Figures: 1
Average size bay: bred by the Shark Hanlon's other half, Rachel: a sibling to amongst other winners, 2020 Grade 1 Tolworth Novices' Hurdle victor Fiddlerontheroof: secured by team McManus at the 2024 Derby Sale for €80,000 and transited to Derek O'Connor for pointing. Sole start was at Ballycahane (LH : Yielding) in March, with Derek on the reins. Held up some way off the leaders, he clicked into gear on the gallop to the second last. Despite conceding upwards of half a dozen lengths to the front running Mister St Eloi, with the race whittled down to a match, Derek squeezed enough out of his charge to poke his head in front in the final strides, the verdict a head. He will make an impact inside the rails proper: he consented to settle and illustrated a most game attitude when the chips were down and the cards stacked against him. One might come to the conclusion, true run races would offer him comfort. Not necessarily a bumper type, he could evolve into one of those 120-140 staying handicappers liable to harvest some upper grade handicaps.

HARRY LOWES (IRE) 4 b g Walk In The Park (IRE) – Dazza
Trainer: Dan SKELTON Form Figures: 41
Angular bay with two white rear socks: €75,000 store acquisition for J.P.McManus, his dam won on the Flat at trips of five and six furlongs for Gary Moore, as a broodmare she has already produced the 120 rated hurdler Coniston George (an individual prone to flatter to deceive). The green/gold via the Derek O'Connor yard, fielded four of the nine runners in the 2m 4f maiden at Oldtown (RH : Yielding) in February, and with DO'C aboard, Harry was the number one string on the day. In truth, he let the side down: on the back foot once the pace was injected running

downhill from three out, he failed to bother the principals, not unduly punished in fourth, beaten by a lesser fancied stablemate amongst others. Then given a near two-month break, his next engagement was on local turf at Quakerstown (LH : Yielding) for a maiden containing a selection of fancied types. On this occasion, stepping up to three miles, he was put into the race entering the closing half mile. He attacked his market rival, Mighty Park, on the run to the final fence, and with a slick jump took the lead and held on to score by a length and a half. The time of the race was the fastest of the day and one senses once on his game he is talented. An individual liable to confuse: two somewhat indifferent point performances: all told when you consider his dam was a 5/6 furlongs sprinter, pigeonholing the offspring presents problems. For now, his optimum trip is up in the air.

HERNANDO DE SOLO (IRE) 4 b g Affinisea (IRE) – Gouyen (IRE)
Trainer: Gordon ELLIOTT Form Figures: 1

Tall, elegant bay: unraced dam a full sister to the 145 rated Western Ryder. Purchased by the Holdens at a price of €90,000 at the 2024 Goffs June sale, he proved to be one of two winners from the four-year-old age group, the Kilkenny based stable saddled in points during the spring and easily the best of the select team. Out in action, once, at Monksgrange (LH : Yielding/Soft) in late March: anchored at the rear, he gradually picked off his rivals and coasted to challenge rounding the home bend. Jumping with accuracy, he had the measure of his main threat, Chase The Moon, when said rival fell at the last, and Hernando De Solo kept on powering clear to score by eight lengths. A fine unit with loads of scope, he attracted attention at the Aintree Goffs sale, it took a bid of £230,000 for the hammer to fall in favour of team Elliott and KTDA Racing. An old-fashioned resolute galloper, with some natural speed, he can win Graded staying hurdles as a novice and he is bound to mould into a competitive 140+ staying chaser, a lovely loose mover with that critical appetite for action.

HIDDEN FORTUNE (IRE) 4 b f Soldier of Fortune (IRE) – Lady Pippa (IRE)
Trainer: Dan SKELTON Form Figures: 1

Rangy bay mare from a modest jump family. Reported for action once in the spring, lining up for a mares' maiden at Ballyraggett (LH : Good/Yielding) under the banner of Wexford handler Gary Murphy. Barry Stone rode and slotted in a pocket behind the leaders, until slipping through the inner at the third last to take the pole position. Hungry to please in the closing stages, he rolled out with conviction to score by five lengths. A mare with plenty of potential, no issue on the count of stamina and one with a fair future not just as a hurdler but also when heading chasing. Bought privately by Dan Skelton on behalf of owner Jarlath Patrick Conway.

HITINTHEHEADLINES (IRE) 4 bb g Harzand (IRE) – Larnalee (IRE)
Trainer: Dan SKELTON Form Figures: 1

Athletic bay with white markings on face: sibling to three track winners, Tom Cloke a long-time deputy to Denis Murphy, purchased him competitively for €16,000 at the 2024 store sales. He locked horns with some talking horses in an early spring four year old maiden hosted at Tallow (LH : Yielding): parked out rear in a race run at a good lick, he was six lengths down on the market leaders away from the third last: making steady headway, he was pulled out to challenge and appeared to hold all the aces, when his two rivals fell independently at the last, allowing Hitintheheadlines to land the prize by fourteen lengths. Dan Skelton was quick off the mark to purchase privately on behalf of Eventist Group Limited and there is nice scope and potential attached to the youngster. He did display a slight knee action, a hint soft/heavy will give him comfort. For now, a career as a handicapper in the 120-140 range is on the cards, with the possibility of more, if fortune visits him.

HOMEGROWN HERO (IRE) 4 b g Jukebox Jury (IRE) – Shesafoxylady (IRE)
Trainer: Olly MURPHY Form Figures: 1

Medium sized bay with white star in face and white rear sock. A €36,000 store, his dam was a three-times winner. Handler Tom Keating was confident pre-race and a market move (4/1 into 6/4) reflected same as the runners headed to post at Bartlemy (RH : Good) in May. Ridden with confidence, and also sited close to the leaders, his jockey, Adam Feeney, kicked for glory approaching the second last. Given a squeeze, Homegrown Hero put the race to bed and strode away to score by a non-flattering two lengths. It is positive to watch a young horse on his debut justify hype: he can lower the colours of talented rivals and has a fair crack at transitioning into a Listed/Graded standard track horse. He enjoyed the good summer ground at Bartlemy and it may be a vital ingredient for his future battles.

HOT TO GO (IRE) 4 bb g Maxios – Taylor (IRE)
Trainer: Nigel & Willy TWISTON-DAVIES Form Figures: 2

Chunky bay, €30,000 store half-brother to Custom Taylor. Under his trainer, Rob James, he forced an honest pace in one of the divisions of the four year old maiden staged at Lisronagh (LH : Heavy) in February: he was pressed by different rivals from halfway: on the way to the second last he held a small lead, which was wiped out when he blundered, allowing the Bowe trained rival, Cooltobecareless to wrestle the lead. Two lengths down at the last, Hot To Go, found for pressure and almost pegged back the Bowe trained winner. As happens, the winner Cooltobecareless and Hot To Go are both sons of Maxios: I take the view, the winner enjoyed the run of the race, whereas Hot To Go was a sitting duck and his mistake two out was pivotal in the result. I admired the manner in which he rallied close home and he has steel in his belly: qualities which certainly convinced the Twiston Davies team to offer a successful bid of £165,000 at the Cheltenham Festival Sale on behalf of owners Options O Syndicate. It was deep winter ground at Lisronagh, and he handled it.

JET TO MONTE CARLO (IRE) 4 b g Jet Away – Overnight Success (IRE)
Trainer: Emmet MULLINS Form Figures: 1

Racy bay with lots of white markings, especially on face: home bred by Douglas Taylor, the owner of the sire Jetaway. He is the first foal of an unraced mare, who is a sibling of Samcro. Taylor retained a share in his ownership when the young horse debuted out of the Nicky Stokes stable for a maiden at the Ballynoe (RH : Soft) fixture in March. In a nutshell, he was kicked out into an early lead by Finny Maguire, and posted an exciting aggressive all the way win, scoring by 14 lengths. He was flagging a little in the last couple of furlongs, and a case can be advanced, his style of racing may be better suited to shorter trips (2m - 2m 4f). He enjoyed an uncontested lead, and one wonders how he would function if pestered at the head of affairs. Willie Mullins liked his performance, yet a private deal apparently hit the buffers: the horse then failed to reach his reserve of £200,000 at a Tattersalls auction. He apparently has ended up with Emmet Mullins, and some suggest Paul Byrne is involved in the ownership. Hard to nail down a prediction for this lad: he has an engine, and my inkling is, he will be a boom or bust sort of campaigner.

KAKA'S COUSIN (IRE) 5 b g Mahler – Dancing Baloo (IRE)
Trainer: Jonjo O'NEILL Form Figures: F2

Muscular bay: €62,000 Monbeg store from the family of Oscar Whiskey. Raced twice for Sean Doyle: fell in the early stages at Loughrea (RH : Good/Yielding) on debut in the spring of 2024. Next appearance was for a decent maiden at Boulta (LH : Yielding) in December. He slowly made progress on the final circuit and loomed up travelling sweetly at the second last: from that juncture to the finish, he had a real ding-dong battle with Clay Pigeons and at the winning post, he came out the wrong side of a short head photo finish. With the race producing three subsequent winners, the form is reliable. Although he exits the Irish pointing code as a maiden, he is talented: Jonjo O Neill paid £160,000 for his services and decided to put him in cold storage: now acclimatised, he can kick on and win a 2m 4f – 3 miles maiden hurdle in the first half of the winter and one capable of making an impression as a fair 125-135 handicapper (hurdles or chases): could imagine he may land a punt one day.

KALKBRENNER (IRE) 5 b g Getaway (GER) – Coillte Alainn (IRE)
Trainer: Ben PAULING Form Figures: 14

Athletic bay: €45,000 store, several ordinary winners in immediate family. The December fixture at Tattersalls Farm (RH : Soft) saw the four-year-old geldings maiden divided and the Fogarty yard managed to win the two events. In the slower time, Kalkbrenner bagged the second division. He shared the lead from four out and in dogged workmanlike style outstayed his rivals. It earned him a visit to the sales and a £130,000 move to Ben Pauling. I found it odd, new connections lobbed him into the bumper at Ayr on Scottish National day, as the fast ground was a negative for staying types. And so it proved, Kalkbrenner was rather one paced in the closing stages, finishing fourth, though not punished. Perhaps, it was a run for extra experience. Still immature, 2m 4f and above over hurdles and fences will be his stomping ground, especially when there he encounters testing conditions.

KANZLER (FR) 4 b g Tai Chi (GER) – Kiss Me Lena (GER)
Trainer: Willie MULLINS Form Figures: 1

Medium bay gelding: cheap €4,000 foal when bought in France by J.D. Moore for Mick Goff. Sire a little-known entity, the dam won two modest flat races in France, and in general, the gelding has a Flat biased pedigree. One of three runners in a disappointing turn out for a maiden at Kirkistown (LH : Good/Yielding) in February: held up behind his two rivals, he played his cards at the second last and in a matter of strides he quickened away to secure an impressive win. Sold to the Mullins yard for £165,000, he strikes me as a horse likely to focus on races at the minimum two miles or 2m 4f as a hurdler and chaser. The change of gear on show at Kirkistown, if repeated will guarantee racecourse success, guesswork how far up the ratings ladder he will climb.

KINDLY PRINCE (FR) 5 b g Great Pretender (IRE) – Belle Princesse (FR)
Trainer: Emmet MULLINS Form Figures: 1

Tall lanky bay with broad white face: €100,000 two-year-old store from France: member of respectable jumps clan, his full brother has been Grade 1 placed. Competed for the Fogartys in a division of the four year old maiden at Lingstown (RH : Soft) in November: a contest run in blustery weather, saw him move from mid pack to lead four out: niggled along heading to the second last: once into a rhythm he really stretched out and increased his advantage to score by 16 lengths: on what was a decent fixture, Kindly Prince clocked the fastest time of the day, all the more remarkable given the weather he confronted during the race. A syndicate owned him when he won his point and they dispatched him to the Goffs November sale held at Newbury: the auction details suggest he sold to David Mullins for £320,000: in contact with David a few weeks later, he told me he had in fact bought back the horse for the owners (so no real sales transaction), and they were trying to organise a new syndicate and initially the horse was heading to Emmet Mullins. A maiden at Lingstown the previous pointing campaign unearthed Final Demand: Kindly Prince is of that ilk: strong galloper once he clicks into stride and therefore 2m 4f to 3 miles will suit. One harbouring live ambitions to capture a Graded hurdle as a novice and bound to become at least a 130+ chaser later in his career, though may be reliant on juice underfoot to be in his pomp.

LARGY GO (IRE) 4 b g Poet's Word (IRE) – Jo Go (IRE)
Trainer: Jonjo & A.J.O'NEILL Form Figures: 1
Chunky bay, €15,000 foal, dam won three track races in the care of Tony Martin. It was testing conditions at Loughbrickland (LH : Yielding/Soft) for the late March meeting: with eleven runners clashing in the four-year-old maiden, it turned out to be an oddball race: one of the runners steamed off a long way in front, which stretched out the field. As the front runner ran out of fuel around the third last, the complexion of the race changed: a few, including Largy Go took over. From two out to the finish, Largy Go battled away with Seven Towers for the gold: both fought honestly, with Largy Go claiming the prize by a couple of lengths. A taking victory from an honest broker: he raced for the Crawford team and they were quick to cash in their chips, selling via Aintree sales to Jonjo O Neill for £305,000. Poets Word is a new stallion on the jumps roster with stock on the ground and he has had positive reviews: Largy Go was his top performer from his first crop of pointers and all eyes will be on his produce going forward. One would expect Largy Go to develop into a smart novice hurdler and a 130+ staying chaser. Of note, the runner up, **SEVEN TOWERS**, a Walk In The Park, closely related to Cheltenham Gold Cup winner Lord Windermere, was later sold privately by the Ger Quinn stable and transfers to **Gavin Cromwell**: he too will make an impact on the track and it would not surprise if his new handler were to trace a path to getting him on an exploitable handicap mark over hurdles and fences.

LAZARE DE STAR (FR) 4 b Masked Marvel – Urbissa (FR)
Trainer: Gordon ELLIOTT Form Figures: 2
Well defined muscular bay, one white rear sock: €48,000 Derby Sale store in 2024: dam a French Flat winner. Raced once at Fairyhouse (RH : Yielding) in April: figured in a race which concluded with a mini dash after the second last: steered by his handler, Rob James, Lazare De Star was caught flat footed and in tight quarters when the tempo was injected: too far back to win as they advanced to the final fence, once extracted and having room to manoeuvre, he picked up and kept on making late headway and secured the runner up spot. Much promise in defeat. From the same sire as Teahupoo, he made appeal to Robcour who invested €190,000 to snap him from the Goffs Punchestown Sale. He has potential and enough raw material to offer a degree of promise.

LE FRIMEUR (FR) 4 b g Gemix (FR) – Ty Perrine (FR)
Trainer: Harry DERHAM Form Figures: 1
Lanky bay with white face: €50,000 store from modest French stock. First horse I have witnessed Pat Doyle handling on behalf of the double green partnership. Turned up at Nenagh (LH : Good/Yielding) in March for a seven-runner maiden. Held up, he survived a poor jump with a mile to travel: back on an even keel, once he met the uphill climb to the second last, his bit of class counted: he swaggered through to lead and jumping the last with his ears pricked, he strode out and won by seven lengths. Those behind have not done much to date to advertise the form, meaning one can simply gauge Le Frimeur on style over substance. He moves like an animal with gears and will win his quota of track races. Whether he becomes a mere bridle horse or has more depth and character will be answered in the fullness of time. He handled the sound underfoot Tipperary sod at Nenagh and given his pedigree ought to perform on softer terrain. Could be an ideal middle distance candidate over fences.

LEGENDARY LUKE (IRE) 5 b g Soldier of Fortune (IRE) – Mo Bury (IRE)
Trainer: Jamie SNOWDEN Form Figures: 1

Rangy bay with white marks on head and nose: €68,000 store, dam a sibling of Cheltenham Gold Cup winner, Native River. Sean Doyle turned him out at Ballycrystal (LH : Good/Yielding) in March to start off in a five-year-old maiden. Prominent all the way, from the home turn, he engaged in a duel with Eclat De Marvel, and both showed guts and resolve as they battled to the finish, with Legendary Luke claiming the glory by a length: the head-to-head shootout certainly assisted in producing the fastest time at the fixture. Sold to Jamie Snowden for £100,000, he can mould into a 130+ handicapper, with stamina tests his forte.

LIME ON GIN (FR) 4 b m Doctor Dino (FR) – Eminence Rouge (FR)
Trainer: Henry De BROMHEAD Form Figures: 1

Imposing bay mare: dual winning dam, a half-sister to Gin On Lime and Lord Rouge, purchased for €95,000 by Robcour at the 2024 store sales. Sent to the Denis Murphy nursery for her pointing education and commenced action at Curraghmore (RH : Soft) on Easter Sunday. In a 14 runner mares' maiden where they went a proper clip from the start, having settled out the rear, she advanced forward heading down the back straight the final time. Rounding the final bend on the approach to two out, she tackled the leaders: striking the front between the last two fences, she attacked the last and eased away to score in style, defeating what looked like a decent rival in Halftheworldaway. Judged on the performance, she may be a superior product than her sibling Gin On Lime, and for starters, she has more in the way of stamina. One of the top four-year-old winning efforts amongst the mares of the age bracket: she has the class and attributes to become a Listed/Graded level winner over hurdles/fences within the mares only category.

LOVE SIGN D'AUNOU (FR) 4 b g Goliath Du Berlais (FR) – Ossun (FR)
Trainer: Willie MULLINS Form Figures: 1

Chunky bay with a white star on head: €70,000 store, son of a three-time French winner, his dam has produced some average winners already. Running for Ger Quinn, he was popped into one of the competitive maidens for four-year-olds staged at Loughanmore (LH : Good/Yielding) on Easter Saturday. It is a race which has a tradition of unmasking above average talent: for example, the 2023 edition was won by Jasmin De Vaux. All the trainers in the north/Ulster region save a decent horse for the race. Love Sign D'Aunou raced up with the pace, though his jumping was messy: still upsides in a battle heading off the final bend with one to jump, he was left clear when his main threat ran out through the wing of the final fence (It's Party Time) and he kept on to win by over a length. He has natural toe, the same cannot be said about his jumping technique. Moved on a private sale to join Willie Mullins and he looks like he has the necessary goods for a bumper, and more if the Closutton maestro can nurture him to the maximum.

MASKED MAN (FR) 4 b g Masked Marvel – Mangenie (FR)
Trainer: Nigel & Willy Twiston-Davies Form Figures: 1

Muscular bay: €70,000 store purchase for the double green partnership out of an Arqana Sale in 2023: dam a three-time winner. Sibling to three winners, including another successful in the double green silks, Batman Girac. Handled by the Crawfords for his sole point, at Stowlin (RH : Good/Yielding) in East Galway at the start of May. In a race run at a consistent pace, he was initially dropped out the rear. On the closing circuit, he crept into contention and by the second last he was challenging for the lead. In a matter of strides he took control and swept clear to score by a dosen lengths. A silky smooth and polished display. He enjoyed the manner in which the race unfolded: he settled and relaxed and was suited to attacking off a nice pace. He has an engine and lots of potential, traits such as battling quality under pressure has yet to be tested. Nonetheless, lots of promise from his first run.

MIDTOWN MANHATTAN (IRE) 4 b g Order of St George (IRE) – Clara Allen (IRE)
Trainer: TBC **Form Figures: 1**
Racy bay with white sash on crown: dam five times winner, she has bred Major Destination (125 rated chaser). €40,000 store in 2024 for Colin Bowe. Travelled from the Bowe base in Wexford, across country to Ballysteen (LH : Yielding) in Limerick and pitched for a maiden won by Faugheen in the past. The opposition looked modest, and Barry O'Neill assumed an early lead aboard Midtown Manhattan and with his mount razor sharp in the jumping department, they were in control at all times and once travelling downhill to the penultimate fence, a winning lead had been established and he won unbothered by over six lengths. It could be tight tracks, fast ground and the ability to dominate may be his desirable requirements. He fetched a price of €205,000 when sold to Noel Fehily: might a sound surface be key to his optimum output?, if so, he may excel in summer jump racing and find life more complex in the higher quality winter fare. Ought to be able to win a moderate bumper at the beginning of his track career.

MIGHTY PARK (IRE) 4 b g Walk In The Park (IRE) – Knotted Midge (IRE)
Trainer: Willie MULLINS **Form Figures: 2**
Athletic bay: €105,000 store, that price linked to the fact, Might Bite (2018 Gold Cup runner up), is an older sibling. Housed with the Monbegs and touted as smart early in the spring, it was not until Easter Sunday at Quakerstown (LH : Yielding) that he was introduced to competitive action. Partnered by Rob James, Mighty Park bided his time in midfield before he moved to the lead at the second last: instantly tackled by Derek O'Connor on Harry Lowes, they had an exciting battle to the winning post, with Harry Lowes, having the advantage of previous racing experience, edging the verdict. I gather Mighty Park impressed Derek O'Connor and he advised team green/gold (J.P.McManus) to buy the gelding in a private transaction and the plan is for Willie Mullins to take him under his wing. Loads of scope with this gelding and he could be a fair article going forward. Might Bite possessed some negative quirks and regressed with age, and one could reason the first half of his track action was the best. Will this apply to Mighty Park?, he will win track races, more evidence will be needed to form a sounder verdict on his ability range.
NB: The four year old maiden at Quakerstown on Easter Sunday has been won by The Big Breakaway (2019), Brewin'upastorm (2017), Next Destination (2016), Bacardys (2015) and Champagne Fever (2011).

MINELLA MACHINE (IRE) 4 b g Blue Bresil (FR) – Queen Alphabet (IRE)
Trainer: Henry DE BROMHEAD **Form Figures: 1**
Rangy bay: dam seven-time winner, she liked good ground: her progeny to date includes two upper class mares, Four Clean Aces and Jubilee Alpha. A €62,000 store acquisition by John Nallen from the 2024 store sales. Stepped out for a 12-runner maiden at Curraghmore (RH : Soft) on Easter Sunday, encountering a selection of quietly fancied rivals. Settled off the early pace, he advanced from five out and rounding the home turn with two to jump he was firmly in contention. He charged to the front between the last two fences and had matters in hand when the second placed, Bande Organisee, decked at the final fence: his departure resulted in a 24 lengths margin of victory for Minella Machine. He certainly enjoyed the proper test of three miles offered by Curraghmore and we have seen smart horses emerge from the Waterford

estate point fixtures in recent times, such as Gentlemansgame and Nick Rockett and the track promotes genuine staying types. Minella Machine falls under this banner. He can evolve as a better than average staying novice hurdler and chaser and should enjoy a fair degree of success on the track. Sold at Goffs/Punchestown to Robcour for €350,000. **BANDE ORGANISEE** (son of Bande) indicated he too would be a smart cookie in time: despite his late fall, he made a price of €125,000 at the sales and moves to **Rebecca Curtis** and I am certain he will be an individual who leaves the Irish point world a maiden, but will showcase his talent on the track proper and pay to follow in the middle grades.

MISTER ST ELOI (FR) 4 b g Jeu St Eloi (FR) – Miss Frog (FR)
Trainer: Olly MURPHY **Form Figures: U2**
Tall athletic bay: dam French Flat winner. Well punted in the ring for his debut in the 2m 4f maiden staged at Knockanard (RH : Heavy): running for the Alan Ahern stable, he was tracking the leader when he was basically knocked over at the fourth last and exited proceedings. He made a relatively quick reappearance, eight days later at Ballycahane (LH : Yielding), this time racing at the three miles trip. He forced a nice pace from the drop of the starter's flag: he had all of his rivals in trouble advancing towards two out, save for Derek O'Connor aboard the McManus newcomer, Hardly Surprising: in front to the tune of about three lengths away from the last, Mister St Eloi either idled or his tank was running dry, and it was not until the final stride he surrendered the lead, cruelly denied by a head. With the winner, he drew 14 lengths away from a subsequent four-year-old maiden victor, giving substance to the form. The simple fact he ran twice in eight days, hints he is a hardy customer and clearly talented. Recruited by Olly Murphy for £180,000, it could be, he will be in his pomp in the 2m-2m 4f range, and he may not be a pure three mile stayer. He handled the softer terrain in his two races and such underfoot conditions may be his bag. He is a 130+ hurdler/chaser in the making with upside.

MOMENTS IN TIME (IRE) 4 gr g Kingston Hill – Wyndham Rose (IRE)
Trainer: Dan SKELTON **Form Figures: 1**
Muscular grey: dam unraced has produced 2024 hurdle winner A Perfect Day: €20,000 store for Gary Murphy. Posted an exciting win at Borris House (LH : Yielding) in March: jumping with accuracy, and always to the fore, he turned the screw after two out and burned off his rivals, rocking up to win by 24 lengths. With the runner up and fourth home winning their own maidens later in the campaign, the form looks reliable. He has the traits of an exciting front running grey over fences, and one due plenty of respect until he is exposed. Sourced privately by Dan Skelton, he is owned by Jarlath Patrick Conway.

MOSSY FEN COOLIO 5 b g Kayf Tara – Little Acorn
Trainer: Jonjo & A.J.O'NEILL **Form Figures: 1**
Sturdy bay gelding, €80,000 store for the Monbegs, grandson of Cheltenham Festival winning mare, Whiteoak. Without question he posted one of the slickest and most taking winning efforts by a five-year-old during the spring and rightly earned a high p2p.ie rating. At Tallow (LH : Yielding) in February, he coasted through a maiden, and for minimum persuasion drew right away from three out and scored by 25 lengths with plenty left in his tank: on visuals, well above average. Virtually doing a solo for the closing half mile, and winning eased down, it was noteworthy he clocked the day's fastest time by seven seconds, no mean feat. Joined Jonjo & A.J.O'Neill in a private transaction and he will win some valuable pots over hurdles or fences and will either mould into a candidate for premier handicap chases or even higher up the ladder in the elite staying chases. He functioned smooth as silk on the good/soft or yielding surface

at Tallow and as a tall individual, some element of juice in the ground may be vital for him to produce of his best.

NO WALKOVER 4 b g Poet's Word (IRE) – No Pushover
Trainer: David PIPE Form Figures: 2
Chunky muscular bay, dam half-sister to Wishfull Thinking, she won a bumper for Nicky Henderson and already has produced the winner Laganhill. Running for the local Andy Slattery yard on his debut at Lisronagh (LH : Heavy) in February, positive pre-race vibes was reflected in market support as he traded odds on as they left the start. He ghosted through from mid-pack to lead three out, and was still in front when tackled at the final fence by Cristal D' Estruval: No Walkover ploughed through the fence, losing momentum and his jockey also lost the irons: about two lengths down with fifty yards to race, he rallied to tremendous effect and closed to a neck at the line. A most unlucky loser, the moral winner of the race. It was admirable with the odds attacked against him, he was prepared to battle back close home. Certainly, the premier pointer from the Slattery farm in 2025, he sold privately to David Pipe and rates as his best young recruit, one who has genuine prospects of elevating to Graded class as a hurdler/chaser. He is owned by Mr G.Thompson.

RISKY OBSESSION (IRE) 4 b g No Risk At All (FR) – Dual Obsession
Trainer: TBC Form Figures: 1
Robust bay sporting a white face and two white socks: a €70,000 store, half-brother to nine-time winner, Ask Paddington. Racing for Matt O'Connor, he was to the fore in the betting market for one of the four-year-old maiden divides at Ballyknock (RH : Good/Yielding). Brian Lawless had confidence in his mount as he allowed the gelding to pop away in front: in the closing couple of furlongs, he managed to maintain a decent tempo and resisted two late challengers, ultimately scraping home by a head. As a smooth slick jumper, he may be seen to better effect, should he in time, drop down to two miles or 2m 4f over fences. Sold to Noel Fehily for €170,000, and another customer of the 120-140 variety.

SALVADOR LORD (IRE) 5 ch g El Salvador (IRE) – Lady Wagner (IRE)
Trainer: Rebecca CURTIS Form Figures: 1
Chunky chestnut: €16,000 store, plain pedigree. Tipperary based handler Eddie Power handled the gelding and they travelled up to Fairyhouse to contest a maiden for five-year-olds in April on yielding terrain. Ridden from the front and crisp with his jumping: he quickened away from the second last to establish a winning advantage and kept on to win by six lengths. He looked a sharp customer, and the type likely to enjoy courses like Wincanton or Kempton, which favours freewheeling front runners. Sold to Rebecca Curtis for €125,000, and will probably achieve more as a chaser than over hurdles.

SOOMAROY (FR) 4 ch g No Risk At All (FR) – Version Toujours (FR)
Trainer: Nicky HENDERSON Form Figures: 1
Bulky and flashy chestnut: dam Flat winner, another offspring a half-sister has twice won 1m4f flat handicaps in France. Norman Williamson sold him for €42,000 to Jim O'Neill at the 2024 Goffs Summer sale. Ran for O'Neill (brother of jockey Barry), at Ballyragget (LH : Good/Yielding) in March, facing up against nine others. Dropped in for two miles, keeping his powder dry, he made good headway during the closing mile and pressed for the lead three out. He was left with a clear advantage after two out, due to a runner upsides falling: to the finish he drove along merrily to prevail by four lengths. A fine natural jumper, despite possessing French Flat

bloodlines, he has the shape of an old fashioned three mile chaser. Sold to Nicky Henderson at a price of £190,000, and his long-term targets may be the premier staying chases at Doncaster or Newbury.

STARMOUNT (IRE) 5 b g Mount Nelson – Sparky May
Trainer: Ben PAULING Form Figures: F1
Chunky bay with white blaze on face and distinguishing white rear socks: fair pedigree, dam (Sparky May) was a four-time winner and his half-brother is Grade 1 winner Stage Star. The Fogarty's had him under their charge for two Autumnal points in 2024. On debut at Damma House (LH : Good/Yielding) in November, he was held up, before closing ranks on the final lap: a few lengths down and sitting second when he fell at the penultimate obstacle. Different tactics were deployed four weeks later at Tattersalls Farm (RH : Soft) in December: booted out in front, from the third last he had three different threats to contend with, yet to his credit, he dug deep and managed to find enough on the extended run in (normal last fence omitted) to secure a two lengths win. Sold to Ben Pauling for £82,000, I suspect he may not be the complete physical package, because given his page, he probably ought to have commanded a bigger transfer fee. Should win races for new connections and it could be 2m 4f and some cut in the ground will be his preferred playground.

TALES OF BRAVERY (IRE) 5 b g Affinisea (IRE) – Hannah Maud (IRE)
Trainer: Dan SKELTON Form Figures: 1
Muscular bay, €50,000 store for Monbegs, full brother to four-time winning mare, Bluey. Handled by Eamonn Doyle, he made his only appearance at Ballinaboola (LH : Soft) in February in a five-year-old maiden. His jumping was indifferent, yet he had the engine under his bonnet to power to the front two out and post a six lengths win, in the fastest three-mile race on the card. Far from the finished article, he had a knee action and soft/heavy terrain may be vital ingredients for him to prosper. A stout stayer.

TAURUS BAY (IRE) 4 b g Poet's Word (IRE) – Tea Time Tilly (IRE)
Trainer: Ben PAULING Form Figures: 1
Well defined/muscular bay with white spot in head: unraced dam, €26,000 store. Represented Denis Murphy for the four year old maiden at Comea (RH : Yielding) in February (7 runners). He settled in rear was asked to close at the third last: soon he picked up to lead away from the second last and kept on willingly to score in workmanlike fashion by two and a half lengths: in winning he became the first victor for his sire between the flags. Sold to Ben Pauling for £155,000 at the Cheltenham February Sales and hard to evaluate as the form remains rather hollow. Should perform to a decent level as a 2m 4f novice hurdler and his comfort zone may be 125-140 handicaps.

THE BURREN MAN 4 b g Maxios – Ryme Bere (FR)
Trainer: Harry DERHAM Form Figures: 2
Fine big bay: sibling to three winners, €68,0000 store shared by Donnchadh Doyle and Paurick O'Connor with the former winning the toss to train the gelding. Paurick managed to convince his brother, Derek, to partner the horse for a maiden at Dromahane (LH : Yielding) in April. In truth, it was a steer which allowed the horse to show his wares without having six bells knocked out of him. He progressed through the field to challenge from three out and, try as he might, he could not peg back the front running Wyoming Line: a four lengths second his lot. Very impressive from a physical stance, he needs time to muscle up his immense frame and in 12 -18

months, he may be primed to yield better outcomes. Acquired by Harry Derham for €180,000, he is a fair prospect, if allowed the time to flourish.

THE IRISH AVATAR (IRE) 4 b g Poet's Word (IRE) – Dinaria Des Obeaux (FR)
Trainer: Willie MULLINS Form Figures: 2
Chunky and muscular bay: €100,000 store, his dam won five races for Gigginstown House Stud. Pointed for Colin Bowe just the once, at Dromahane (LH : Good/Yielding) in April and contested one of the season's rock-solid maidens: a race with an earnest gallop throughout. He moved up to dispute the running after four out: rounding the final bend, a fleet of horses were in the picture for the top prize. He shared the lead two out and at the climax from the final fence, he failed to master Ballycommon Boy, going down by two and a half lengths. Plenty of encouragement from the performance and I felt he had the scope to bring more to the party in due course. Spotted by team Closutton, they forked out £200,000 at the Cheltenham April Sales and, given the dam was seen to best effect racing at 2m - 2m 4f, her son could follow suit. Whilst he remains a maiden as he exits the pointing domain, he has bright prospects of winning a bumper and could even book a spot in the Mullins bumper team for the Cheltenham Festival 2026.

TRINITY STREET (IRE) 4 b m Mahler – Boskill Lady (IRE)
Trainer: Henry DALY Form Figures: 1
Attractive and athletic bay: €38,000 store for Timmy Hyde, unraced dam, she has produced multiple winners from previous offspring. Handled by Sam Curling and with Josh Williamson riding in his grandfather's colours, the mare commenced action in the four-year-old mares' maiden at Ballindenisk (RH : Good/Firm) in May. She crept through the pack to post her challenge at the second last: producing a gear too high for her rivals, she opened up a lead and was untaxed to score by five lengths. She rattled off the firm underfoot conditions and sold to Henry Daly for £115,000, ought to figure in a mares' bumper and can bag mares' novice hurdles and more.

UN SENS A LA VIE (FR) 5 b g Muhtathir – Kpalime (FR)
Trainer: Nigel & Willy TWISTON-DAVIES Form Figures: 3 - 11
Rangy light bay with white face: €50,000 store, dam winner in France and lots of winners associated with equine clan. Showed a glimpse of ability when a well held third to Theflyingking at the 2024 Loughanmore (LH : Good/Yielding) Easter fixture. Returned in the Autumn for Denis Murphy and managed to shed his maiden tag in a four-year-old maiden at Loughrea (RH : Yielding). As a race which unfolded as a late dash, he arrived to press for the lead taking the widest berth: and in a driving finish managed to win by a neck. Following a mid-winter sale to Twiston Davies (£180,000), he track debuted in February at Market Rasen (2m : Good/Soft): he led the bumper with a circuit to travel and resisted all threats and won going away by over three lengths. Now a winner at two and three miles and successful on yielding and good/soft, he is talented and versatile and seems to have progressed from age four to five. He will succeed in the maiden/novice hurdle ranks and capable of placing at Grade 2 or 3 standard as a novice hurdler.

VANDERFLIER (IRE) 5 b g Milan – Maiden City (IRE)
Trainer: Jonjo & A.J.O'NEILL Form Figures: 31
Strapping bay with white star on head: €52,000 store, produce of an unraced dam. Housed with Sam Curling, he lost no honour in defeat on his Boulta (LH : Yielding) debut in December:

he was amongst the leaders over the second last and failed to match the lethal finish of Gee Force Flyer, a four lengths third his lot. He was the full package next time at Bellharbour (LH : Good/Yielding): steered with confidence by Derek O'Connor, he made a decisive late move at the final fence to outkick Talk To The Boss. Switches to Jonjo & A.J. O'Neill at a £155,000 tariff and can emerge as a fair 125-140 staying handicap chaser.

WITH NOLIMIT (FR) 4 b g Bande (IRE) – La Pampalina (FR)
Trainer: Gordon ELLIOTT Form Figures: 1
Medium bay: dam half-sister to Welsh Grand National winner, Le Beau Bai. Brought by the Fogartys to commence point action at Liscarroll (LH : Yielding) in late March. He bombed out in front and freewheeled: Liscarroll suits aggressively ridden horses. Generally, four to six lengths ahead of the chasing pack, rounding the top bend and swinging downhill to the penultimate fence, it appeared as though his pursuers would reel him in: it was not to be, he found again after the second last, and kept on rolling to the winning line and won by ten lengths. It was notable, it took his jockey a further half mile to pull him to a standstill after the winning post. A freak performance or perhaps a rare gem...difficult to say. Bought by Gordon Elliott for £250,000 at the Aintree Goffs sale; with his natural speed winning a bumper should not be a problem: could be mould into a contender for the Cheltenham Festival bumper in 2026?, possible, I suspect he will have to tone down his bold attacking style to conserve energy against top bracket opponents or else he will be found out. The most prominent member of his immediate family is a premier marathon winner, this gelding may locate 2m 4f as his optimum distance as a chaser.

STABLE SWITCHERS

The following section highlights horses who have changed stables since last season, either being transferred or acquired at a public sale.

Following the retirement from the training ranks of North East based Pauline Robson during the summer, her string have been relocated. They include stable star **DOYEN DU BAR** who has joined **Nicky Richards**. Owned by Eric Elliott, father of bloodstock agent Alex, he is a talented but fragile nine year old. Successful in half of his twelve career runs, he won twice over hurdles during the 2023/2024 season acquiring a rating of 120. The Doyen gelding has taken his form to another level though since sent over fences winning three out of four last winter. Ironically, he defeated his new stablemate The Kalooki Kid (won twice since) by a length in a novices' handicap chase at Ayr (2m : Good) in November off 120. He then followed up in a similar event at Aintree (2m : Soft) on Boxing Day defeating the subsequent Greatwood Gold Cup winner Booster Bob by a length and a quarter off a three pounds higher mark. Runner-up at Sandown in January, he rounded off his second season over fences with a six and a half lengths victory at Ayr (2m : Heavy) in February making all under Craig Nichol. Raised five pounds to a mark of 131, he ought to be a force in the decent two miles handicap chases in the North. Despite the fact he has won on good ground, his form figures on soft/heavy ground are 121148121. The Castleford Chase at Wetherby (27th December), which is a 0-150, looks tailormade for him. Even though he has yet to race beyond two miles one, there is a feeling he will stay further, too.

The Cumbrian trainer has also taken charge of three ex-James Ewart inmates after the Borders based handler relinquished his licence earlier this year. The trio includes **JO COKO** who has made the relatively short journey (49 miles) from Westerkirk near Langholm to the outskirts of Penrith. He won an Irish point before being acquired for a six figure sum (£105,000) in the spring of 2024. The Cokoriko gelding gained an official rating of 112 following three runs over hurdles for Ewart last term. Former champion jockey Brian Hughes was at the wheel on each occasion finishing a length and a quarter runner-up behind Ski Lodge at Haydock (3m : Soft) in early December. Third next time behind the 125 rated Ayiko at Ayr under similar conditions the following month, the six year old was beaten in excess of thirty lengths at Newcastle (2m 4f : Good/Soft) over three weeks later. Officially rated 112, there is a feeling **he is well handicapped and shouldn't be missed in novice handicap chases this term for his new trainer**.

Dan Skelton forked out £11,000 for the ex-Ewart trained Beat Box in May 2024. The gelded son of Cokoriko arrived in Warwickshire with an official rating of 89 over fences and proceeded to win six of his next seven starts for his new connections. He is now rated 129. Paul Nicholls' former assistant has returned to the same source to acquire the lightly raced **THISTLE ASK** for the same amount. Having begun his career with Stuart Crawford in Northern Ireland, the eight year old won twice for Ewart, including on his second run over fences at Musselburgh's Trials meeting (2m : Good/Soft) in early February. A four and a half lengths victor of a 0-125 handicap chase off a mark of 108, he doesn't look overburdened off 115. Skelton is eyeing some of those valuable two miles handicap chases and with only a couple of runs over the larger obstacles in his log book, there could be plenty of improvement forthcoming.

A winning pointer in Ireland when trained by Andrew Latta, **KEPLER'S LAW** is a fine looking gelding by Jack Hobbs. Purchased privately by owner Alan Rogers, he was sent to Laura Morgan in Leicestershire. Having seen him in the flesh on his hurdles debut at Aintree (2m 4f : Good) last Autumn, he is a striking individual and, while no match for Mister Meggit, Adam

Wedge's mount shaped encouragingly in third having been hampered before the hometurn. He filled the same position in the The French Furze Novices' Hurdle at Newcastle (2m 6f : Good) three weeks later. Given a break of 52 days, he shed his maiden tag under Rules when defeating five opponents by upwards of 30 lengths at his local track Leicester (2m 4f : Heavy) in January. Leading before the second last, he sauntered clear with his trainer waxing lyrical afterwards: **"He is a gorgeous horse who we are so excited about going over fences next season. He is one of the best I have ever had and we have schooled him over fences – he was class."** A remote eighth in the EBF Final at Sandown (2m 4f : Good/Soft) in March, he reportedly got struck into and is better than he showed that day. Officially rated 127, the six year old has been transferred to **Christian Williams** and rates a cracking prospect for novice handicap chases.

Anthony Bromley has been a huge supporter of *One Jump Ahead* and the *Updates* over the years and the leading bloodstock agent has forwarded some information regarding a few promising youngsters owned by Simon Munir and Isaac Souede, for whom he is racing manager.

LOOK ME was denied by half a length in the valuable Tattersalls Ireland George Mernagh Memorial Sales Bumper at Fairyhouse (2m : Soft/Heavy) on Easter Sunday. Trained by Stuart Crawford, the Jeu St Eloi gelding led over a furlong out only to be headed inside the final 100 yards by Robert Tyner's I'm Slippy – the race's roll of honour features subsequent Grade 1 winners Brighterdaysahead (2023) and Kopek Des Bordes (2024). Transferred to **Willie Mullins** since, he looks a smashing prospect for novice hurdles for team Double Green.

Another once raced Crawford inmate on the move is **TALK THE TALK** who is now residing at Piltown, Co.Kilkenny, the home of **Joseph O'Brien**. A four year old by Born To Sea, he was a £70,000 store and is from the family of Cheltenham Festival winner Elimay and Goshen. Fitted with a tongue tie on his racecourse bow in the Goffs Hundred Grand Bumper at Newbury (2m : Good) in March, James Bowen's mount stayed on well in second behind the more experienced winner Kadastral. Beaten three and a quarter lengths, he was two lengths ahead of the third. It will be disappointing if he can't win a maiden hurdle before going on to better things.

CUSHENDALL also began her career with Stuart Crawford and she is now owned by Million in Mind and in training with **Alan King**. A cheap store (€8,000), the daughter of Getaway is a fine big filly with scope and she was strong in the market on her debut in a small field mares' bumper at Kelso (Good) towards the end of May. Brian Hughes' partner was held up during the early exchanges before making ground in the homestraight. Leading a quarter of a mile out, she readily pulled away to record a two lengths win. The form amounts to very little but the five year old demonstrated speed – covered the third last furlong in 12.34 seconds, according to *Race Iq*. Anthony was keen to point out that the partnership have had a successful connection with the Crawford family over the years with nine of the ten purchases from them winning in the Million in Mind silks, including The Organist, Largy Poet and A Moments Madness. Their latest transaction is expected to make an impact in mares' novice hurdles this time around.

POETISA beat some well regarded opponents in an eighteen runner mares' bumper at Cheltenham (2m 1f : Good) in April when trained by Thetford based Toby Bulgin. A four year old filly by Poet's Word, she was a £42,000 store and is a half-sister to Grade 2 hurdle winner Queenohearts. Still unfurnished, she did plenty wrong during the race – raced keen and didn't come down the hill particularly well – but took off in the closing stages under Brian Hughes to lead a furlong out and prevail by a neck. Sent to the Goffs UK Spring Sale at Doncaster the following month, she had reportedly thrived physically and was bought by **Gigginstown House Stud** for £300,000 and will go mares' novice hurdling with **Willie Mullins**.

Staying in Ireland, impressive Thurles bumper winner **TIM TOE** was bought privately by **Robcour** and has joined **Henry De Bromhead** to go novice hurdling. A four year old by Joshua Tree, he was trained by Pat Doyle and ridden by his son David on his debut in March (2m : Good). Despite being hampered on the hometurn, he quickened up readily to lead a furlong out before stretching clear to win by a length and three quarters (third has won twice since). Blessed with an abundance of speed, he hit a top speed of 38.22mph and covered the penultimate furlong in 11.94 seconds, according to *Race Iq*. Doyle snr said afterwards: **"He is a very smart horse and had been showing us that the whole time. He was too pacey and probably hadn't enough height to go point to pointing so we decided to wait for a bumper. He is big enough though, has always been showing a lot of gears and is a very good horse. It's only now I have him ready and I'm sure he'll handle bad ground as well."** Timmy O'Byrne and his father John, of The Lodge Stud in County Waterford, have educated Grade 1 winners At Fishers Cross, Banbridge, Carlingford Lough, Inothewayurthinkin, and Spillane's Tower and the former commented in April: **"I think we sold a very nice horse to Robcour recently called Tim Toe. I bought him for Roddy (O'Byrne) from Kieran Cotter and he could be a very good horse."** Two mile novice hurdles will be on his agenda.

Finally, as discussed in Rich and Susannah Ricci's interview, their famous pink and green silks will be sported by the ex-Paul Nolan trained **KARA SACRE** for the first time this campaign. A five year old by Karaktar, he was an impressive winner of his point-to-point when trained by Sam Curling (Heavy) in April 2024. Bought soon afterwards by Nolan, he was absent for nearly a year before finishing runner-up in a nineteen runner maiden hurdle at Naas (2m : Good/Yielding) in early April. Inclined to race enthusiastically, he was fitted with a hood next time when third behind Black Soul at Down Royal (2m 1f : Good) a month later. Reported to have hung left throughout, it is possible he will always be at his best racing left-handed. Stepped up to middle distances at Listowel (2m 4f : Good) last time, he didn't appear to get home in fourth. Now under the guidance of **Venetia Williams**, he needs to learn to relax but there is no doubt he has potential, especially over fences. Rated 116, he is one to watch out for in two miles novice handicap chases this winter.

ONE JUMP AHEAD & AHEAD ON THE FLAT *UPDATES*

"MERCHANT (William Haggas) *represents Highclere Thoroughbreds Racing (won it four times) and William Haggas (won it with Desert Hero in 2023) and is rated 90. Bred by Jim Bolger, he was a €135,000 yearling and improved in each of his three races last year. A narrow winner over an extended mile at Wolverhampton over Christmas, he was held up on his handicap debut at Newmarket's Guineas meeting (1m 2f : Good/Firm). Lacking the acceleration to get involved, the Teofilo colt stayed on in third behind Lightning Mann (runner-up in the London Gold Cup since) off 82. Eleven days later, he tackled a mile and a half for the first time at York (Good/Firm)and the improvement was marked. Ridden more prominently, he led going easily quarter of a mile from home before putting the race to bed quickly. A two and a half lengths winner, he beat the Queens Vase bound Rahiebb (third won since) decisively. Raised eight pounds since, this has been his target all season. Baghdad won the same York handicap prior to following up here off the same mark (90)."* **Advised @ 13/2 WON the King George V Handicap Stakes at Royal Ascot @ 3/1**

"ETHICAL DIAMOND (Willie Mullins) *is one of two leading contenders for Willie Mullins who is bidding to win the race for a third time (Sesenta (2009) & Absurde (2023)). Purchased for 320,000gns in July 2023, the five year old is rated 104 on the Flat and 143 over hurdles. A two lengths winner of the Duke of Edinburgh Stakes at Royal Ascot off 96, he finished fourth in the same event in 2024. Kept fresh since (64 days), he was fourth in the County Hurdle at the Cheltenham Festival in March and is accustomed to the hussle and bustle of large field handicaps. His record over twelve furlongs is 141 and handles any ground. If he stays, the Awtaad gelding looks set to play a leading role – he hasn't raced beyond a mile and a half on the Flat and is inclined to race keenly. With William Buick likely to be on board for the first time, the key to his chance could be how he settles early on.* ***Best Price: 8/1 (Bet365, William Hill).*** **Advised @ 8/1 WON the Sky Bet Ebor at York**

BIG RACE SUCCESSES

GREATWOOD HURDLE – BURDETT ROAD Advised @ 5/1
KING GEORGE – BANBRIDGE @ 7/1
WILLIAM HILL HANDICAP HURDLE – JOYEUSE Advised @ 8/1
CORAL CUP – JIMMY DU SEUIL @ 16/1
GRAND NATIONAL – GRANGECLARE WEST (3rd) Advised @ 66/1
9 WINNERS @ ROYAL ASCOT 2025
***SKY BET* EBOR – 1st & 2nd ETHICAL DIAMOND Advised @ 8/1 & ASCENDING Advised @ 25/1**

For full details of the *One Jump Ahead Updates* see pages 191-197 and the *Ahead On The Flat Updates* pages 199

APPENDIX

The purpose of the *Appendix* is to highlight those horses who are expected to make a major impact in the top prizes - both over hurdles and fences - during the 2025/2026 campaign and are discussed in the various categories.

Two & Two and a Half Mile Chasers

MARINE NATIONALE is the reigning holder having won the Queen Mother Champion Chase at the Cheltenham Festival (Good/Soft) by eighteen lengths. Barry Connell's stable star benefited from his rival's jumping frailties before following up at the Punchestown Festival. A seven lengths winner from ten year old Captain Guinness, El Fabiolo hit the deck at the second last, while stablemate Fact To File looked in trouble a long way from home. His trainer said afterwards: **"I think this horse has all the attributes to be a multiple Champion Chase winner. Our target is to win three and equal Badsworth Boy. He is only eight. He grows an extra leg at Cheltenham."** The French Navy gelding is a four times Grade 1 winner and unbeaten at the Cheltenham Festival but remains vulnerable to a top notch two miler.

There hasn't been a home trained winner of the Queen Mother Champion Chase since Politologue in 2020. Nicky Henderson has won the coveted prize on six occasions and the Seven Barrows team may hold the key to the 2026 renewal provided **SIR GINO** can regain full fitness and confirm the brilliance we witnessed last winter. The five year old has only raced once over fences producing an awesome display on his chasing debut in the Grade 2 Wayward Novices' Chase at Kempton (2m : Good/Soft) over Christmas. The ex-French gelding, who had won the Grade 1 Fighting Fifth Hurdle at Newcastle on his previous start, had reportedly schooled exceptionally well over fences with Henderson commenting: **"He's a very, very talented horse and we've always known that. He's so good at it chasing, you haven't seen a horse over a fence like that. He's unbelievable. He's like all those good two milers we've been lucky enough to have, he's as good as we've seen."** He jumped beautifully at the Sunbury track treating triple Grade 1 winner Ballyburn with disdain and winning hard held by seven and a half lengths. His jockey Nico De Boinville remarked: **"He's got an enormous engine. The fences come up fast here, you have to stay but you have to be able to jump at speed, and it suited Sir Gino. He's improved for a fence."** Due to contest the Game Spirit Chase at Newbury in February, he reportedly suffered a bang on his hind leg which was sore. By the 10th February, the It's Gino gelding had got an infection in a wound to a near hind leg and was ruled out for the remainder of the season. While it appears unlikely Sir Gino will be running before Christmas and he lacks chasing experience, he is one of the most talented horses in training and it is hoped he returns to action at some stage this term. If turning up in March, he will be a major threat to all. Voy Por Ustedes (2007) and Master Minded (2009) were the last two 6yo's to win the Champion Chase.

Paul Nicholls has also won the two mile championship event on six occasions and he is hopeful **KALIF DU BERLAIS** will be a force in the top events over the minimum trip this winter and beyond. The Masked Marvel gelding is officially rated 156 having won three of his five starts over fences last season. Unlucky not to be unbeaten over two miles over fences, he skipped the Arkle Trophy at Cheltenham and was kept fresh for Aintree. The five year old provided Team Ditcheat with their eighth win in the Grade 1 Maghull Novices' Chase when making all and scoring decisively by three and a half lengths. **"He's a seriously good horse. I'd have loved**

to have run him in the Arkle because I think he would have gone very close, but he came here fresh. He's a very smart horse and I thought he'd win today. He's been working great, he's maturing – the world's at his feet. I'd like to think that he's real Champion Chase horse for next season," enthused his trainer afterwards. His jockey Harry Cobden added: **"Jumping was the name of the game there, and Kalif Du Berlais was foot perfect all the way round. He's very forward going – he's what you want, he's an out and out galloper. I can't believe how much he's improved this season. He's one we're really excited about."** The ex-French gelding is expected to reappear in either the Grade 2 Haldon Gold Cup at Exeter (7th November) or Shloer Chase at Cheltenham (14th November) before a tilt at the Tingle Creek Chase (6th December). The fourteen times champion trainer has won the Sandown showpiece a record twelve times. His form figures over two miles are 111F111.

J.P.McManus has never won the Queen Mother Champion Chase and, having fluffed his lines in March, one can't help feeling **JONBON** has missed his chance. Despite the fact he is a dual winner at Cheltenham, his record at the Festival is 222 - beaten 22, 5.5 and 18 lengths. There has speculation this Autumn that the nine year old could be aimed at the King George but connections will find it difficult to resist the temptation of the Tingle Creek once again as he bids to emulate Flagship Uberalles and win it for a third time. His form figures at the Esher track are 111112.

Even though he finished a remote fourth in the Champion Chase at the Punchestown Festival (2m : Yielding), it is not beyond the realms of possibility **FACT TO FILE** will be tried over the minimum trip once again - form figures 224. The Poliglote gelding has produced two brilliant displays at the Cheltenham Festival, including when trouncing Heart Wood by nine lengths in the Ryanair Chase in March (2m 4f : Good/Soft). Willie Mullins said afterwards: **"On that performance he's a Gold Cup horse. J.P. (McManus) didn't want him to have a real hard race in a Gold Cup this year. Sometimes that can ruin a horse's career. I'd imagine the Gold Cup is where he'll be aimed next year."** Mark Walsh did the steering and reported: **"That sort of distance suits him, as you can let him gallop on and let him use his jumping. He never missed a beat today, he winged everything and he's just happier going on that stride. I was struggling to pull him up at the finish, so there's loads left."** His overall record at the Festival is 211. The John Durkan Memorial Chase at Punchestown (23rd November), which he won last year, is likely to be his first port of call. That performance will determine his Christmas engagement with the King George at Kempton a possibility. Regardless of which race he contests in March, he will be a leading player because, along with Sir Gino, he is one of the most gifted horses in National Hunt racing at present.

That comment also applies to one of my favourites **MAJBOROUGH**. Still only five, he is already a triple Grade 1 winner, including twice over fences last season. Prior to his chasing debut at Fairyhouse in December, Willie Mullins commented: **"Being a Triumph Hurdle winner, I think he will go on to be a three miler, may be even a Gold Cup horse later in his career."** A nine lengths winner of the Grade 1 Irish Arkle Novice Chase at Leopardstown (2m 1f : Yielding) at the DRF, his trainer said: **"He's only five and does things so naturally. Funnily enough, last week I wanted to school him and Mark Walsh wasn't around. I just made up my mind on the spot that I wanted to school him one morning, so I told Paul (Townend) to get upon him, which he wouldn't normally do, but I told him that I'd like to see him sitting on him anyway. Paul got down off him and couldn't get over the power of him. He said when he got down to a fence, he couldn't believe the power he had, he just shot forward. When**

he impresses someone like Paul, I thought that was a big statement, especially on just a schooling morning." Sent off 1/2 favourite for the Arkle Trophy at Cheltenham, he blundered away his chance with two crucial errors in the homestraight and, yet was still only beaten three parts of a length. According to *Race Iq*, the J.P.McManus owned gelding was travelling at 32.03mph when making his mistake at the second last. Despite showing a tendency to jump to his left, the former Daniela Mele trained gelding made amends with a comprehensive victory in the Barberstown Castle Novice Chase at the Punchestown Festival (2m : Yielding) - one of 15 winners, including 9 at the highest level, at the meeting for his trainer. Following his fourteen lengths victory, Mullins said: **"He has similar attributes to Fact To File. They're tall and athletic with huge strides, and hopefully can keep improving. He's well over seventeen hands. He's huge but light framed and the moment he stepped off the lorry at home, I thought he could be some article. He's still only five and a summer's grass will help him come back bigger and stronger again. I'm looking forward to what he might be able to show over the next two years."** It remains to be seen whether he is campaigned over two miles to begin with - the John Durkan Chase is an option if stepped up in distance, although his preference for racing left-handed tempers enthusiasm for Punchestown. There aren't many options over two miles on left-handed tracks in Ireland before Christmas. Yet to race beyond two miles one, I remain convinced he is a stayer provided he learns to relax and will be even better over longer trips. J.P.McManus has an abundance of top staying chasers, including the reigning Gold Cup holder Inothewayurythinkin, but **I wouldn't put any reader off backing the former Triumph Hurdle winner at 25/1 for the Cheltenham Gold Cup in March** (Betfred, Ladbrokes, Paddy Power, Skybet, Unibet). Best Mate, War of Attrition, Kicking King and Kauto Star were all campaigned over two miles during their novice chase careers.

Staying Chasers:

Gold Cup winners **GALOPIN DES CHAMPS** and **INOTHEWAYURTHINKIN** will continue to be hard to beat in the big staying chases with the Savills Chase and Irish Gold Cup at Leopardstown in late December and February respectively on their agendas before returning to Cheltenham in March.

Willie Mullins has won the King George VI Chase at Kempton twice (Florida Pearl (2001) & Tornado Flyer (2021)) and it is hoped **GAELIC WARRIOR** lines up in the Christmas showpiece on Boxing Day. Following a difficult first half of the season, the Maxios gelding came good in the spring recording his fourth Grade 1 victory in the Bowl Chase at Aintree (3m 1f : Good/Soft) under a fine ride by Patrick Mullins (2121), who was having his first experience of the Mildmay course. A three lengths winner from Grey Dawning, his jockey said afterwards: **"I don't think we've ever had a horse with the attributes and foibles he has. He's so unique and such a character."** Paul Townend (211111U1231) took over in the saddle in the Grade 2 Oaksey Chase at Sandown (2m 6f : Good) on the final day of the season and the seven year old outclassed eight opponents winning by five lengths. His form figures over three miles are 11 and his record racing right-handed is 1111121.

Rebecca Curtis has trained four Grade 1 winners but none since 2020. The Pembrokeshire based handler tasted Cheltenham Festival glory for a sixth time in March when stable star **HAITI COULEURS** won the National Hunt Chase (3m 6f : Good/Soft) by four and a half lengths. Ben Jones (22121) was on board and said afterwards: **"It was a walk in the park really. I didn't really ask him to quicken until we turned for home. I felt like I had loads left and he galloped all the way to the line. I still don't think we've seen the best from him."** His trainer added: **"I always felt the further he goes, the better. He'll definitely stay four miles, no bother. He loves Cheltenham, stays well and has got a high cruising speed."** The eight year old produced an even better display to win the Irish National at Fairyhouse (3m 5f : Soft/Heavy) beating thirteen year old Any Second Now by three and a quarter lengths off a mark of 141 and becoming the first British trained winner for eleven years. Sean Bowen (411131) did the steering and said afterwards: **"He was just doing a half speed the whole way around and I was hacking. Haiti Couleurs got into such a good rhythm, he jumped amazingly. He sweated up and it wasn't smooth beforehand but as soon as we jumped he got into such a good rhythm."** Equally impressed was Curtis who remarked: **"It's a big jump from winning a handicap to becoming a Gold Cup horse but there's no reason why he can't keep progressing to that level. I'll train him with that goal in mind. We'll try him early in the season in races like the Charlie Hall or the *Betfair* Chase, and the horse will tell us how good he is. If not, we'll look at races like the Welsh National or the Grand National. He's still a novice, so I think there's lot of improvement to come."** A winner of four of his five races over fences, his official rating climbed from 122 to 152. His record on stiff/undulating tracks is 21211. The Charlie Hall Chase at Wetherby (1st November) looks a suitable starting point.

Few novice chasers made a bigger impression during the first half of last season than **THE JUKEBOX MAN** until injury robbed him of the opportunity of competing at the spring Festivals. The seven year old suffered a hairline fracture of his cannonbone in January. Placed three times in Grade 1 company over timber, including when narrowly beaten in the Albert Bartlett Novices' Hurdle in 2024. Ben Pauling's charge jumped superbly on his fencing bow in the Grade 2 John Francome Novices' Chase at Newbury (2m 4f : Good/Soft) in late November winning by two lengths. **"I always thought I hadn't had one as good as Barters Hill. He was an exceptional talent and I think this lad might be the same. At home, he's as slow as a hearse, but on the track he finds another gear."** Owned by Harry Redknapp, he gained his first Grade 1 win when defeating Hyland by two and a half lengths in the Kauto Star Novices' Chase at Kempton (3m : Good) on Boxing Day. Leading two out, Ben Jones' mount strolled clear to win comfortably. **"He got better as the race went on and I do think there is a lot of improvement to come. He's had a few sore heels in behind all week, so I've been working on that all the time. Going down to the start he was never moving with the exuberance he would've wanted and I was watching the race and wondering when he was going to let fly. Ben said he was so much quicker and accurate, and almost a better jumper today. He was probably feeling those heels early in the race before warming into it."** Off since, his first target is expected to be the Grade 2 Copybet 1965 Chase at Ascot (22nd November) followed by the King George VI Chase at Kempton. His record over three miles is 1221.

MYRETOWN is rated 142 having won three of his five races over fences. The former pointer, who cost £135,000, won a handicap at Wetherby (2m 3f) on Boxing Day off 121 before taking a crunching fall at Windsor's Million Festival when still in front. None the worse, Lucinda Russell's charge made all before beating three rivals by upwards of nine and a half lengths at Kelso (2m 7f : Soft) in mid February. The eight year old then provided his stable with their third win in the Ultima Handicap Chase at the Cheltenham Festival (3m 1f : Good/Soft) in the last four years. By the same sire as Grade 1 winning stablemate Ahoy Senor, the Dylan Thomas gelding was partnered by Patrick Wadge for the first time and he never saw another rival before staying on strongly to defeat fellow novice The Changing Man by eleven lengths off 127. His trainer commented afterwards: **"We knew that if Myretown jumped round, he was phenomenally well handicapped. I just didn't know if he was going to be man enough. He's a novice, his**

jumping has been a bit hit and miss, he turned upside down at Windsor, but then we ran him at Kelso and he's got his confidence back. He's a bit different to Corach Rambler – he jumps so exuberantly." Raised fifteen pounds since, the eight year old is set to reappear in the £50,000 Edinburgh Gin Chase at Kelso - 2 from 2 at the track - on Saturday 25th October followed by a crack at the Coral Gold Cup at Newbury (29th November) - the aforementioned Corach Rambler finished fourth off 147 in 2022. Expect the lightly raced chaser to make an impact at the Berkshire track before contesting Graded events.

Staying Hurdlers:

Willie Mullins has won the Stayers' Hurdle twice (Nichols Canyon (2017) & Penhill (2018)) and, despite winning at Grade 1 level over fences, **BALLYBURN** is likely revert back to timber. Rated 162 over hurdles compared to 159 over fences, the Flemensfirth gelding looked a superstar during his novice hurdle career winning four of five, including three Grade 1 victories at Leopardstown (2m), Cheltenham (2m 5f) and Punchestown (2m 4f) in 2024. Things didn't go to plan over the larger obstacles finishing a disappointing fifth in the Brown Advisory Novices' Chase in March. Bred to stay well, the seven year old is a half-brother to a 3m 4f winner and he could emerge as a Stayers' Hurdle candidate next March.

Former Cheltenham Festival bumper winner and stablemate **JASMIN DE VAUX** was a slow burner over hurdles last term before coming good in the spring. The Tirwanako gelding finished fourth in Grade 1 novice hurdles at Naas (2m 4f) and Leopardstown (2m 6f) before stepping up to three miles in the Albert Bartlett Novices' Hurdle at the Cheltenham Festival (Good/Soft). With the headgear dispensed with, the six year old was given a patient ride by Paul Townend before running on powerfully to beat the mare The Big Westerner by two and a half lengths. Around seven weeks later, the Simon Munir and Isaac Souede owned runner did well to overcome a mistake at the last before denying Aintree winner Honesty Policy by half a length in the Grade 1 novice at the Punchestown Festival (3m : Yielding) with the pair six lengths clear of the rest. Unbeaten at Cheltenham and over three miles, he isn't always easy on the eye but is a triple Grade 1 winner and has a lot of ability.

Gordon Elliott has indicated **THE YELLOW CLAY** will head down the staying hurdle route and could reappear in the Grade 2 Lismullen Hurdle at Navan (16th November) - 2 from 2 at the track. A faller at the Punchestown Festival last time, the six year old won four times over hurdles, including the Grade 1 Lawlor's of Naas Novice Hurdle (2m 4f : Soft) in January. Three parts of a length runner-up behind The New Lion in the Turners Novices' Hurdle at Cheltenham (2m 5f : Good/Soft), it was a career best effort by the Yeats gelding. Yet to run beyond two miles five, his form figures in Grade 1 company are 6212F. The Cullentra team have won the Stayers' Hurdle twice and he has strong credentials.

Grade 1 winning novice **POTTERS CHARM** will remain over the smaller obstacles and tackle three miles for the first time under Rules. Rated 145, the six year old needs to improve to make a splash in the staying division but it is possible he will progress over longer trips. The Nigel & Willy Twiston-Davies trained gelding was in excellent form during the first half of last season winning his first four races over hurdles, including the Grade 1 Formby Novices' Hurdle at Aintree (2m 1f : Soft) on Boxing Day. Prior to that, he had won twice at Cheltenham (2m 4f & 2m 5f) in October and November. **"We haven't had one like this for a while I don't think. I've always said this horse is the apple of my eye,"** enthused Willy Twiston-Davies in late October. Past his best by the time he lined up in the Turners Novices' Hurdle at the Festival, he looks tailormade for the Grade 2 West Yorkshire Hurdle at Wetherby (1st November) - his stable won it with Redemption (2006) and Pettifour (2008) - before contesting the Grade 2 Long Distance Hurdle at Newbury (29th November). Later on, the Grade 2 Cleeve Hurdle at Cheltenham in January is likely to be on his radar.

Finally, **MISTER MEGGIT** is a very talented performer but has hadn't much luck during his short career. The seven year old suffered a fractured skull when getting hampered in the championship bumper at Aintree last year. Most impressive on his hurdles debut at the same track (2m 4f : Good) in November, the Jonjo & A.J.O'Neill trained runner was then sidelined until the spring due to a setback. Returning from an absence of 146 days, the Hemmings Racing owned gelding had reportedly only been back in training five weeks prior to the Grade 1 Sefton Novices' Hurdle at Aintree's Grand National meeting (3m : Good). Last off the bridle, Jonjo O'Neill jnr's mount travelled beautifully until making a mistake at the final flight and losing his momentum. Eventually beaten two and a half lengths in fourth, his run at Perth next time should be ignored. Granted luck and a clear run, the son of Shantou can bag a big prize off his rating of 136 - **he is tailormade for the £100,000 *Betfair* Stayers' Handicap Hurdle at Haydock** (22nd November). By all accounts, he will be schooled over fences in the Autumn and then a decision will be made whether to stay hurdling or go chasing. Either way, he has a lot of ability.

ONE FOR HANDICAPS

JUBY BALL is rated 129 over hurdles and remains unbeaten over the smaller obstacles. Well bought at €38,000, he is a younger sibling of the *Betfair* Hurdle second Fifty Ball and Willie Mullins' exciting youngster Kaiser Bell. A bumper winner at Ffos Las the previous campaign, the Nom De D'La gelding returned from a break of 343 days to win on his hurdles debut at the same venue in January having missed an intended engagement at Sandown's Tingle Creek fixture (travel problems) in early December. Travelling well in behind the leaders, he moved up after the third last before leading at the final flight. Pushed clear to register a four lengths win, the runner-up Lud'or won next time. Less than a month later, he produced an even better display under his penalty at Chepstow. The six year old raced enthusiastically before putting his stamp on the race in the homestraight. Still on the bridle after the second last, he stretched away to score hard held by half a dozen lengths from the 119 rated Ben Solo.

Due to a dry spring, Juby Ball hasn't been sighted since and has only raced four times during his career. Favourably treated over hurdles, his future lies over the larger obstacles, but it is possible his connections will attempt to win a valuable handicap over timber beforehand. Granted suitable conditions, the Greatwood Hurdle at Cheltenham (16th November) is an option. His stable sent out Quoi De Neuf to finish fourth off the same mark in 2019, while Silver Streak was runner-up off 145 the previous year. There is a big prize to be won with Juby Ball.

ANTE-POST ADVICE – GRAND NATIONAL 2026

Irish trained runners have won 7 of the last 9 renewals of the Grand National at Aintree with Lucinda Russell being responsible for the two home trained successes, One For Arthur (2017) and Corach Rambler (2023). The official ratings of the last six winners have been 159, 146, 147, 146, 159 and 163 and all of the last ten winners have been aged between seven and nine.

Willie Mullins has won the last two renewals, including with Nick Rockett last season. The eight year old was only having his ninth run over fences and was a second season chaser. He began the campaign rated 150 having finished seventh in the Irish National and third in the Bet365 Gold Cup as a novice. Last term, he followed the traditional Closutton Grand National route, namely the Thyestes Chase at Gowran followed by the Bobbyjo Chase at Fairyhouse. The Walk In The Park gelding won at Aintree off a mark of 163. I like his prospects of his stablemate **QUAI DE BOURBON**. Officially rated 151, the ex-French gelding has only raced a handful of times over fences winning at Gowran Park (2m 4f) in January. He failed to complete in Grade 1 novices at Cheltenham and Aintree in the spring but was travelling well on both occasions. The six year old was particularly unlucky at the latter when getting brought down by the fatal fall of his stablemate Dancing City who impacted on Handstands six out. Patrick Mullins was on board and commented afterwards: **"Quai De Bourbon is jumping and travelling well. We had a chance, we had a big bloody chance."** Sent off 11/2 favourite and the mount of Paul Townend in the Irish National at Fairyhouse on Easter Monday, he finished less than ten lengths third behind potential Gold Cup candidate Haiti Couleurs conceding seven pounds having held every chance between the last two fences. While his jumping still needs attention, the raw talent is there and he remains lightly raced and unexposed over staying trips. Expect him to follow a similar path to Nick Rockett this winter.

MONTY'S STAR has only won one of his eight races over fences and realistically isn't going to win the Cheltenham Gold Cup. Therefore it is hoped the eight year old is steered towards Aintree next spring, especially with the same connections Minella Indo now enjoying a well earned retirement. Officially rated 159, he jumps and stays and five of his eight races over the larger obstacles have been in Grade 1 company. Restricted to four outings last term, he finished seven and three quarter lengths fifth behind Galopin Des Champs in the Grade 1 Irish Gold Cup at Leopardstown in February. The second, third and fourth that day were Grangeclare West, Fact To File and Inothewayurthinkin. Henry De Bromhead's eight runners at the DRF produced form figures of 75467009. Fourth in the Cheltenham Gold Cup, it was creditable run considering the Walk In The Park gelding made a bad mistake at the ninth and was then hampered by the fall of Ahoy Senor. His last run in the Punchestown Gold Cup behind Galopin Des Champs when a distant third of four should be ignored because, once again, the stable's runners performed poorly at the Festival - 0 from 29 with only two placed. With only fourteen career starts, he remains low mileage and will have a new jockey this term following the retirement of his regular partner Rachael Blackmore (rode him nine times).

Advice: **QUAI DE BOURBON** (40/1 Bet365, 33/1 Ladbrokes, Paddy Power, Skybet) & **MONTY'S STAR** (40/1 Bet365, Unibet, William Hill).

INDEX

SELECTED HORSE = BOLD *Owners' Enclosure & Talking Trainers = Italics*

Don't forget to read my Diary @

www.mhpublications.couk

ONE JUMP AHEAD UPDATES

I shall be producing **5 One Jump Ahead *Updates*** throughout the 2025/26 National Hunt season. Each *Update* comprises information about the horses in ***One Jump Ahead,* Ante-Post Advice** (recommendations for the major races), **Big-Race Previews**, **News from Ireland** from one of the most informed Irish experts Declan Phelan and **Significant Sales. Please note, the *Updates* are ONLY AVAILABLE VIA EMAIL (Not Post).**

It is £12 per *Update* (except £15 for the Cheltenham Festival version) or £63 for ALL 5 via **EMAIL**.

Summary of the 2024/2025 *Updates:*

What The Clients Said:

"Congratulations on your King George advice Banbridge at 33/1. Tremendous tipping and well deserved for the work you put in." **M.S.**

"Congratulations on nominating Banbridge for the King George in OJA. What an inspired ante-post selection from yourself. The trophy price of 33/1 was gratefully taken. Keep up the good work!" **S.H.**

The PADDY POWER MEETING 2024

6 WINNERS FROM 12 SELECTIONS: TRANSMISSION (11/4), DOYEN QUEST (Advised @ 3/1), HAMSIYANN (Advised @ 5/1), PEAKY BOY (9/5), ABUFFALOSOLDIER (Advised @ 6/1), BURDETT ROAD (Advised @ 5/1). Plus: LETS GO CHAMP (Advised @ 14/1 – 3rd @ 15/2), SURREY QUEST (14/1 – 2nd)

Quote: *"Tony Martin won this a couple of years ago with Unanswered off a mark of 111 and stablemate* ***HAMSIYANN*** *lines up here off an identical mark. The four year old has only raced four times over hurdles having been bought for €250,000 in July 2023 out of Jean-Claude Rouget's yard in France. Twice a winner over middle distances in his native country, the son of Lope De Vega was placed over hurdles at Ludlow and Ascot (1m 7f : Good) last spring. A length and a quarter behind Royal Way on his handicap debut at the latter track in March off 109, he stayed on strongly suggesting a longer trip will suit. Back on the level, he stayed on strongly in second behind stable companion Alphonse Le Grande in the Chester Cup consolation (2m 2f : Good/ Firm) off 87 in May. The winner subsequently 'won' the Cesarewitch at Newmarket only to lose the prize in the stewards' room (has been reinstated since). He was conceding thirteen pounds, too. Unexposed, he appears to have been lot in lightly here off a feather weight of 10st 2lb. Speedo Boy won this as a four year old in 2018. Daniel King, who has ridden 42 winners in Ireland (0 from 7 at Cheltenham) will do the steering."* **Advised @ 5/1 WON @ 2/1**

Quote: *"****ABUFFALOSOLDIER (Warren Greatrex)*** *has only raced seven times over fences winning by ten lengths at Newbury (2m 6f : Good/Soft) off 120 in January (wore cheekpieces for the first time). Beaten less than five lengths behind Sharjah in a decent novices' handicap chase at Ayr (3m : Soft) in April, the seven year old shaped nicely under top weight on his seasonal return at Exeter (3m : Good/Soft) last month. Attempting to make all, he jumped boldly out in front and, despite being headed two out, he rallied and stayed on to fill the runners-up berth off 129 conceding twelve pounds to five year old Jupiter Allen. It is worth noting the cheekpieces (134) were left off but expect them to be refitted here. Placed on the New course over hurdles on New*

Years Day in 2023, his four career wins have been gained on good and good to soft ground. His second time out record is 112 and Sean Bowen will take the ride, unless the weights rise, in which case his brother James (105261342) will be on board once again. Yet to race beyond 3m 1f, the Mahler gelding is from the family of smart chaser Kingsmark who was fourth in the Grand National." **Advised @ 6/1 WON @ 100/30**

Quote: *"**BURDETT ROAD (James Owen)** is rated 109 on the Flat having won the Golden Gates Handicap at Royal Ascot last year and the Listed Godolphin Stakes at Newmarket (1m 4f : Soft) by eight and a half lengths (runner-up has won a similar event since) in late September. Sixth behind Kyprios in the Group 2 Long Distance Cup at Ascot on champions day last month, he looks potentially well treated over jumps off a mark of 133. The former Roger Varian (0 from 3) and Michael Bell (3 from 8) trained four year old has only raced three times over hurdles winning twice at Huntingdon and Cheltenham – including a Grade 2 juvenile hurdle at this meeting last year. Ten lengths runner-up behind Sir Gino on the New course in January, he was ruled out of the Triumph Hurdle due to a minor setback. However, he has looked better than ever on the Flat this summer/ autumn and James Owen has his string in splendid form – 12 winners from 43 runners in the last fortnight. Four 4yos have won the race this century with Old Guard (2015) being the latest. Harry Cobden (2 from 3) is expected to be back on board. **Best Price: 5/1 (generally)**."* **Advised @ 5/1 WON the Greatwood Hurdle @ 5/1**

French Revolution – Part II: **KURASSO BLUE (9/2), LADY VEGA ALLEN (2nd in Grade 2 at Leopardstown (26/12/24) on his Irish debut @ 10/1 & 4th in the Triumph Hurdle), LIVE CONTI (Runner-up in the Grade 2 4YO Hurdle at Aintree (3/4/25) @ 16/1), LULAMBA (4/5, 11/10), MISS ALTEA BLUE (4/5), ZAOCHEN ENKI (Evens).**

Quote: **LULAMBA**: *"Another Auteuil winner who has found his way to the UK, he is a cracking type who is residing at Seven Barrows in Berkshire. Arnaud Chaille-Chaille, of Galopin Des Champs fame, trained him to win the Prix Isopani (2m 2f : Heavy) at the Parisian track last month. A big scopey gelding by Nirvana Du Berlais, he was positioned on the outside in mid division by Florent Bayle before making a move halfway down the backstraight. Switched to the inside, he jumped upsides at the final flight before pulling away on the run-in to register a five lengths victory. The form has yet to be fully tested, although the fifth won at the same track last week, and the Chaille-Chaille horses tend to improve with experience. He could be top-class. As discussed in the Introduction, Nicky Henderson has won the Triumph Hurdle on seven occasions but not since 2019, although Sir Gino would have gone close last spring. The former champion trainer may have unearthed another major contender for March. Like Sir Gino, he belongs to Joe and Marie Donnelly."* **Grade 1 winner at the Punchestown Festival and runner-up in the Triumph Hurdle at the Cheltenham Festival**

Talking Trainers: **JAMES OWEN: WINNERS: BURDETT ROAD (7/2), EAST INDIA DOCK (4/5 & 1/2), JUBILANT (2/1), LAVENDER HILL MOB (Evens), ONE BIG BANG (11/2), OPEC (9/2).**

Quote: **BURDETT ROAD**: *"He is in great form at home and runs in the Greatwood Handicap Hurdle at Cheltenham on Sunday (3.30). Lightly raced over hurdles, he has been running very well on the Flat this summer/autumn winning the Listed Godolphin Stakes at Newmarket by a wide margin. The form has been franked since with the runner-up winning a similar event on the all-weather. We have been riding him more positively on the Flat and I think he has enjoyed that. Sixth in the Group 2 Long Distance Cup at Ascot on champions day, I thought it was a hell of run behind Kyprios considering it was two miles on heavy ground and he is only a four year old. It is easy to forget he is only four. If he translates his Flat form to jumping, he should be very competitive on*

Sunday. He won a Grade 2 juvenile hurdle on the Old course at Cheltenham last season and we know he stays well. A well run handicap ought to suit him and his preparation has gone well. I think he will be progressive over hurdles." **WON the Greatwood Hurdle @ 7/2**

Quote: **OPEC**: *"A full-sister to Allmankind, she was unlucky on her hurdles debut when falling at the second last at Market Rasen during the summer. She made amends winning nicely at Wetherby next time and then we decided to give her a bit more experience at Fakenham a fortnight later. Despite the fact the track didn't suit her, she won well enough and the handicapper has given her a mark of 107. Her target is the Listed fillies' juvenile hurdle at Newbury (29th November). She is a nice progressive filly."* **WON Listed fillies' juvenile hurdle at Newbury (29/11/24) by 8 lengths @ 9/2**

Other **WINNERS**: **GIBBS ISLAND (100/30 & 4/1), HELLO NEIGHBOUR (9/4 & 85/40), KEPLER'S LAW (7/4), LAVENDER HILL MOB (Evens), MELON (8/15 & 4/1), MISS CYNTHIA (11/4), ST PANCRAS (33/1 & 1/5), THEY'RE CHANCERS (13/2), WENDROCK (3/1)**

Quote: *"It is 28 years ago since Rough Quest won the Grand National for owner **Andrew Wates** and trainer Terry Casey. The same patron paid 95,000gns for the improving three year old **ST PANCRAS** who has joined **Toby Lawes**. Bred by Cheveley Park Stud and out of a Group 2 winning mare, he raced three times for Richard Hannon before being transferred to Martyn Meade mid summer. A dual winner at Pontefract (1m 4f : Good) and Southwell (1m 6f), the son of Siyouni scored by seven lengths at the latter venue and is a strong stayer. Rated 86, he has only raced seven times and appears suited by decent ground."* **WON twice, including the Listed Scottish Triumph Hurdle at Musselburgh (1/2/25) @ 33/1**

CHRISTMAS SPECIAL 2024

KING GEORGE CHASE: WINNER: BANBRIDGE (7/1)

Talking Trainers: **OLLY GREENALL & JOSH GUERRIERO: WINNERS**: **JAGWAR (4/1 & 3/1), MELON (4/1)**

Quote: **JAGWAR**: *"A progressive young chaser who is a much stronger horse this season, he jumps fences very well. A winner at Wetherby and Bangor, we don't think he was at his best last time when finishing third at Uttoxeter. He was quiet afterwards and it explains his slightly lacklustre effort. He was strong at the finish in both his wins over fences but that wasn't the case at Uttoxeter. We have given him a break since and may bring him back for the novices' handicap chase at Cheltenham's Trials meeting (25th January). Two and a half miles suit him, although I think he will stay three miles eventually. He is learning to settle now because he was quite keen over hurdles last season."* **WON twice at Cheltenham, including the Festival @ 4/1 & 3/1**

The Irish Angle by Declan Phelan: WINNERS: HERON IN THE PARK (4/1), KOVANIS (Evens), KSAR FATAL (Evens), ROAD EXILE (4/9)

Quote: *"As ever, the Monbeg brand produced smart winners: out of the 15 maidens exclusively confined to mares in the four year old age category, the most taking victor was **HERON IN THE PARK**: she oozed class when scoring at Borris (good) in December: she has gears and in winning she clocked the fastest time on a card which also included two 4 year old gelding maidens and a decent Open lightweight: a mare with size, she is a sibling of the 2022 Betfair Hurdle winner*

Glory And Fortune and she commanded a price of £280,000 at the Tattersalls Sale in December and has joined Tom George. She is a mare I advise you pay respect to." **WON on Rules debut in mares' bumper at Newbury (1/3/25) @ 4/1**

Quote: *"A steel grey gelding called* ***KOVANIS*** *maintained a strong gallop at Portrush (good ground) in October, pulling clear from two out to defeat a stacked field readily, clocking a fast time. Sold to Gordon Elliott and Gigginstown for £330,000, he looks a readymade Graded class jumper and more than capable of winning an ordinary bumper. Entered at Leopardstown & Limerick on Saturday (28th December): he will give a good account in his chosen engagement."* **WON at Leopardstown (28/12/24) on his Rules debut @ Evens**

Other **WINNERS: BIOLUMINESCENCE (4/5), CASUAL OBSERVER (6/4), LA ZOUBIDA (5/2), LE TIEP'S SACRE (100/30), THEY'RE CHANCERS (13/2)**

Quote: *"**BIOLUMINESCENCE** featured in Declan Phelan's Irish Pointers section last season and the J.P.McManus owned mare justified her inclusion winning twice including a Grade 3 mares novice hurdle at Limerick (2m 6f) in March. A big strapping six year old, she is built for fences and returns to the same C&D on Friday for the Grade 2 mares' novice chase (1.27). The more rain the better for Gavin Cromwell's mare whose first time out record is 12. The daughter of Walk In The Park is reunited with Derek O'Connor who steered her to her point-to-point win in November 2022. Her course form is 21 and a bold showing is expected."* **WON Grade 2 mares' novice chase at Limerick (27/12/24) @ 4/5**

FEBRUARY 2025

WILLIAM HILL HANDICAP HURDLE: WINNER: JOYEUSE (Advised @ 8/1 – WON @ 9/2)

Quote: *"**JOYEUSE (Nicky Henderson)** is number 39 on the list at the time of writing and therefore isn't guaranteed a run. However, if the daughter of No Risk At All makes the cut, then she is very much shortlist material. From the family of Champion Hurdle winner Epatante, she hails from the same source, namely Armand Lefeuvre for whom she won an AQPS Flat race in October 2022 before being snapped up by J.P.McManus for €235,000 the following month. The six year old has only raced three times over hurdles for Nicky Henderson and looks favourably treated off a mark of 123. A half length winner at Taunton on her UK debut in January last year, she missed the remainder of the season with her stable struggling for form in the spring. Six and a half lengths third in a Introductory Hurdle at Ascot behind Celtic Dino, she was reportedly in need of the run that day. She then made her handicap debut in a mares' event at Cheltenham (2m 4f : Good/Soft) in mid December and ran well in second off 119. Nico De Boinville's mount moved strongly through the contest until meeting a few traffic problems in the homestraight. Staying on well behind the unbeaten Woodhooh (6 from 6 and rated 136), she was beaten a length and three quarters in receipt of eight pounds. The third Take No Chances claimed the notable scalp of Grade 1 winner Kargese in a Grade 2 mares' hurdle at Ascot next time giving the form a very solid look. Raised four pounds since, she remains well handicapped and the drop back in distance is unlikely to pose any problems. A winner on good and soft ground, she has plenty going for her. **Best Price: 8/1 (Betfred, Bet Victor, Ladbrokes, Paddy Power, Skybet, William Hill).**"* **Advised @ 8/1 for the William Hill Handicap Hurdle at Newbury (8/2/25) WON by 8 lengths @ 9/2**

ANTE-POST SELECTION:

GRANGECLARE WEST @ 66/1 for the Grand National at Aintree – 3rd @ 33/1

The other potential runner whose profile I like is ***GRANGECLARE WEST*** *– one of ten entries trained by Willie Mullins. Unfortunately, like Inothewayurthinkin, there is an element of risk of backing him ante-post due to the fact one of the qualifications is that the horse must have raced at least six times over fences and, at the time of writing, the nine year old has only run four times – he is due to have his next run in the Irish Gold Cup on Saturday. A point winner for Denis Murphy, prior to being bought by Cheveley Park Stud for £430,000, he hasn't had a lot of racing – only 10 starts during his career, five of which have been in the highest company – but is a high-class horse. Unbeaten as a novice chaser last season, he beat Heart Wood (rated 159) and Corbetts Cross (163) at Naas (2m 4f) followed by an even more emphatic victory in the Grade 1 Neville Hotels Novice Chase at Leopardstown (3m), beating the latter again by half a dozen lengths. A setback cut short the rest of his novice career and the Closutton runner was reportedly in need of the outing when pulling up in the John Durkan Memorial Chase at Punchestown on his reappearance in November. The Presenting gelding ran much better last time when sixth in the Savills Chase – still in contention after the second last, he couldn't match his dual Gold Cup winning stablemate Galopin Des Champs thereafter but it was a more than satisfactory performance. Officially rated 159 – the same as last year's winner I Am Maximus, he is considered well handicapped by his trainer and his owners will surely be keen to have a runner in the Grand National. Admittedly the trip is an unknown, but he comes from the family of Gunner Welburn who finished fourth in the National in 2003 and won the Foxhunters over the same fences two years earlier.* ***Best Price: 66/1 (Bet Victor, Unibet, William Hill).***"

The CHELTENHAM FESTIVAL 2025

5 WINNERS: KOPEK DES BORDES (Advised @ Evens), HAITI COULEURS (Advised @ 9/2), JIMMY DU SEUIL (16/1), KARGESE (Advised @ 7/1), WODHOOH (9/2).
Plus: IMPOSE TOI (Advised @ 10/1 – 2nd in the Coral Cup)

Quote: "***JIMMY DU SEUIL (Willie Mullins)*** *ran in two French bumpers prior to be bought for €200,000 in October 2022. Absent for 461 days, he developed into a high-class novice hurdler last season winning at Clonmel (2m : Heavy) by nine lengths in January last year before staying on well in second behind stablemate Ballyburn in the Grade 1 Gallagher Novices' Hurdle over C&D. Below par in Grade 1 novice events at Aintree and Punchestown during the spring, the Galiway gelding hasn't been seen since (off 313 days). Good fresh, the six year old makes his handicap debut off a rating of 146. His record on soft/heavy ground is 12 compared to 52245 on good or good to yielding and good to soft ground. Three of his five runs over hurdles have been at the highest level. The Closutton outfit won this in 2018 with Bleu Berry."* **WON the Coral Cup @ 16/1**

Quote: "***KARGESE (Willie Mullins)*** *was a top-class juvenile hurdler last term winning Grade 1 events at Leopardstown and Punchestown and runner-up in the Triumph Hurdle behind Majborough twelve months ago. The five year old has won 4 of her 9 races over hurdles and looks well treated here off 141. Too keen on her reappearance in a Grade 2 mares' hurdle at Ascot (1m 7f : Good), it was her first start for 259 days and she spoilt her chance during the first half of the race. Three parts of a length second behind Take No Chances, she ought to get a strong early pace which will be beneficial. Spirit Leader was the last mare to win this in 2003. Three of her* *stable's seven previous winners of this were five year olds, including ex-French racers Saint Roi (2020) & State Man (2022)."* **Advised @ 7/1 – WON the County Hurdle @ 3/1**

Quote: *"**WODHOOH (Gordon Elliott)** failed to win any of her four starts on the Flat for Sir Michael Stoute (rated 71) before being sold for 50,000gns in July 2023. The Le Havre mare has proved a revelation since sent jumping winning all six of her races for Gordon Elliott. A dual Listed winner at Newbury and Doncaster last term, she returned from an absence of 322 days to win a mares' handicap hurdle at Cheltenham (New course : 2m 4f : Good/Soft) in December. Ridden by Danny Gilligan, she raced handily before running on strongly to score by a length and three quarters off a mark of 130. Rated eleven pounds higher now (could be top weight here), the form of that victory couldn't have worked out much better – the runner-up Joyeuse won the William Hill Handicap Hurdle at Newbury next time and is now rated 138, the third won a Grade 2 mares' hurdle on her next start and the fourth has won a Listed event since. A winner on good and soft ground, she is a terrific mare and lines up here rather than the Coral Cup. Team Elliott have won this three times, including with the 140 rated Better Days Ahead last year. Indefatigable (2020) was the last mare to win the prize."* **WON the Martin Pipe Conditional Jockeys' Handicap Hurdle @ 9/2**

Talking Trainers: **PAUL NICHOLLS: WINNERS: CALDWELL POTTER (7/1 & 11/4)**

*Quote: "**INTHEWAYURTHINKIN (Gavin Cromwell)** has been supplemented (£25,000) and is expected to be the choice of Mark Walsh (11221). Rated 160, he is unbeaten over 3m 1f plus and made a mockery of a mark of 145 when winning the Kim Muir off 12st twelve months ago. The well bred seven year old then followed up in the Grade 1 Mildmay Novices' Chase at Aintree (3m 1f : Soft) defeating Iroko by four lengths. Even though he has failed to win in three races this season, Gavin Cromwell's stable star has run well twice in the Savills Chase and Irish Gold Cup at Leopardstown – both on drying ground – finishing fifth and fourth respectively. Seven and a quarter lengths behind Galopin Des Champs at the DRF, he will relish this longer distance and is unbeaten on the New course. His half-sister Limerick Lace is also a Festival winner and, while easier ground would be a positive, he has strong each-way claims." **WON the Cheltenham Gold Cup** @ **15/2***

*Quote: "**HAITI COULEURS (Rebecca Curtis)** will seek to provide his trainer with her sixth Festival winner and her first since 2020 – Rebecca Curtis won this with Teaforthree in 2012. Bought for £68,000 having run in two Irish points for Harley Dunne (42), the eight year old finished 60 lengths behind Now Is The Hour in a Grade 2 novice hurdle at Haydock (Heavy) last season before winning twice at Chepstow and Bangor. Switched to fences this term, he has won two of his four races scoring at Aintree (3m 1f : Good) and Cheltenham (3m 1f : Good/Soft) off 125 and 130 (now rated 135). A two and three quarter lengths winner on the latter occasion, he beat Transmission who reopposes here (four pounds worse off) – the fourth Moon D'Orange has won since. In order to protect his chase mark, the Dragon Dancer gelding ran over hurdles last time finishing a good third at Newbury (3m) behind Santos Blue. Ben Jones (2212) takes over in the saddle and his record on stiff/undulating tracks is 2121." Advised @ 9/2 – **WON the National Hunt Chase** @ **7/2***

ONE JUMP AHEAD *UPDATES* 2025/2026 ORDER FORM (EMAIL ONLY)

ALL 5 UPDATES £63.00

☐ **CHELTENHAM NOVEMBER 2025** **£12.00**
(Will be emailed on Thursday 13th November 2025)

☐ **CHRISTMAS SPECIAL 2025** **£12.00**
(Will be emailed on Tuesday 23rd December 2025)

☐ **FEBRUARY 2026** **£12.00**

☐ **CHELTENHAM FESTIVAL *UPDATE*** **£15.00**
(Will be emailed on the Sunday before the Festival)

☐ **AINTREE GRAND NATIONAL *UPDATE*** **£12.00**
(Will be emailed on the Tuesday before the Meeting)

Total Cheque / Postal Order value £................ made payable to Mark Howard Publications Ltd. Please send to Mark Howard Publications Ltd. 69 Fairgarth Drive, Kirkby Lonsdale, Carnforth, Lancashire. LA6 2FB.

NAME: ....

ADDRESS: ....

....

....POST CODE: ....

Email Address: ....

If you have not received your UPDATE via email 24 hours before the meeting starts, please contact us immediately.
Alternatively, order via **www.mhpublications.co.uk**

AHEAD ON THE FLAT 2026

The 26th edition of *Ahead On The Flat* will be published in early April for the 2026 Flat season. It will be formulated along the same lines as previous years with a ***Top 40 Prospects* (2025 edition)** included Group 1 winners **JAN BRUEGHAL & OMBUDSMAN, plus other Pattern winners CONVERGENT, ESTRANGE, FALAKEYAH, OPERA BALLO & SARDINIAN WARRIOR,** ***Bromley's Best Buys*** (included unbeaten Group 1 winner **ZAVATERI (11/2, 18/1, 8/1, 15/2) & first time out winner PATHEIN (28/1)) &** ***Maidens In Waiting, Stable Switchers & Unraced Three Year Olds***. In addition, there will be the usual stable interviews with some of the top trainers in Great Britain (this year's included **Andrew Balding, Ralph Beckett, Ed Bethell, George Boughey, Karl Burke, William Haggas, James Owen & Roger Varian).** *Ahead On The Flat* will contain 152 pages and the price is £13.99.

I shall also be producing three *Ahead On The Flat Updates* (EMAIL ONLY). There will be a **Royal Ascot Preview (9 Winners in 2025 – GSTAAD (advised @ 9/2), FIELD OF GOLD (advised @ 5/6), OMBUDSMAN (7/1), MERCHANT (advised @ 13/2), TRAWLERMAN (advised @ 7/2), AMILOC (11/8), HUMIDITY (4/1) LAZZAT (9/2)** and **SOBER (4/5)), York Ebor Preview (Sky Bet Ebor 1st & 2nd ETHICAL DIAMOND (Advised @ 8/1) & ASCENDING (Advised @ 25/1),** plus **STELLAR SUNRISE (100/30) & OMBUDSMAN (15/8)** and **ANTE-POST ADVICE: NORTHERN TICKER (25/1) for the Ayr Gold Cup)**, and an **Autumn *Update*.** The Royal Ascot version is £12 with the other two £10 or £32 for the ALL THREE.

ORDER FORM

- **AHEAD ON THE FLAT 2026 (Book ONLY) £13.99**

AHEAD ON THE FLAT *UPDATES* 2026 (can be ordered individually at £10.00 EACH (£12 ROYAL ASCOT) or ALL 3 updates for £32.00):

- **ROYAL ASCOT PREVIEW 2026 £12.00**
- **YORK EBOR MEETING PREVIEW 2026 £10.00**
- **AUTUMN PREVIEW 2026 £10.00**
- **ALL 3 *UPDATES* (EMAIL ONLY) £32.00**
- **AHEAD ON THE FLAT + 3 *UPDATES* £45.99**

Total Cheque / Postal Order value £............ Made payable to MARK HOWARD PUBLICATIONS Ltd. Please send to: MARK HOWARD PUBLICATIONS Ltd. 69 FAIRGARTH DRIVE, KIRKBY LONSDALE, CARNFORTH, LANCASHIRE. LA6 2FB.

NAME: ....

ADDRESS: ....

....

....POST CODE: ....

Email Address: ....